DI284707

Love You to Death

The Unofficial Companion to **The Vampire Diaries**

Season 4

• CRISSY CALHOUN *and* HEATHER VEE •

ecw press

Copyright © Crissy Calhoun and Heather Vee, 2013

Published by ECW Press
2120 Queen Street East, Suite 200, Toronto, Ontario, Canada M4E 1E2
416-694-3348 / info@ecwpress.com

LIBRARY AND ARCHIVES CANADA CATALOGUING IN PUBLICATION

Calhoun, Crissy, author
Love you to death : the unofficial companion to the
Vampire diaries, season 4 / Crissy Calhoun, and Heather Vee.

ISBN 978-1-77041-184-5 (PBK.)
ALSO ISSUED AS: 978-1-77090-438-5 (PDF); 978-1-77090-439-2 (EPUB)

1. Vampire diaries (Television program).

1. Title.

PN1992.77.V34C344 2013   791.45'72   C2013-902470-0

Typesetting: Kendra Martin
Text design: Melissa Kaita
Cover design and painting: Carolyn McNeillie
Printing: United Graphics   5   4   3   2   1

The publication of *Love You to Death — Season 4: The Unofficial Companion to The Vampire Diaries* has been generously supported by the Government of Canada through the Canada Book Fund for our publishing activities, and the contribution of the Government of Ontario through the Ontario Book Publishing Tax Credit and the Ontario Media Development Corporation.

PRINTED AND BOUND IN THE UNITED STATES

Contents

Foreword

"I was feeling epic." A 350-year-old vampire named Lexi announced this four years ago to her vampire friend Stefan after she placated a very distraught human girl named Elena Gilbert. Elena was falling in love with Stefan. Lexi saw that Elena was afraid — afraid of what Stefan was, afraid of what a relationship with him might mean for herself, afraid for her family and friends — but she saw that Elena was crazy about him and that she couldn't walk away, because that love was real. Such has been my relationship with *The Vampire Diaries* for the past four years. Terrifying and encouraging, frustrating and fulfilling, exhausting and energizing, insomnia-inducing and calming, and *always* tweetworthy.

Through it all Heather Vee and Crissy Calhoun have been there. It started with a simple yet bold social network relationship born out of my co-dependent desire to get people to like me. I was anxious that Vee and Red, the purveyors of a comprehensive fan website for the book series The Vampire Diaries, didn't think Kevin and I effed up the TV series. From little things like them being okay that Elena wasn't blonde, to us changing the brothers' name back to Salvatore from the scripted "Whitmore," our respect of their opinion was paramount (and they had no idea). Their website, Vampire-Diaries.net, evolved into a comprehensive site of show news, media, episode summaries, wikis, and a network of passionate viewers. Then came a legendary book called *Love You to Death* by Crissy Calhoun. I read it and it blew my mind. Insightful essays that dug as deep (if not deeper) into the themes and mythology of the show as any writer of the show. I was so moved and proud to read such smart people writing such thoughtful, intelligent, and analytical breakdowns of elements of season one, and I remember thinking, "Wow, I think we made something really good."

Now, three years later, Heather and Crissy have every one of our 89 episodes engrained in the fiber of their DNA. But more importantly, they understand, above anyone, the extensive stories that need telling from in front of and behind the camera, during the making of the past four seasons of *The Vampire Diaries*. They love to honor the writers, the directors, the cast and crew — and because we've built a family over four years, I always shed a tear or two of pride when I read the praise showered on the other artists who give their hearts and souls to the show.

The entire Love You to Death series stands as an entertaining, exhaustive bible of the character arcs, plot lines, mythology, and the behind-the-scenes happenings of a TV series made by people who are crazy in love with their work. Or just crazy. Hard to say.

I'd like to say thank you to Crissy and Heather for their tireless work, and give a big shout-out to all the vocal fans for continuing to watch. This show cannot exist without you. Even though 89 episodes nearly killed us, everyone at *The Vampire Diaries* is feeling terrified, deeply invested, and as epic as ever. We're humbled and grateful that we get to keep telling these stories in season five of *TVD* and now on the spinoff, *The Originals*. If we're lucky, there will be enough heartbreak, death, tears, smiles, laughs, swelling songs, and shirtless torsos to go around.

With much love and appreciation,
Julie Plec
Co-creator of *The Vampire Diaries*
July 2013

Introduction

During *The Vampire Diaries* panel at the ATX Television Festival in Austin this past June, Julie Plec said that while she was writing season three's "Ghost World," she realized that at its heart this series was about the very human fear of being alone. If you go back to season one, you will see that fear driving the Gilbert kids in the wake of their parents' sudden deaths, in Matt and Caroline's parallel desperation to assuage the loneliness, in the Salvatore brothers' fraught relationship. For four seasons, *The Vampire Diaries* has taken achingly real emotional truths and explored them in mind-blowing and fast-paced supernatural stories, and I've had the honor and privilege of writing about each episode — both on Vampire-Diaries.net and here in the Love You to Death series.

But writing a book? When you're in the thick of it, you can feel as alone as a vampire with an eternity ahead of her. So when *Love You to Death — Season 4* was given a go-ahead from my lovely publisher (thanks, guys!), I did what the Mystic Falls gang always does: I turned to a friend. Enter Heather Vee. She's one of the Originals: a devotee of the L.J. Smith series from back in the day and the co-founder of the insanely awesome and classy Vampire-Diaries .net. Together, we faced down the Big Bad of a blinking cursor on an empty page and whittled our way to this book that you now hold in your hands.

Keeping in the spirit of opening the book up to more voices, we are proud and excited to present invaluable and entertaining behind-the-scenes insight direct from the people who conceptualize, write, produce, shoot, edit, and score *The Vampire Diaries*. Starting with the chapter "Every Episode

Is Huge" and continuing within the episode guide itself, these interviews spotlight the incredible amount of thought and effort the *TVD* team puts into every episode, from mapping out the story arc of an entire season to why a certain scene was shot a specific way to the level of detail that goes into creating the episode that airs each Thursday. We came away from these illuminating interviews with a heightened appreciation for the complexity of the *Vampire Diaries* machine, as well as for the obvious affection and pride of those who keep it moving, and we hope you will too.

In the episode guide, each write-up begins with a bit of dialogue that stood out either because it captures the episode in a pithy few lines or it was just too well written to ignore. From there, we dive into an analysis of the episode, exploring its main themes, the character development, and the questions it raises. Next, we present these sections:

COMPELLING MOMENT Here we choose one moment that particularly stands out — a turning point, a character standing up for herself, a shocking twist, or a long-awaited relationship scene.

CIRCLE OF KNOWLEDGE This is the section in which you'll find all the need-to-know info — the details you may have missed on first watch, character insights, the cultural references, and motifs or recurring elements. If an episode's title is a play on another title (of a film, book, song, etc.), those references are explained here.

THE RULES Any work of fiction with a supernatural element has its own particular spin on how that world operates. Here we catalog what we've learned about what goes bump in the night.

HISTORY LESSON The only class at Mystic Falls High School that ever got considerable screen time is history. History, both real and fictional, is important in this series — so, for the characters' backstories, the town's history, and subtle references, "History Lesson" is your study aid.

PREVIOUSLY ON *THE VAMPIRE DIARIES* History repeats itself in Mystic Falls, and here we outline the incidents, motifs, and key moments that are revisited or echoed in each episode. (Included at the back of the book is a quick refresher on the previous seasons' episodes, if it's been a while since you rewatched.)

OFF CAMERA Here we leave the fictional world behind to hear what the cast and crew have to say about an episode; you'll also find background details on guest stars.

FOGGY MOMENTS Elena, surprised by Stefan in the cemetery in the pilot episode, tells him the fog is making her foggy. "Foggy Moments" is a collection of confusing moments for the viewer — continuity errors, arguable nitpicks, full-on inconsistencies, and conundrums that may be explained later.

QUESTIONS *TVD* fans *love* to theorize about what will happen next or what motivates a certain character. In this section, we raise questions about characters, plotting, and mythology and leave you to consider them as you watch the season unfold.

Make sure you watch an episode *before* reading its corresponding guide — you will encounter spoilers for that episode (but never for any episode that follows). The timeline included in previous volumes of Love You to Death is updated to include season four's info on the past 2,000 years (!) in the *TVD* universe. As well, a song-by-scene guide is included at the back of the book.

After our nearly five years of involvement with *The Vampire Diaries* fandom, as a reviewer and a blogger, we continue to be overwhelmed with the devotion of the show's many fans all over the world. To everyone who has supported, followed, read, or engaged us in conversation, in person and online: Thank you. This book is for you.

We're not crazy — just passionate,
Crissy Calhoun and Heather Vee
July 2013

Every Episode Is Huge

The Making of *The Vampire Diaries*

While every 42-minute episode of *The Vampire Diaries* may seem to be an effortless whiplash of cliffhangers and epic moments viewers have come to expect, what plays out with such breathtaking speed and tension onscreen takes weeks and months of careful crafting from a huge number of people.

We asked writer and co-executive producer Caroline Dries, season four writer and coproducer Jose Molina, producer and director Pascal Verschooris, cinematographer Dave Perkal, editor Tyler Cook, composer Michael Suby, and show co-creator and executive producer Julie Plec to walk us through the process of creating an episode of *TVD*, from the initial breaking of story to the airing of the completed episode. What follows here is a unique peek at the nuts and bolts of the show's creation and an introduction to the passionate people behind the curtain.

What is your background and how did you come to work on *The Vampire Diaries*?

Tyler Cook *(Editor)* Like most people who go into filmmaking, I got into it to be a director. I wanted to be the next Spielberg or George Lucas, and then in film school, when I learned about foreign cinema, I wanted to be the next Ingmar Bergman or Jean-Luc Godard. But when I started making my own movies in film school, I realized that I was only ever directing so I could get into the editing room and play around with the footage. I just loved tinkering with the movie and I saw the whole process of editing as this very big and exciting puzzle.

After making that realization, I started taking a lot of editing-based internships. I worked on a couple of low-budget independent movies as an intern and then as an assistant editor. I worked really hard and met a lot of great people that way. And the movies I worked on did really well. They played at Sundance and all the major festivals around the country and won a lot of awards along the way. When I graduated college, I called up one of the editors that I had worked for just to tell him I would be moving out to L.A. and wanted to grab coffee, and he offered me a job over the phone. I was extremely lucky in that regard. So I moved out and started working on that feature and from that job I was able to get into the [Motion Picture] Editors Guild, and then I transitioned into television, working on *90210*, followed by *Eastbound and Down* for a short time, and finally ended up at *The Vampire Diaries*.

Dave Perkal *(Director of Photography)* I went to school for [cinematography] — undergrad at San Diego State University Film and Television and then graduate at American Film Institute for cinematography. Then after I finished school I started working in entry-level positions in the industry and worked my way up. I was a film loader, 2nd assistant camera, 1st AC, operator, and gaffer.

Pascal Verschooris *(Producer and Director)* I started in radio. One day, a production team walked into Radio Monte Carlo, where I was working, and used our studio for a Coca-Cola commercial. I was mesmerized. I can't really explain what it was: the buzz, the pace, the people. It all seemed so different. I moved to Paris a little later and eventually got a job for a TV show called *The Hitchhiker*. This took me to Vancouver, Canada, for a French-Canadian coproduction called *Bordertown*. The series was about a small town [straddling] the U.S./Canada border; the heroes, a Mountie and a U.S. Marshall. That was great fun.

I eventually moved my way to production manager, but in 2002 I was forced to decide between TV and feature film. In Vancouver, these are very different worlds. I like watching big movies, but I also always feel you can tell the story better in TV. You get to know the characters, you can expand on the stories, their background. So I chose TV and instead of doing a huge feature,

I picked a Showtime series, *Dead Like Me*. This was the real beginning of producing for me.

Michael Suby *(Composer)* I was in a band when I was 19, and one of the guys I lived next to, I used to teach him how to play guitar. We became good friends. He was at USC film school, and he ended up writing and directing *The Butterfly Effect*. He essentially asked me to do his first independent movie, to which I said no, because I didn't know what I was doing. So he forced me to do it, which was great, [because] I went to music school, moved out here, and he had just sold the movie and that was my first project.

And it filtered down from there, because they did *Kyle XY* several years later and Julie Plec was hired on. I think at that point she was head of television at BenderSpink, and she was brought on just as a coproducer originally. Then those guys left the show and Julie took over *Kyle XY*, and then she left that show and went to Warner Bros. with *Vampire Diaries* and Kevin [Williamson]. So she brought me over, and that's how I got on the show.

Jose Molina *(Writer and Coproducer)* The Lady of the Lake, her arm clad in the purest shimmering samite, held aloft Excalibur from the bosom of the water, signifying by divine providence that I, Jose, should write for TV.

That, and I was lucky enough to win the 1993 TV Academy Screenwriting internship, during which I met some great mentors like Michael Piller, Robert Hewitt Wolfe, and René Echevarria [all writers and producers on *Star Trek: Deep Space Nine*]. I would literally not be where I am if not for those gentlemen. I was a little late to the [*TVD*] party, but had been watching pretty religiously since season two. I was most impressed by how quickly and fearlessly the show burned through story. I loved the idea of writing at that breakneck pace — having major plot points every couple of episodes where more timid shows would hoard those ideas until the end of the season. I think *TVD* raised the bar for a lot of other TV shows in terms of pacing.

Caroline Dries *(Writer and Co-Executive Producer)* I was a fan of the pilot script during staffing season — believe it or not, it was the character of Aunt Jenna that really jumped off the page and made me think, dang, this show feels weirdly clever. But, as much as I loved it, I had already committed to working on another show, *Melrose Place*, so I just watched the first part of *TVD* season one as a fan. Then *Melrose* ended, and one afternoon I was home being unemployed, watching DVDs from my new *Dawson's Creek* box set, when my agent called and asked if I wanted to meet with Kevin Williamson.

I was like, "Uh, the guy who created Joey Potter? What do you think?" So I interviewed, got the job, came on for the episode "Let the Right One In" [1.17], and have been here ever since.

Tyler Cook *(Editor)* I came on toward the end of season one ("Let the Right One In") as an assistant editor and I was only supposed to fill in until the end of the season. I even had another job already lined up, but I loved the tone and feel of the show and the story that Julie and Kevin were telling so much that I really wanted to be involved in helping bring the show to life in any way I could. So I quit my other job and came back to *Vampire Diaries* full time. From there I slowly worked my way up from being an assistant, which is more of a technical/administrative job directly under the editor, who makes sure that he/she has everything they need.

What is your job on the show?

Caroline Dries *(Writer and Co-Executive Producer)* I started as a writer/producer, but I didn't do much producing because the show was managed so tightly by Kevin and Julie. As the seasons continued, and as Kevin and Julie got to know me more, and trust my instincts more, I took on more responsibility by producing my own episodes. I also got a chance to write more and spend more time with Kevin and Julie, because they liked my writing and mentored me. Now, going into season five, I'm co-running the show with Julie.

Pascal Verschooris *(Producer and Director)* My job is to serve the vision of the showrunner and protect the financial interests of the financier, which, in this case, is the studio [Warner Bros.]. I get a script every week and a half, and I have to figure out ways to make it for the right money, but I also have to make sure that the vision is protected so that the show looks good. For instance, sometimes directors and writers make demands that can be very costly or not doable in the allowed schedule, so I try to find solutions, alternatives, or — at times — ask for some cuts. (Writers don't like cutting.) Because I have a bit of an artistic heart, I always get torn between art and money so I always try to make things work, otherwise I get heartbroken.

Dave Perkal *(Director of Photography)* The cinematographer's job is to visually tell the story through lighting, lensing, and camera movement. The idea is to support story and character without being self-indulgent or conspicuous, while also incorporating the director's and showrunner's vision for the episode. On *The Vampire Diaries*, this is a huge job because there are so many different looks to the show with flashbacks, the vampire world versus the Mystic Falls world, and the immense amount of special and visual effects. I have to coordinate with all the show's departments like wardrobe, makeup and hair, stunts, production design, the art department, VFX and SFX [visual and special effects], postproduction, and locations.

Tyler Cook *(Editor)* My job on the show has grown quite considerably since I started in season one. I started as an assistant editor and was promoted to editor during season three. The best way I can describe the role of an editor is that of a sculptor. On a given episode an average of 30 hours of film is shot (sometimes as much as 50) and the editor has to shape that raw footage into a 42-minute show.

I think the big misconception about editing is that all we have to do is cut out the bad pieces or that we just push buttons on a computer, which is the furthest thing from the truth. Editors have to be storytellers in the same way writers and directors are storytellers. We take the script that the writers wrote and the film the director shot and we are tasked to create the most compelling hour of television out of those two components.

Michael Suby *(Composer)* Pretty simple: I write all the background instrumental music — which is not very simple on this show. It's a lot of music, *a lot* of music. A lot of complex characters; huge emotional arcs on the show, and they're more than on most television shows because the nature of the vampire [means] everything is magnified. So the love is intense love, the sadness is overwhelming, and whatever emotion these guys are feeling it's magnified by a tremendous amount. My job is to help navigate all the emotional arcs, and help make the action exciting and scary. So I write music day and night.

Tyler Cook *(Editor)* The role of the editor has also considerably expanded over the years. It used to be that the editor was just required to cut the picture. But now, we have to deliver something that could air, so that means we are now responsible for adding all of the music, whether that be score or songs, as well as doing the sound design and even some rudimentary VFX.

Julie Plec's Epic To-Do List

The showrunner details her duties for each episode, from inception to air date.

Oh boy, you asked for it. Here it goes:

1) Stare at blank whiteboard in writers' room in a dull panic. Blank boards are terrifying.

2) "Blue sky" the episode with the writers, which means asking and answering the following questions:

    a) Where did we leave our characters in the last episode? Where do we want them to get to by the end of this one?

    b) Where are we in our mythology? What's the big move we want to make in this episode to push it forward?

    c) What are the "holy shit" moments we want to try to hit?

    d) What are the romantic "wows" we want to try to hit?

    e) What's Elena Gilbert's freaking drive? (Meaning, as the "heroine" of the show, in every episode she needs to have a want that drives her actions. This is often the hardest part of breaking the story, as writers ironically instinctively prefer passive/reactive characters who observe, reflect, and emote, as opposed to having to constantly move the plot forward.)

    f) What event or "big idea" can bring everyone in the episode together? The power is in the ensemble — how do we get our ensemble interacting together as one?

    g) What "kind" of *TVD* episode will this be? A hostage crisis? A romantic event where things go perilously awry? Elena in jeopardy? Magic-driven? Flashback? The gang has a mission? etc.

3) Take all of the above and "break" the story. Lay out plot moves and story beats in a six-act structure. Find good act outs.

4) Once you have a handle on the basic story, write a "story area," an approximately two-page document that puts it in pitch form for studio/network notes.

5) After receiving approval from studio/network, internally "scroutline" the episode. (A script outline using Final Draft with temp dialogue and temp scene descriptions so we don't forget what we talked about.)

6) Write episode.

    a) Rewrite episode.

    b) Re-break the story and rewrite yet again.

7) Deliver the script for studio/network notes.

8) Rewrite based on studio/network notes. Deliver script to production.

9) Day 1 of prep: Concept meeting. Talk through script scene by scene with all department heads (stunts, props, costumes, special effects, visual effects, etc).

10) Throughout prep: Sign off on location photos, wardrobe photos, stunt

rehearsal videos, set photos, etc. Watch casting sessions, choose guest actors.

11) Also throughout prep: Fight with production. The script's too long, it's unproduceable, it's too expensive, blah blah blah. The most annoying part of the process for all involved.

12) Listen in on cast read-through. Make final tweaks to script based on production needs, schedule needs, and actor thoughts.

13) Last two days of prep:
    a) Production meeting (same as concept meeting only with everyone giving answers instead of asking questions).
    b) Tone meeting. A two- to three-hour phone call or meeting with director and writer to go through every moment in the script, discuss important character moments, intentions, visual requests, etc. Basically, the writer's chance to have an open dialogue with the director about every single thing on the page.

14) Shoot. Anywhere from eight to 10 days, often 12–15 hours a day. The writer on set needs to be there to defend the script and make sure nothing gets missed.

15) Watch dailies, the videos you get every day of the previous day's work.

16) Approximately 10 days after the episode wraps, receive first cut from the editors.

17) Have a private meltdown over how much you hate the episode.

18) Give notes on the edit, wait for re-edit, give more notes, etc., etc., until we're happy (and we can proudly say that 99.9 percent of the time we always end up happy).

19) Deliver cut to studio/network for notes.

20) Music and sound spotting. Once the episode is complete, we screen it with the editor, composer, sound designer, sound editor, and music supervisor and call out places that will need ADR (dialogue replacement), different music cues, sound effects, etc.

21) Sign off on visual effects and color-timing (the process of color correcting the footage so it looks as lush and beautiful as it can).

22) Attend final mix playback, which is a week after the sound spotting, where we get to watch the episode and give notes on music and sound levels, sound effects, the new ADR that's been dropped in, etc.

23) Air date. Read both loving and hateful feedback on Twitter. Swear to quit Twitter forever.

That's what we go through for each episode, and we do it 22–23 times a *year*. At any given point, there is at least one episode in the "blank board" stage, an episode in the writing stage, prep stage, shoot stage, and post stage. So take the above list and imagine doing it again and again and again, like poor Sisyphus trying to push that freakin' rock up the mountain.

And that's our job in a nutshell. God help us all.

Mapping the Season

Caroline Dries *(Writer and Co-Executive Producer)* We meet for five weeks after each season ends and before the next season actually starts to map out the [coming] season. So, while my other writer friends are on hiatus and Instagramming pictures of their daytime cocktails, I'm eating ice from my Starbucks coffee in our windowless writers' room. As much as I huff and puff about it, it's incredibly helpful. Our seasons are long — season four was 23 episodes. That's an insane amount of story to brainstorm. We break down the season into four chapters to a) make things sane and manageable and b) give us mini-arcs within the overall spine of the season. In theory, these mini-arcs build on each other and push us to the end with a bang.

Jose Molina *(Writer and Coproducer)* The senior writers gathered to start discussing season four while season three was wrapping up. We spent weeks brainstorming the broad strokes of the year — a luxury I've never even *heard* of other shows having — and cracked the spine of the whole year in that short a time. [The entire season] was all planned out before we gathered the entire staff in June. Unheard of.

Pascal Verschooris *(Producer and Director)* The writers meet at the end of the previous season and discuss the direction to go for the next season. They hopefully take a short break and gather again very early on for the new season. I get an idea of what [that narrative direction] will be. It does evolve, so I also have to use my instincts as to whether to invest in sets, locations, etc.

Dave Perkal *(Director of Photography)* I [have] meetings about where the show's story would go for the entire season. These are just beats about the trajectory of the season's arcs but it gives you a sense about what will happen over the course of the year. I use this information to assemble a team and we make adjustments to make the production more efficient while maintaining the *Vampire Diaries* look.

From the Writers' Room to the Screen

Caroline Dries *(Writer and Co-Executive Producer)* Picture a group of the best-looking people you know, sounding like the most charming people you know. And then think of the opposite. You've got a writers' room. So there's the writers' room, and then there's the actual process of writing — they're two totally separate things. In the room, usually Julie or I will be in charge of discussion and coaxing ideas from the genius staff. Then together we'll all organize the ideas and then shape them into a story. There's a lot of banging heads against walls and crossing out ideas, and feeling lost, but we ultimately get it to a good spot. That takes about a week.

Jose Molina *(Writer and Coproducer)* The biggest novelty for me [coming to *TVD* after writing for other series] was how monstrously collaborative the writing had to be, simply because every story affects every other story. There's no such thing as a standalone *TVD* episode; writing any series is a team effort, but this one required that the entire staff have a certain level of telepathy with each other.

Caroline Dries *(Writer and Co-Executive Producer)* Then we go off to write the script alone. Here we're free to get lost in the characters and be *writers* who get to arrange words in clever ways. That takes about a week. Then we all read it and realize it's all wrong and take what nuggets we like from the story, and build on it, and reshape things, and de-complicate it and rewrite everything. That takes about three or four days. It's a hellish process (unless you compare it to a real-person job, in which case, it's a dream) because sometimes you feel like you're living with an episode forever. But it's actually very rewarding once the script is delivered to the studio and network because you know it's pretty much the best it can be.

Jose Molina *(Writer and Coproducer)* There are three basic stages to writing/producing a *TVD* episode: breaking down the story from a concept to a six-act structure, outlining/scripting that idea, and supervising set to make sure everyone is on the same page about the story. Each stage is pretty time-consuming, so we all tend to be far more involved in our own episodes than in everyone else's. That said, we all pitch in as much as we can, and it's not rare for non-credited writers to write scenes in someone else's script or have a huge influence on their stories.

Tyler Cook *(Editor)* The show is a six-act structure. Act 1 consists of a teaser or cold open, which is meant to pique the audience's interest and tee up the rest of the episode. From there Act 1 sets up the rest of the show (where the characters are in the overall story, resetting important information) and then ends on the new problem that the gang will have to deal with. Acts 2 and 3 usually involve figuring out the plan/arguing about the plan, and then acts 4 and 5 are about executing the plan (or failing to execute the plan, in some cases). Act 6 is about dealing with the aftermath and setting up the next episode. As far as act breaks are concerned, we always try to break each act at its most exciting place or the next turn in the story. We always try to leave at the highest note so people will stick through the commercial breaks and come back for more.

Pascal Verschooris *(Producer and Director)* [I become involved with an episode] as soon as we get the script. Often I try to get information prior, to find out if we need to build a set, a prosthetic, a prop, etc. Do we need to scout for a new location? Once we have the script then I work with the UPM [Trish Stanard, unit production manager] and the ADs [assistant directors] and we come up with a schedule. The schedule defines our episode. We usually need to make it work with nine days (eight, plus one second-unit day). I pass along information that I have, I help with the design of the sets, the logistics of the schedule, and also communicate with the writers about our production needs.

Dave Perkal *(Director of Photography)* I start to get involved as soon as a "beat sheet" or rough draft is released to production. My first move is to start a dialogue with our production designer, Garreth Stover, about what kind of sets he envisions and how we can work together to make them shootable. During the first few days of that prep, the director will usually start formulating an idea about where and how they would like to visually convey the episode's story. My job is to help support their vision and elevate the material. I will then go with production to scout locations. Together with the production designer, 1st assistant director, and location department, we will formulate the best time of day and direction to shoot a particular location. The 1st assistant director and I will go over schedule plans and work out a shootable plan for the episode. We will have production meetings with all departments, from a concept meeting (a rough draft of our intentions) to a final production meeting (our final plan), to make sure that we are all coordinating with the same vision for the episode. During this prep time, I am in constant contact with my key departments, lighting, grip, and camera, so that the heads of these departments can be prepared when we start shooting.

Tyler Cook *(Editor)* I get involved with an episode usually the day before it starts shooting. The script is distributed to the entire cast/crew and there is a meeting to talk about the overall story direction of the script, what are the most important moments of the episode, and the best way to convey those through the direction, photography, and editing.

Pascal Verschooris *(Producer and Director)* This show is amazing because everyone listens to everyone, so it makes it easier to come up with solutions, alternative ways to make the show. It is not always the case on every series, so it is important to point this out. But I think on *TVD* we've developed a reciprocal trust between production and creatives, which helps the process tremendously and allows for us to make a better show.

Jose Molina *(Writer and Coproducer)* We sacrifice a basket of kittens to the Egyptian god Set before the start of every shoot.

Dave Perkal *(Director of Photography)* Once we start shooting we are simply executing our plan. While we are shooting the episode, I am also in contact with our post department to make sure we are getting everything we need. Once shooting is completed, the episode goes into editing.

Tyler Cook *(Editor)* We start getting in the footage the day after they begin shooting the episode and that's when we start assembling the show. The episode shoots for eight days and once the shooting is done we have another week to finish putting it together. That's the editor's cut. Then the director will come in and spend some time with the episode for a few days, and give his/her notes on what we've done. That's the director's cut. And then from there it goes to Julie and the rest of the producers. They watch the show and start to figure out if the moments of the show are working as well as they can be and if the show is as exciting and interesting as it needs to be. Or if we're running too long, she suggests places where we can lift out scenes or lines of dialogue to get us to time.

It's really during this time that Julie goes over the show in very fine detail to make sure it's great. That process usually takes anywhere from one week to two, depending on the schedule and the strength of the episode. From there we show the episode to Warner Bros. and The CW and they weigh in with any final thoughts and we're done picture editing the episode. That whole process usually takes a month. But the show's not done. The composer starts to work on the episode along with the sound designer, and other elements such as color timing, VFX, and audio mixing take place.

Dave Perkal *(Director of Photography)* Once the cut is locked they send it back to me to supervise final color. Final color is like the Photoshop or printing portion of photography where we fine-tune the look of every frame of the show.

Michael Suby *(Composer)* I never read a script; I like to watch it when it's completely finished. So I basically just get it and do it — right before the mix and right before it airs pretty much! It's a very tight schedule. I just finished the season finale: I got it on Wednesday, I started Thursday, and they mixed it

Julie Plec on Finding Her Stride as Showrunner

Season one was brutal. Absolutely, hatefully brutal. We were never on schedule, always on the ugly side of a past deadline, struggling to figure out what the show was and how to actually write it. The voice didn't come naturally, we had to find it.

Season two was almost as brutal, because we wanted it to be even better than season one.

The beginning of season three for me, specifically, was excruciating because Kevin was off on *The Secret Circle* and I didn't want the show to suffer in his absence. I worked myself into a state of near insanity.

Once the middle of season three hit, however, things started to get easier. I tried to micromanage less, be less controlling, less insecure, and set out to do my best to give the other writer-producers more ownership over their material. The "team" really took shape and other writers came out of their shell and started to really blossom and find their own confidence and their own voice.

Season four was very functional and very enjoyable. My favorite season as far as the process goes. I loved watching Caroline Dries, specifically, come into her own as a soon-to-be showrunner.

yesterday [Sunday] and they're doing the playback today. So it's three or four days. This show, that's just the way it runs, it's been normal for a long time on this show. I do other shows; *Pretty Little Liars* — that does not happen on that show. I can't speak to other shows, but *Kyle XY* was not like that, I had about a week usually. They usually try to give you a week to 10 days because of the amount of work. So this one's particularly tricky because it's probably twice the amount of work in half the amount of time [laughs].

Tyler Cook *(Editor)* Postproduction can seem very small but it's actually quite large. At its most basic there are three teams of editors and assistant editors (six people total) that are in rotation editing episodes of the show. In our office there is also the post producer, post supervisor, post coordinator, and post PA and they are in charge of running the postproduction office and juggling all of the various aspects of the process from the way dailies are transferred to scheduling when all of the cuts have to be delivered. Outside of that there are all of the VFX artists, the sound designer, the music supervisor, the music editor, the composer, the colorists. And they all have their own teams, so it's a big operation.

Michael Suby *(Composer)* I do the whole show by myself. No one helps me, I don't want anybody to touch it. [*laughs*] That doesn't happen a lot on television these days either; most guys have a team and that sort of thing. I just get up, have coffee, and write music. That's it. I write on my computer, I have a microphone set up, I'll play guitar, I'll sample things . . . mostly it's on the keyboard, on the guitar, or I'll get some vocals and record some chants. For this show, I've spent a lot of time off-season creating new sounds, new palettes. It's a heavy-lifting show.

Tyler Cook *(Editor)* I think the biggest challenge of editing *Vampire Diaries* is that every episode is *huge*. I've never seen a dull episode of the show, it doesn't exist. There is just always something gigantic going on and we go through seasons worth of story in the span of five episodes! And that's what makes the show great. But it takes a lot of work. The way I always put it is that normal TV shows operate on a 5–7 intensity for their normal episodes and then crank it up to 10 for their premiere and their finale. We operate on a 8–10 for every episode and then crank it up to 15 for the premiere and the finale. But that's what makes it so successful and why it's so rewarding to work on. It's hard work but you get this incredibly exciting product at the end of it that you can be really proud of.

Jose Molina *(Writer and Coproducer)* One significant difference between *TVD* and many other shows I've worked on was the level of trust we had from the studio and the network. By virtue of being a big hit and a critical success, the show earned the right to take chances, and Warner Bros. and The CW were behind us 100 percent, no matter how crazy we got.

Caroline Dries *(Writer and Co-Executive Producer)* I am proud of every episode because so much work goes into it — not just from me, obviously, but from the director, actors, makeup folks, props, editors, sound guys, etc. *So* many decisions need to be made and everyone works toward the same goal. It's unbelievable how much gets done in such a short period of time.

Pascal Verschooris *(Producer and Director)* Almost everyone on the show is an unsung hero. This show could not function without the dedication of many. Our prop master, Joe Connolly, is probably the best I ever worked with; our 2nd AD, Brandon Leonard, who has to produce a call sheet every day and make sure that everything comes together, is genius; Trish Stanard, our UPM, who calls herself a workhorse, is an inspiration to all; Garreth Stover, our production designer, always comes up with incredible ideas, amazing-looking sets, but he could not do it without Karen, our set decorator, or Jamie, our construction coordinator, who himself could not do it without Billy and Tommy, etc. We have amazing drivers, incredible craft service people who keep the spirit high . . . Just everyone is important, and if one falls through then it shows, but thankfully it rarely happens.

Caroline Dries *(Writer and Co-Executive Producer)* I could go on about things I'm proud of on this show, but I don't want to sound arrogant.

I wonder if I have been changed in the night? Let me think: was I the same when I got up this morning? I almost think I can remember feeling a little different. But if I'm not the same, the next question is, Who in the world am I? Ah, that's the great puzzle.

— *Alice's Adventures in Wonderland*

Episode Guide

Season 4
October 11, 2012–May 16, 2013

CAST Nina Dobrev (Elena Gilbert/Katherine Pierce), Paul Wesley (Stefan Salvatore), Ian Somerhalder (Damon Salvatore), Steven R. McQueen (Jeremy Gilbert), Kat Graham (Bonnie Bennett), Candice Accola (Caroline Forbes), Zach Roerig (Matt Donovan), Michael Trevino (Tyler Lockwood), Joseph Morgan (Klaus Mikaelson)

RECURRING CAST David Alpay (Professor Atticus Shane), Charlie Bewley (Galen Vaughn), Nathaniel Buzolic (Kol Mikaelson), Matt Davis (Alaric Saltzman), Torrey DeVitto (Meredith Fell), Alyssa Diaz (Kim), Daniel Gillies (Elijah Mikaelson), Jasmine Guy (Grams Bennett), Claire Holt (Rebekah Mikaelson), Arielle Kebbel (Lexi), Marguerite MacIntyre (Liz Forbes), Grace Phipps (April Young), Paul Telfer (Alexander), Phoebe Tonkin (Hayley), Susan Walters (Carol Lockwood), Todd Williams (Connor Jordan), Rick Worthy (Rudy Hopkins)

> *Elena (to Stefan): How did you . . . ?*
> *Damon: Save you? He didn't.*

4.01 *Growing Pains*

Original air date: October 11, 2012
Written by: Caroline Dries
Directed by: Chris Grismer
Guest cast: Michael Reilly Burke (Pastor Young), Neko Parham (Council Member), Lex Shontz (Deputy Adams)

Stefan and Bonnie have one day to find a way to save Elena from becoming a vampire, while the newly proactive Founders' Council, led by Pastor Young, rounds up vampires for the slaughter.

You feed or you die. "There is no door number three," says Damon near the beginning of the episode, and it turns out he's absolutely right. But the absence of an 11th-hour save at the end of "Growing Pains" doesn't mean we're left with an Elena Gilbert in despair. She's resolved to persevere, one day at a time, as she embarks on her afterlife as a vampire and as the series takes a step into uncharted territory. *The Vampire Diaries* sticks with its twist from the finale of season three: Bonnie has no magic solution to save her best friend from what Elena once considered, literally, a fate worse than death. As Stefan reminds us, in "The Last Day" (after Damon force-fed her his blood on the precipice of the sacrifice), Elena would have rather died than become a vampire, but here — after a terrible transition day — Elena chooses to be a vampire rather than die. What will this mean for the series, now that it no longer has a beating-heart teenager at its core, a mortal without the strengths (or weaknesses) of a vampire and whose humanity has been the show's guiding force?

As Elena goes through her transition — not a girl, not yet a vampire — the episode explores several key themes of *The Vampire Diaries*, primary among them the importance of choice and the inevitability of consequence.

Each character's choices during last season have borne consequences here, but in Mystic Falls, that favorite word "choice" is often loaded with irony — being forced to select the slightly better of two truly awful options is hardly a celebration of free will. Take the resident town leaders. Carol Lockwood and Liz Forbes have a sworn duty to protect Mystic Falls as its mayor and sheriff, respectively, but they are also driven by the bonds of family to protect their children from persecution. Their deception of the very council members who are tasked with ridding the town of supernatural horrors bears major consequences in "Growing Pains": Carol is arrested (albeit briefly), Liz is stripped of her badge, and their children are under threat from a crazed group led by the explosive Pastor Young. As much as they had struggled at first with their decisions, ultimately Carol and Liz chose to take a different tack than their forefathers once they learned that their own kids were among the supernatural denizens in town, and they made a tentative peace with the Salvatore brothers and even with the Originals. But here the old-fashioned Mystic Falls mindset kicks into high gear, and the pastor "makes his move" . . . unsuccessfully. He unleashes death for his own followers, those who are killed by the Salvatores and those he kills himself when he inexplicably (for now) blows up the farmhouse (along with a good pile of vervain). What further consequences will come from Pastor Young's choice? And what motivated him to commit multiple murders and suicide?

Just as Meredith Fell is out of work, busted for using vampire blood to save human lives, Bonnie finds herself punished for her by-any-means-necessary approach to saving her friends' lives. In "The Departed," Bonnie chose to work secretly with Klaus to perform the body-jump spell — thereby protecting his sire line, which includes her mother, Tyler, Caroline, Damon, and Stefan — but that choice had unforeseeable consequences. Overcome with grief and fear that she'd lose another brother, Rebekah caused Matt's truck to go over Wickery Bridge. As a result, Bonnie is faced with another vampire problem: how to save her best friend from a terrible fate. As a powerful but untrained witch, Bonnie is almost always pulled in multiple directions. She feels loyalty to her witch ancestors, primarily her Grams, and the spirits have the power to punish her for abusing magic. She is also loyal to her human friends, willing to do "unnatural" magic to save them. And she is also at the mercy of those ruthless enough to force her hand, like Klaus who doesn't for a second hesitate to dig his hybrid paw into Tyler's chest and threaten a fatal cardiectomy. Bonnie's actions in "Growing Pains" illustrate how rarely this very moral witch gets to exercise her free will. Her attempt to save Elena is made at great risk to herself (she temporarily kills herself to drag Elena back from the Other Side) and she's immediately upbraided by Grams's spirit. But that warning to stay away from black magic collides with Klaus's demand that he be put back in his own body — and Tyler's life hangs in the balance.

© David Gabber/PRPhotos.com

What's a girl to do? What she sees as the only path before her is strewn with dire consequences: Bonnie will be cut off from the spirits' power, Klaus will be scot-free, Elena will become a vampire, and Grams is thrown into some sort of mystical otherworldly torment. Bonnie's thanks for trying to protect her loved ones is a pain akin to when her Grams died in "Fool Me Once."

In circumstances like these, how can any of them make a clear-cut "right" choice? Stefan respected Elena's choice that Matt should be saved, even though it meant she would die — and Elena is grateful to Stefan for that — but Stefan is saddled with regret and feels at fault that she's on the precipice of her worst nightmare. And his big brother isn't too shy to let him know just how terrible a choice he thinks Stefan made. When Damon is pissed off, he is at his quippiest. His wonderfully sardonic "And now the world has one more quarterback. Bravo, brother" runs counter to Stefan's more emo reaction. Damon's furious that Elena has lost her mortal life and the future it promised her. It's a reaction that he describes as "selfish," but we know better. And as Elena begins to recollect what he compelled her to forget in season two's "Rose," she knows better too: there's nothing selfish about trying to give Elena what she's too selfless to take for herself. If Damon had been in Stefan's position, the quarterback would be dead but Elena would still have her chance for human happiness. In Damon's grief — which manifests itself quite violently, especially if you ask the guy who was stabbed to death with his own shotgun — he punishes those he deems responsible for her death, going after everyone but Elena herself. His reaction gives voice to the guilt Stefan and Matt feel. Damon tells Matt, "It should've been you," and that's exactly what Matt feels. As Matt tells Caroline in the hospital, he was the one driving, he's the one who escaped the accident unscathed, and he hates himself for that. Reassurances from Caroline don't help assuage his survivor guilt, and when Damon is poised to kill him at the end of the episode, Matt welcomes it.

And that's another kicker of this episode: putting aside the importance of choice on this show, the less-talked-about but ever-present reality is that sometimes horrible things just happen to you. Matt didn't choose to live and let Elena die. Elena didn't ask to be healed by vampire blood. Their loved ones have been killed, and their lives turned upside down by powers far outside their control. Stefan kills that deputy — a guy who was, presumably, trying to protect his town from those he considers bloodsucking monsters — but would Elena have made the same choice: her life over Deputy Adams's? Any action done on someone else's behalf can be just as life-changing as those which are self-directed, so even though Damon's quip "Your choice, Elena, as always" has its desired effect, it's not quite accurate. Elena was "ready to die" and she made the choice to drown in "The Departed," and yet she lives to face another life-or-death moment. With the pool of the deputy's blood just wide enough for her to reach, Elena chooses an afterlife.

The other big choice Elena made in "The Departed" was which Salvatore brother was her #1 dream hunk. (To one segment of the fandom, this was of greater import than whether Elena lives or dies.) Damon's emotional state in this season premiere is in part a response to *not* being the chosen one — his snark when he and Elena talk about what she now remembers makes that clear enough. But Elena's choice, interestingly, has the greatest effect on Rebekah, who witnesses Stefan and Elena's touchingly romantic exchange in the barn. Though Elena is on death's door, she tells Stefan that her choice to come back to him — the choice that snowballed into her finding herself in her current predicament — was the "best choice I ever made." It's a tragic scene not only for the lovers separated by the barrier between the stalls, unable to see each other or touch, but also for Rebekah. She once loved Stefan, and she sits opposite them in her prison, without a single, solitary person willing to come to her rescue. She feels how empty her life is in comparison to Elena's. Sure, she's rich and basically unkillable, but she lacks the things that truly matter. Her life is loveless, whereas Elena is surrounded by love. Rebekah sees how connected the Mystic Falls gang is, how they are literally willing to die for each other, and sees herself alone with only a cruel brother who takes her for granted and repeatedly devalues her. In perhaps the most selfless moment of the episode, without a word, Rebekah decides to help Stefan save Elena. She scares the deputy into Stefan's range, so he can spill blood for Elena to feed on. And when Rebekah is finally free, what does she return home to? Klaus fussing over his precious hybrid blood. He didn't bother to save her, but he will disown her for destroying the blood bags. Where will Blondie Bex go from here?

Both Rebekah's and Caroline's worst fears are assuaged when the loved one they believed was dead in "The Departed" is "resurrected" — and in an odd, only-on-*TVD* way, it happens when Klaus is in Tyler's body. But the happiness is tainted. Rebekah is left behind with her captors and must face the fact her brother doesn't care a whit about her. Caroline accidentally makes out with Klaus and unwittingly suggests having some hot hybrid-vampire sex with him. ("Wrong equipment" is a wonderfully pithy Klausism to explain the situation.) For both characters, it is all a bad supernatural practical joke: Tyler is alive and well, and Klaus is returned to his own body thanks to Bonnie's magic. For them, there is a way out of the nightmare.

Not so for Elena. Despite living in a world with supernatural loopholes, this time there is no escaping the consequences. The Salvatore brothers take very different stances on the question of hope in "Growing Pains." Damon's firm belief that there is no "door number three" illustrates his famous practicality: feed now, get it over with, move on. Stefan, on the other hand, risks getting Elena's hopes up, as Damon puts it, about some as-yet-undiscovered way to reverse the transition to vampirism. Where does the line between hope and delusion lie? Damon knows about false hope, particularly given the century and a half he waited to be the dashing hero to rescue Katherine from her entombment. To Damon, that way lies disappointment, heartache, and failure. But for Elena, hope — even though it ultimately bears no magical fruit — is just what she needs. And though Stefan uses every available opportunity to help Elena find another way, he has a backup plan — a daylight ring in his pocket thanks to Bonnie — and he doesn't hesitate to kill the deputy to get some blood for his lady. Hope for the best, prepare for the worst.

In the scene in her bedroom, Elena placates her little brother by assuring him she's okay, and though Jeremy sees through the lie, knowing that's what his sister always says to protect him, he hopes she's right. At the center of this episode is Elena in transition, definitely experiencing growing pains. As our human heroine becomes the thing she least wants to be, we get visual cues from her perspective to show her newly heightened senses and emotions. Extreme close-ups, jump cuts, and disorienting shifts in focus help the viewer feel Elena's new and overwhelming world, a reality she's never experienced before — like how annoyingly buzzy lightbulbs are, and how intense her need is to smash 'em. Nina Dobrev's performance is masterful as Elena ranges from manic laughter to the stillness of near death. This episode (and the series as a whole) simply would not work without an actor of her caliber at its heart.

What prevents this episode from getting maudlin is Elena's firm grip on hope. Even in her darkest moment, she is still surrounded by love and is a believer in hope. It makes her embrace Stefan's later honesty that being a vampire will be the worst thing she's ever lived through, and it's the reason she resolves to take it "one day at a time."

Stefan tells Matt that he now has an obligation to make Elena's sacrifice worth it in how he chooses to live his life. And the finality of their situation fuels Stefan and Elena as well. Their chorus of "everything will be okay" resounds in that rooftop scene with the ever-so-symbolic dawn of a new day, as Elena has her chin up ready to begin again. However unrealistic it may be, they are hopeful about the forever that now lies ahead of them both.

COMPELLING MOMENT Elena reaching desperately for the blood that will keep her from finally dying, and her single tear falling as she completes her transition into a vampire.

CIRCLE OF KNOWLEDGE
- "Growing Pains" is a popular choice for TV episode titles; it's also the name of the 1985–1992 ABC sitcom about the Seaver family.
- The premiere of season four marked a new (if short-lived) opening sequence for the series: the "Previously on *The Vampire Diaries*" format was replaced with a montage of clips from previous episodes and accompanying narration from a number of *TVD* actors.
- The soundscape that Elena hears as she wakes up at the beginning subtly prepares us to meet Pastor Young later in the episode. She hears lawnmowers and birds chirping . . . and an ominous church bell ringing.
- Back in "Family Ties" (1.04), Vicki joked about giving "Pastor Bill" a lap dance; Pastor Bill is not Pastor Young, Bill is the man in a clerical collar seen at the Founders' Ball talking to Liz (who is also in uniform) as Caroline arrives.
- In a strange funhouse-mirror version of the end of "The Departed" (3.22), Klaus-as-Tyler has to make a choice of who to rescue from the totaled van, Caroline or his sister, just as Stefan had to choose between rescuing Matt or Elena from the submerged truck. Klaus opts for Caroline, later telling Rebekah he made that choice since the Original sister couldn't die at her captors' hands. Unbeknownst to Stefan, this was also true of Elena as Matt's truck sank in the water — with vampire blood in her system, she was spared final death.
- Rebekah tells a guard that her family has "money, castles, apartments, and jewelry." Though the Original family's wealth has been repeatedly demonstrated, this is the first time one of them has made direct reference to the extent of their property.

- In lockup at the Young farm, Stefan and Elena talk to each other from either side of the wall that separates them, just as Pyramus and Thisbe did. The tragic lovers from Greek myth, and one of the sources for *Romeo and Juliet*, whisper to each other through a crack in the wall that separates their houses. Their story also ends in bloodshed (but not in mutual vampirism).
- Before blowing up the cabin and everyone in it, Pastor Young says they will soon be free to "pass through the gates," a phrase used in the New Testament in Isaiah 62, a verse that goes on to describe a holy and redeemed people reaching a city that is not forsaken. Presumably the opposite of Mystic Falls, which seems totally 100 percent forsaken.

THE RULES Bonnie dips into dark magic, stopping her own heart so she can visit the Other Side. While there, she sees Elena's living physical self (imprisoned at the farm), but she also sees her Grams's spirit. When Bonnie uses dark magic again to put Klaus back into his own body, the spirits punish her abuse of magic by hurting Grams, which demonstrates that it is possible for spirits on the Other Side to feel physical pain. Klaus-as-Tyler changes just one part of himself into wolf form, as opposed to other hybrids and werewolves who we've only seen make a full wolf transformation.

PREVIOUSLY ON *THE VAMPIRE DIARIES* Stefan reminds Damon that he wasn't there the day Elena told him how desperately she did *not* want to become a vampire, referring to their conversation at the top of the mountain in "The Last Day" (2.20).

Jeremy recalls watching Vicki go through her transition in "Lost Girls" (1.06), which also took place, in large part, at the Gilbert house. Like Elena in this episode, food didn't satisfy Vicki, she was sensitive to light and noise, and her teeth felt super freaky. In that season one episode, Elena told Jer, "It'll be fine. It'll all be fine," just as she tries to reassure him now.

Elena describes the consequences of Bonnie's previous appeal to the witch spirits as "horrible." When Bonnie brought Jeremy back from the dead in "As I Lay Dying" (2.22), there remained a residual crack between the world of the living and the Other Side that led to (among other things) Esther's resurrection and, eventually, to Alaric's death.

Bonnie used dark magic in "Before Sunset" (3.21) to stop Jeremy's heart in order to perform a desiccation spell on Klaus; she does the same to herself here in an attempt to drag Elena back from near death.

Tyler Cook on Editing for *TVD*

Everything in editing is situational. You make the best decisions based on the footage that you have. Within that, though, there is a certain feel that you have to achieve. We often talk about constructing and maintaining this heightened sense of emotion (these are vampires after all) so the editing has to really support that. Julie and Kevin describe it as having an epic quality. That's really the only "rule." How you do that is really dependent on the scene you are cutting and the way it was filmed. But each editor does have a slightly different style and approaches the show from a different point of view. As far as experimentation goes, I think that there is ample room for that within the framework of the show. I look at the underwater sequence in the finale of season three as a big example of that. They shot *a lot* of film and there could have been 50 different versions of that sequence. But they really empower the editors to be creative and take risks because that's really the only way you can discover something new. No one came in and sat over my shoulder and told me how to construct that sequence. It was my decision on how and when to transition from the present day to the flashbacks, and it was my decision to play it haunting and ethereal. When I dropped in [music by] Sigur Rós on top of the whole sequence, I realized that we had something really special.

    That sequence could have easily been action packed and exciting with drumming music, but I thought we could really capture something bigger than that by playing it more emotional and operatic. And, of course, Julie could have said do it the other way but she thought it really worked and I ended up hitting exactly the emotion and tone she wanted, but I was just following my own instincts and trying something different.

As Elena transitions, she remembers what Damon compelled her to forget in "Rose" (2.08), and present-day Elena touches where her necklace would be, just as she did in that original scene after Damon disappeared. The other memory Elena gets back is meeting Damon the night of the car accident with her parents, shown in "The Departed" (3.22).

Caroline and Klaus-as-Tyler's passionate forest makeout was reminiscent of Caroline and real Tyler's reunion in "Heart of Darkness" (3.19).

Pastor Young reminds Elena that she used to read her short stories to his daughter and asks if she still wants to be a writer. In "The Turning Point" (1.10), Elena tells Stefan that writing was once her ambition, but after her mother died, her interest in it waned.

Elena tells Pastor Young that Stefan would never hurt her (and she means it, despite his actions during the season three ripper days, and putting aside the fact that he let her die in "The Departed"). She said a similar thing to Alaric back in "Under Control" (1.18), "Stefan is different. He would never do anything to hurt me."

The Donovans are made of sturdy stuff: in this episode, Damon says of Matt that the "guy just won't die" and in "Lost Girls," he said to a reviving Vicki, "You just don't want to die, do you?"

To thwart Klaus, Rebekah destroys the three bags of blood that were painfully drawn from Elena in "Before Sunset."

The rooftop scene with Stefan and Elena is reminiscent of their middle-of-the-night Ferris wheel moment in "Brave New World" (2.02), which occurred the day Caroline became a vampire. Stefan and Elena say they'll take it "one day at a time," which is what Stefan recommended to Vicki in "Haunted" (1.07).

OFF CAMERA This episode marks the first *TVD* season premiere not written by Julie Plec and Kevin Williamson. Writer Caroline Dries was proud of how it turned out. Her favorite moments include: "all the stuff in the stable between Elena and Stefan and the way their heartbreaking situation was landing on Rebekah," "the part where Elena had to strain to reach the guard's blood so she could feed," and "the moment where Elena stopped Damon from killing Matt and we learned she was a vampire." Julie Plec told *ET Online* that director Chris Grismer called her after filming the scene where Elena strains through her cell bars to reach the blood and complete her transition. "He said it was so spectacular and harrowing and exciting when they shot it, that the crew just burst into spontaneous applause."

According to Pascal Verschooris, "Every season premiere is a challenge because it sets up the tone for the entire season and everyone is more attentive to it, so of course it puts a lot of pressure on us to deliver magic." This premiere was no exception: "It was particularly difficult with the weather. At [Pastor Young's] farm, we had a big showdown, but every time we scheduled this day, we were faced with a storm, rain, etc. We had to constantly reschedule. We finally set up this day as a stand-alone day [outside of the production of the rest of the episode], so that we could adjust to the weather. It worked."

FOGGY MOMENTS In the opening narration, Elena says, "And then there's me. I'm human. At least I was." Except she wasn't, technically: she was a doppelgänger, supernatural enough that the Gilbert ring wouldn't work on her. The council's deputies wouldn't have told Carol Lockwood where they were taking Caroline, so how did Klaus locate the van holding Caroline and Rebekah? Pastor Young wasn't shown in the inner circle of the Founders' Council in previous seasons, and yet he's been a town fixture long enough to know Grayson and Miranda and for Elena to babysit his daughter.

QUESTIONS

- Pastor Young tells Elena that it was Grayson and Miranda Gilbert who advocated for the Founders' Council's emergency plan. How violently anti-vampire were Elena's parents?
- Pastor Young makes a point of saying that they've gathered up the council's vervain supply as well as that at the Salvatore house, and we see a big pile of it on the table at the farm — right before it exploded. Is there no more vervain in Mystic Falls?
- Rebekah destroys Klaus's three bags of Elena's blood — does this mark the end of Klaus's hybrid-making era? What will the estranged Original siblings do now?
- What would have happened if Grams hadn't interrupted Bonnie as she tried to pull Elena's Other-Side self back to the land of the living?
- Jeremy says to Elena that he needs his sister, "not another one of them." Now that Elena is a vampire, how will that affect her relationship with Jeremy?
- Why did Pastor Young hunt down and imprison the vampires if he was just going to blow himself and his fellow council members up? Why did he blow them all up? "We are the beginning," he says. Of what?

Elena: All of the hurt, I feel like it's trying to explode out of me.

4.02 *Memorial*

Original air date: October 18, 2012
Written by: Jose Molina and Julie Plec
Directed by: Rob Hardy
Guest cast: Michael Reilly Burke (Pastor Young), Randall Taylor (Pastor McGinnis)

Mystic Falls mourns the 12 dead council members as Elena struggles with her vampire status and a new formidable hunter arrives in town.

"The challenge always has been and always will be tone. How to keep it honest, grounded, and real in the midst of some pretty extraordinary circumstances." So said Julie Plec when asked what was the greatest challenge in creating *The Vampire Diaries*. And "Memorial"? It's a master class in how to combine the heartbreakingly human with the action-packed supernatural without sacrificing a drop of the impact of either element. This episode reaches back to the series' thematic roots in its exploration of grief and loss, while racing forward with Elena's transition story and the problem of a new slayer in town. "Memorial" also manages to toss in the sexy, the funny, and the traditional genre moments. Plus Elena barfs a ton of blood.

In addition to being horrifying, Elena's inability to keep blood down — but her shocking proficiency at bringing it back up — hits at the heart of one of the episode's subtler threads: the stark contrast between an idyllic hoped-for best scenario and the harsh and dark reality. Stefan wants Elena's transition to go smoothly — bunnies and bubbly and romantic getaways in the forest — but what it descends into for her is sickness and starvation followed by secrets and lies. In the same vein, April Young is nervous before the memorial, hoping that people will say nice things about her dad at his funeral despite the circumstances, that he'll be beautifully remembered for his life, not his death. Hope for a successful memorial takes a backseat as she lies bound and gagged and gushing blood, as Tyler is shot and the service descends into chaos.

Driving the action and ratcheting up the tension are two traditional vampire-story plot lines: there's a slayer in town and there's a newly turned vampire having "adjustment issues." Connor's presence in Mystic Falls makes it even more treacherous territory for newbie vamp Elena. While, of course, this is a show about vampires, it rarely walks the well-trod path of vampire stories, and here too we get a spin on the usual tale: the determined lone-ranger slayer is not the good guy, he's the enemy. The one chasing down monsters, devising clever booby traps for his formidable foe, and attacking without hesitation is not the protector of the innocent but a guy willing to gut April Young at her father's funeral in order to draw out the vampires he knows are in attendance. This is a man who barges into the mayor's mansion and shoots Tyler in his own front hall. He's relentless, vicious, and *strong* (if Damon's failed attempt to go "old-fashioned on the new guy" is any indicator). Connor doesn't operate by the same set of rules as those who've tried to eradicate the town's vampire problem in the past. Whether Connor's human or has a touch of the supernatural, there's inhumanity in his choice to target April and to disrupt the memorial for 12 dead.

Of course, that he does attack at the memorial means there is a dramatic standoff in a church setting, which is a great way to bring in symbols of faith to an agnostic show without making any big statements about whether or not there's a man upstairs (or another one downstairs). Instead, "Memorial" trots out the traditional vampire tropes to both humorous and horrific effect: Damon Salvatore, smirking and sauntering, crosses himself with holy water. Blood drips from the church ceiling into said holy water, while Elena battles a hunger she's never known before. It's about as vampy as you get.

The story of a human becoming a vampire is another cornerstone of the genre, and Elena's transition story takes a different path from those we've seen with Vicki or Caroline, or even the Salvatore brothers in flashback. The intensity of her thirst, her grief, and her horror at herself makes being "normal" — volunteering at the memorial, being a friend to April — a herculean task for Elena. In the opening scenes, she's crying while feeding from the deer (which Stefan assures her is hardy enough to recover) and he sees that her compassion will be her Achilles' heel as a vampire. That struggle is perfectly depicted in Elena's reaction to April: the old Elena could be there for April and help her with her speech, but this Elena wants to take a bite. In the church restroom, it's a veritable bloodbath and Elena is frantic and trapped, terrified by what's happening to her and of being caught. Damon, Stefan, and Elena are all asking the same question: how will she survive this?

The brothers Salvatore have conflicting ideas about how to approach her transition, about the "right" way to be a vampire. Damon thinks that Stefan's method is a cheat, that a vampire cannot find true control of their bloodlust without first going through certain difficult steps, using the analogy of giving a kid a calculator before they've learned basic math. Damon wants to reduce the risk of her going blood-crazy through carefully controlled feeding, but Stefan wants to keep her off the human stuff entirely so she won't have to deal with the guilt of hurting someone. Stefan and Damon also faced off over Vicki in "Haunted"; in the end, she took Damon's way and ultimately ended up dead. While Damon wanted to stake Caroline and get her out of the picture after she turned, it was Stefan who guided her to become the self-possessed model vampire she is today. So it's no surprise these guys butt heads again over Elena, and it seems like Elena is leaning more and more toward Damon's way of being, thanks to her inability to keep anything down save for human blood. But the motivation behind both strategies is the same: neither brother wants Elena to suffer from the other brother's vice. Stefan has a moderation problem brought on, in Damon's opinion, by avoiding human blood, while Damon has finished off a lot of people in his time and, while he has admirable blood control, he lacks compassion, in Stefan's opinion. How to keep Elena from becoming like their darkest selves? If compassion is Elena's Achilles' heel, how will she cope if she hurts someone? Would she flip the switch on her humanity as Stefan fears?

Elena's an "everything's going to be okay" type, and in this episode that manifests in her trying to give Stefan what he wants — a seamless transition to a bunny diet. Faced with a smiley Stefan and a bottle of celebratory champagne, who would mention a blood-barfing session in the forest? And Stefan's made similar choices in the past: he's kept his monstrous side hidden from Elena. What can be a natural instinct in a relationship — to protect the one you love from ugliness — often backfires, as it does here. Elena has always wanted the truth from Stefan, and now, truth is what Stefan wants from her: to share in her darkest and fearful moments, and for her to be open with him. But in "Memorial" Elena feels more able to do that with the "bad brother"; Damon understands her bloodlust without disappointment or judgment, and so she turns to him for an alternative food source and for comfort.

Secret-keeping is a way of life in Mystic Falls. Matt makes a joke about how they'll cover up the memorial shooting with an "altar boy goes postal" story but, as witnessed by the newspaper headline about the Young farm "accident," the powers-that-be in Mystic Falls perpetrate cover-ups all the time, keeping the townsfolk in the dark for the "greater good," to keep the peace. The community is full of secrets, and at the individual level, Elena follows

© Frank Micelotta/PictureGroup

that same instinct and keeps the truth from Stefan. That betrayal creates a seam of tension that runs through the unified, team spirit of "Memorial," and that contradiction breeds pressure, emotion, and consequence.

As much as Damon betrays Stefan by bloodsharing with his girlfriend, and Elena hides her critical problem from Stefan, it's crystal clear how integral *both* of these relationships are to Elena — as are her bonds with her friends. She is part of a true community that cares for and protects its members. (This group within a group is wonderfully represented as they stand separately in the church pews but are able to communicate, thanks to their superhuman hearing.) Damon is there for Elena as she struggles with her hunger. Stefan, in his singularly Stefan way, guides the whole gang toward what they need — a time to grieve. Tyler literally takes one for the team when he redirects the hunter's attention away from Elena. Caroline prevents Elena from making the mistake of a lifetime when she helps her friend control her bloodlust and teaches her compulsion. And dear darling Matt gives her what she needs the most — guilt-free blood straight from the vein — to keep her from falling into the clutches of Connor, the new environmental clean-up man in town. How do you evade a clever and public trap? With a little help from your friends.

In "Memorial," the value of friendship and community isn't only felt in how-to-evade-psycho-hunter scenarios, but in a much more relatable way: in mourning. This is a show filled with corpses, but not so filled with funerals. Season one saw the Gilbert kids faced with the difficulty of going back to normal life after losing their parents, and the essential truth that life goes on even in the wake of loss is brought back to the fore here. With a name that suggests spring and youth and innocence, April Young acts as a sort of avatar of Elena from a year ago — newly orphaned, freshly grieving, scribbling in her journal, and suddenly pulled into a world of blood and horror and secrets. April has to contend with her father's legacy as the guy who "accidentally" killed himself and 11 others, and she's awkward and alone. She doesn't know what to say when people offer her condolences, and has no one to guide her, to model the rites of grieving, and so she's left feeling like "a freak."

As her former babysitter, Elena tries to step up, to act as caregiver and someone who's been through the same kind of trauma. But Elena's increasing bloodlust, starvation, and heightened emotions make it impossible for her to be the compassionate, generous Elena she used to be. Caroline makes the connection between Elena and April explicit: "She's an orphan. Just like you. And she's scared just like you were." What Elena says to April when she compels her — that April will get through it, just like she did — is just what Caroline is saying to Elena in that moment: You'll be okay, you'll survive this, just like I did. The ties that bind these friends, this community, help them through each tragedy. Matt's comment that he wants to "pay it back or forward or whatever" is the Donovan way of saying just that.

And that same spirit is what inspires Stefan to reach out to his friends and give them a moment to grieve, for people they've all lost and for their former selves. Though (nearly) every loss in Mystic Falls has been thanks to supernatural causes, the paper lantern memorial (and Damon's rejection of it) was powerfully relatable to us human viewers. Like for our Mystic Falls gang, life is often too busy for us to acknowledge our own grief, whether for loved ones lost, relationships gone, or (like Elena) imagined futures no longer ours to dream of. And in that moment with the lanterns, Stefan gives his friends a way to manage that grief, which otherwise just builds up beneath the surface. In that ceremony honoring the dead, they embrace what still makes them human and what enables them to keep on going and get through that worst day of loving someone.

In stark contrast to Elena's heightened emotions and her breakdown is

Writer Jose Molina on the Damon Cemetery Moment

I'd have to say my favorite moment [that I wrote in season four] is Damon's "eulogy" of Alaric at the end of "Memorial." A lot of the things Damon says are things I didn't get to say when a dear friend of mine died a few years ago, and it was enormously cathartic to get some of those things off my chest.

As a fan, I always connected with Alaric because he was a grown-up surrounded by children, but he was never superior about his maturity. And you can never go wrong with a bromance between two taciturn guys. The less they say, the more you read into the silences. That's one of the reasons I think the scene worked: Damon never tells Alaric how he feels, he actually does the opposite. He gives him grief and calls him a bad friend, but we all know what he means.

The scene almost never happened. We had something very close to the final version from the very first draft — and I never actually rewrote it — but there was a lot of talk about how to make it more relevant to both the episode and the arc of the season. We ultimately refined Damon's arc in "Memorial" to make the scene fit a little better, but at one point we were just going to cut it from the script . . . which would've made us all very sad. Then, once we figured it out creatively, the production of it almost derailed us. We only had Matt Davis for one day before he had to leave to go join his cult (you know . . . the TV show), and about five minutes before the cameras rolled it started to drizzle. Then rain. Then pour. We did one take of Ian's speech before we had to pull the plug. Rained out on a damn Friday. Luckily, Matt somehow reshuffled his schedule and we were able to shoot the scenes inside on our stage on Monday. But for a while it felt like the fates were against us.

the short scene with Bonnie and Stefan. In the wake of her dark magic spell, she is grieving for her Grams, isolating herself and feeling broken. There is an honesty and subtlety to Kat Graham's performance in this moment, which communicates how quietly destroyed Bonnie is at the thought that she is once again party to hurting her Grams. It is Bonnie's habit to isolate herself in her grief (particularly from Elena), and the way she's holed up alone at home now, even breaking things off with Jamie, speaks to her way of handling hardship.

As for Damon, he doesn't want anything to do with the big group cry. He rejects the paper lantern memorial and claims he is focused on more pressing matters on the to-do list: find the hunter, kill the hunter, figure out who blew up the council. Of course, he doesn't ditch the gang to do any of that; as Stefan says, it's not a list that needs to be tackled that night. Instead Damon continues to mourn in his own way. As he talks to Alaric's grave, drinking his bourbon, he calls the others "delusional" for thinking that prayer or lighting candles or pretending everything will be okay will make anyone feel better for more than the briefest moment. Because the undeniable truth will still be there when it's over: the person you love is gone. That hole is still there. The bar stool at the Mystic Grill remains empty. Though Damon mocks the cultural appropriation of the Japanese lanterns, he's not without his own ways of mourning: he hits the bourbon hard, he makes choices he *might* not have otherwise (a little erotic bloodsharing with his brother's girl), and he talks to his dead friend, because he doesn't want to "consider the alternative" — that Alaric is really and truly gone. (Neither do we, Damon.) Alaric's death means Damon has to carry on living — and taking care of the kids — without him, without the guy who understood his Damon-y ways and loved him for them and in spite of them. And, cue the tears, because this is a supernatural world, and though Damon can't see him or hear him, his buddy is right there with him, always and forever, and missing him right back.

The combination of deeply relatable moments and the tension of the supernatural high stakes was perfectly balanced in "Memorial." Here is a story driven by character and complemented by established mythology — and punctuated by insane scenes of blood vomit. A highlight of the series.

COMPELLING MOMENT Alaric, graveside with Damon: "I miss you too, buddy."

CIRCLE OF KNOWLEDGE
- No Klaus in this episode.
- Connor has a lengthy list of Founders' Council members among his papers; the list includes some familiar names — Giuseppe (misspelled "Guisseppe") Salvatore, William Forbes, and Thomas Keeping Fell; the rest of the names appeared on the registry from the first Founders' Ball seen back in "Family Ties" (1.04).
- Using sky lanterns to memorialize to the dead is a variation of a Buddhist tradition. It is the Chinese who use sky lanterns, not the Japanese as Damon says. The Japanese use floating lanterns, or *toro nagashi*, in the Bon Festival, which honors the dead. *Bon* derives from *obon*, meaning to

Meanwhile in Fell's Church: Bloodsharing

In L.J. Smith's *The Fury*, Stefan and Damon realize Elena needs to feed on human blood or she won't survive her transition; since Stefan doesn't want to hurt or kill an innocent person, he suggests taking Elena to someone who would help her willingly: Matt. Julie Plec revealed to *Zap2It* that Elena feeding from Matt during the memorial service was definitely a book shout-out. "Ultimately, we decided that [Elena's] transition feed should be a stranger, but we wanted to honor this great moment in the books, which is what informed our decision to have her feed from Matt in the second episode."

Bloodsharing plays a critical role in the book series; it's considered a form of intimacy between a vampire and a human. When still-mortal Elena allows Stefan to drink her blood and, in turn, drinks Stefan's blood, there's a clear undercurrent of sex, just as there's a clear undercurrent of sexual assault when Damon threatens Elena's sister so that Elena will drink his blood. When vampire-on-vampire blood drinking is portrayed — Damon attacking Stefan, Katherine with both Salvatores — the act is considered violent and humiliating to the victim. The TV series reimagines bloodsharing as a highly intimate act, which is why Stefan is so upset to learn that Elena drank from Damon.

hang upside down, the painful state the dead are in in purgatory. To ease their suffering, the living must remember the dead and make offerings to them. When the tradition first spread from Buddhist India to China and Japan, it was believed the souls of the dead returned home during this time; they found their way by the light and were guided back to their resting places by the lanterns (traditionally floated down a river) on the last night of the festival.

THE RULES Bloodsharing between vampires is "personal" (read: sexual) for the vampire whose blood is consumed. Caroline tells Elena that the key to successfully compelling a human is to believe in what you're saying.

PREVIOUSLY ON *THE VAMPIRE DIARIES* Stefan and Damon had a "disagreement about process" when they were dealing with newbie vampire Vicki in "Haunted" (1.07): Damon advocated for feeding from humans while Stefan wanted to keep her on a strict diet of animal blood, as he does with Elena here.

As she is here, Bonnie was blocked from doing magic in "Bloodlines"

(1.11) after the trauma of being attacked by Damon (and finding out that vampires are a thing).

The dynamic between Stefan, Damon, and Elena at the memorial plays out like a reverse "Miss Mystic Falls" (1.19): it's Elena who has the secret about her blood-drinking habits, and Stefan who feels betrayed that she was keeping secrets from him. Damon? He's still spilling the beans.

Stefan tells Elena that booze helps with the cravings, but Elena already learned that from Lexi back in "162 Candles" (1.08), who said it makes for "a lot of lushy vampires," and Elena heard it from Stefan himself in "Under Control" (1.18) — granted Stefan was pretty wrecked at that party.

Stefan gathers the gang to finish the memorial service, following the same instinct that Elena had when she held an impromptu funeral for Caroline on her birthday in "Our Town" (3.11); both realized that their friends needed a moment to grieve.

February 4, 1976, is the birth date engraved on Alaric J. Saltzman's tombstone, but Damon's pretty sure it's incorrect. But the date is right: in "Break On Through" (3.17), Alaric's birth date was visible on the paperwork he gave to Elena, just in case something happened to him.

OFF CAMERA April Young, the now-orphaned teenage daughter of Pastor Young, is played by Texas native Grace Phipps. Before being cast on *The Vampire Diaries*, she was best known for her role as Amy, best friend to the main character in ABC Family's *The Nine Lives of Chloe King*, another adaptation from a young adult book series. "What's actually really fun to play about April, and what drew me to her when I first read the part, is that she's not a depressed person," Phipps told *Zap2It*. "She's not a person who goes around blaming. I mean, she's 16, so you're not entirely stable at that point, you're a teenager, but she's not a tragic person, she just got thrust into a tragic situation."

It wasn't until the fourth season of *The Vampire Diaries* that the characters set foot in a church; Julie Plec explains, "This was the first year we allowed ourselves to embrace a tiny bit of spiritual underpinnings. Because after the terribly tragic deaths in the first three seasons, there was something comforting about churches, angel statues, and the like. But mostly we try to stay out of the religion zone or avoid any reference to heaven or hell or god or the devil."

Producers went to great lengths to keep Matt Davis's return as Alaric a secret. "Really, this moment was for us," Plec told *Zap2It*. "Of course it's for fans too, but it was a moment for us to write a love letter to Matt, because he's really such an important part of our family, and will always be. He's part of the heart of *The Vampire Diaries*, he's part of the core." She admitted to *Entertainment Weekly* that the episode's final scene makes her cry. "I cried when we pitched it. I cried when it was written. I cry every time I see it."

FOGGY MOMENTS Elena runs away from Stefan — mid-makeout — and vomits blood, but Stefan doesn't seem to know that when he's later popping champagne and minimizing her feeding trouble. He also doesn't overhear her voicemail for Caroline about "adjustment issues," despite his vampire hearing. At the Young farm, Connor almost immediately looks in the oven and finds the note to April: did the fire department not think to look in there? In Tyler's moving speech at the memorial, he says he learned the importance of teamwork and community as a first grader from Pastor Young, but he must have forgotten by high school because he was a selfish jerk and crappy team player in season one. Elena compels April to believe that people said lovely things at the funeral, but if April talks to anyone about the service, they might just mention that it was awkwardly cut short by Tyler being *shot*.

QUESTIONS
- Mikael fed exclusively on vampires — does that mean that every vamp he fed on, including Katherine and Stefan, experienced the euphoria of bloodsharing that Damon does with Elena here? Or is Mikael exempt from this bit of mythology as some special Original hunter-vampire?
- Why was April sent away from Mystic Falls to boarding school? How did her mother die?
- Jeremy can see Connor's tattoo, but Matt can't. Is the tattoo related to the Other Side, or to black magic, which Bonnie used on Jeremy in "Before Sunset" (3.21), or is it something else entirely?
- What does the symbol on Connor's bullets mean?
- Why can't Elena keep animal or blood-bag blood down?
- What was Pastor Young warning April about in his letter? What "great evil" is headed to Mystic Falls?

Stefan (to Elena): Rage is a really powerful feeling,
but guilt — take it from me — it'll destroy you.

4.03 *The Rager*

Original air date: October 25, 2012
Written by: Brian Young
Directed by: Lance Anderson
Guest cast: Nicci Faires (Heather)

Elena returns to Mystic Falls High and faces Rebekah, the party-throwing mur-
deress; Connor the Vampire Hunter targets high schoolers and hospitals, while
Damon tries to kill him.

Just days after dying, Elena Gilbert returns to school . . . Bad idea? Most
assuredly, but it makes great fodder for an episode about figuring out how to
be "normal" when you feel anything but. In "The Rager," Elena's adjustment
issues continue, and she's not alone.

Relying on Stefan and Caroline to guide her, Elena tries to find a new
way to handle her dramatically changed circumstances. A common enough
problem taken to supernatural heights, Elena's status as high school senior
turned vampire means experiencing things from a new perspective. Her old
makeout spot with Matt is now where she tentatively feeds from him, and
her history classroom is a reminder of her dead guardian. And Elena's emotions can turn on a dime: she is hit with a wave of sadness in Alaric's class,
but in an instant she's seeing red when Rebekah waltzes in. Rebekah offers
Elena a casual peace, by inviting her to the party and suggesting they bury
the hatchet, but Elena rejects it. The two fall into battle mode instantly, and
Rebekah realizes just what an easy target Elena is; it's almost too effortless to
get a rise out of her.

Hats off to the Original sister: she knows how to play this game. When
Rebekah watched Elena and Stefan say their would-be goodbyes in "Growing
Pains," it almost seemed like she had changed her mind about them, but the
continued animosity from Elena's side makes Rebekah ratchet up her aggres-
sion, and we see even more clearly her own stinging isolation. Rebekah tries
to unhinge Elena — taunting her about Alaric's death and about her past
romance with Stefan, smearing blood on her face when there's a hunter down
the hall, and making her sizzle by snatching away her daylight ring — while

Elena gets so riled up as to become murderous. Stefan cautions Elena against giving into the powerful nature of rage: it will feel good to kill Rebekah, but the *very long* lifetime knowing she killed her entire sire line will kinda outweigh that rush. He reminds her that there's a power in deciding someone is not worth it and walking away.

In "The Rager," characters face that choice between getting even or letting it go. After nearly chasing after Rebekah with the white oak stake, Elena comes to see that the way out is to refuse to engage. Once the game stops escalating, gaining little attention and no rise out of Elena, it's no longer fun for Rebekah. Elena intuited this about Rebekah back when Bex was flicking matches at her in the cave in "All My Children": the fun is over when the victim is killed. What's left after that? Emptiness.

And that's exactly what drives Rebekah. Her brother disowned her in "Growing Pains," and she's all alone in her big new house. She's decided (for whatever reason) to try to make a go of it in Mystic Falls, but she has no one. Like April Young who would rather pick up garbage than go home to her own empty house, Rebekah is trying to stave off loneliness by throwing parties and pestering Elena. Her crisis is heightened by the werewolf-venom-dosed beer; her subconscious yearning takes the handsome shape of Matt Donovan, whose forgiveness Rebekah earnestly seems to need. Instead, her hallucination delivers a cutting blow, telling her she's alone because she doesn't deserve love. Rebekah seems truly horrified to find she's torn the heart from the chest of imaginary Matt, revealing how much she cares what he thinks of her. Her situation finds a parallel in Meredith's advice to Damon: don't let your pride leave you all alone.

Elena has a hallucination of her own: of Damon. All her dark, violent instincts make her feel more connected to Damon (despite Stefan's proven capacity to get uberdark and uberviolent). Stefan's control issues prevent him from being "fun" in a vampire way: he can offer her a joyride on the motorcycle and sex, but he doesn't dare go beyond that. Damon's biting "those who can't do, teach" judgment of his ability to be freewheeling and fun-loving is bang on. Stefan wants to teach Elena what it took him "decades" (like maybe 15 of them?) to learn: before she can let go of an emotion, she has to come to terms with it and confront it.

Elena and Stefan individually recognize Stefan's limitations as a tutor for her. Stefan can't take any pleasure in his vampirism for fear of unleashing the ripper, and Elena feels a greater vampire kinship with Damon than with

Stefan. Like Rebekah's hallucination expressing her fear that she's undeserving of love, Elena's flashes of Damon reveal her desire to turn to him for guidance. Nothing like werewolf-venom hallucinations to reveal a girl's secret feelings! And with Elena's attack on Matt, and Damon's timely intervention, it seems like her wish is coming true.

Stefan, meanwhile, is on the same mission as last episode: to help Elena enjoy her transition — without guilt or regret or murder — but he's up against Rebekah's attempts to make Elena lose her mind. How do you sublimate extreme feelings? Finding a way to do that is a part of being human, and a bigger part of being a vampire who holds on to their humanity, rather than giving into impulse. As the poster behind Jeremy in the math classroom advises, "Don't Hate, Calc-ulate!" Matt is willing to be a "human blood bag" because he feels he owes Elena his life, and he doesn't hesitate to help her survive, hoping like Stefan to ease her transition. With Rebekah, Matt shows his own ability to hold a grudge. He does not let her off the hook for causing the crash that turned his best friend into a vampire. He stonewalls her, and then he lies, naming her as the vampire who's been feeding on him to Connor (a nice, non-fatal payback, since Matt knows Rebekah can't be killed). But in the process of getting revenge, Matt unwittingly puts his friends in danger.

To Klaus, Tyler first suggests they "call it even." Yes, he and his friends tried to desiccate Klaus and throw him in the ocean, but Tyler's body was used as a vessel in which Klaus made out with his girlfriend. But Klaus won't call a truce. He sees an opportunity with the arrival of Hayley, who may or may not have had a fling with Tyler in the Appalachians as he was breaking his sire bond. Klaus is pleased to have a secret to lord over Tyler, one that could lend him an advantage in his ongoing interest in Caroline.

Klaus was halfway to Chicago when he returned to protect the last of his hybrids, and he has a twisted sense of paternal duty that runs parallel to Damon's "taking care of the kids" joke from the previous episode. A sense of duty also drives Damon's actions in "The Rager." Damon wants to leave town but can't until the threat to his loved ones has been dealt with.

Without Alaric, Damon doesn't have a go-to buddy for his investigations, and in "The Rager" he's reaching out to a variety of people, since he and his brother are at odds. He calls up Meredith when he's stuck in an explosive situation (good use of her surgical skill set, really), he rings up Tyler for a wingman (perhaps impressed with Tyler's stand-up action at the memorial), but in the end winds up stuck with Klaus. Despite Elena's protestation,

Damon doesn't hesitate to rope in Jeremy (and Meredith) to his trap-the-hunter-at-the-hospital plan. And it very nearly works. He's developed relationships — maybe not *friendships* — beyond Stefan and Elena, people who will step up and fight alongside him and trust him.

Of course, Damon's still doing everything Damon-style — unnecessarily dangerous and maybe not as effective in the end as he hopes. (Like, did he even look for remnants of Connor post-explosion, or what?) But as Meredith says, he's being a good brother, and by the end of the episode he decides he can't leave Elena behind in his brother's care. He tells her not to feel ashamed of the feelings she's having, or of how she lost control while feeding on Matt; that kind of impulse-control issue, that darkness, is part of being a vampire. Damon sees that *he* needs to help her learn how to be a vampire. Instead of leaving town, he'll be helping her adjust.

Klaus as Damon's wingman isn't the only strange pairing in this episode. Connor attempts to team up with Jeremy, who is a potential hunter. Oddly, Jeremy opts to join Team Damon and Klaus, putting aside the fact these are two guys who've been responsible for a lot of heartache and death in his life. And by episode's end, Klaus has taken up the protection of Connor (for reasons yet to be revealed) and he shows renewed interest in preserving Elena's life, despite her vampire status.

Just as Damon doesn't turn to Stefan for help nabbing the hunter, Stefan doesn't feel he can turn to Damon for help when he feels his ripper instincts rising. Instead, he turns to Caroline, the vampire who wobbled at first but quickly found her balance, and her control, thanks to Stefan's guidance. She seems touched and honored to be able to return the favor, happy to be there for the Salvatore who guided her to a happy afterlife. Will Damon be able to do the same for Elena?

COMPELLING MOMENT The two solid friendships showcased here: Caroline and Stefan, and Elena and Matt.

CIRCLE OF KNOWLEDGE
- No Bonnie in this episode.
- "The Rager" is also the title of an excellent season two episode of *The O.C.*, which features a huge party and a near-death.
- When Klaus meets Hayley he calls her a "new face," and in reply she calls him "an old one," which, in addition to a comment on Klaus's

extreme senior citizen status, happens to be the term L.J. Smith used for "Originals" in The Vampire Diaries books.

- Stefan and Elena are such goody two-shoes: they wear helmets on their motorcycle joyride, despite the fact that as vampires they can't die or suffer any permanent injury from a crash. But they're actually still breaking Virginia state law, which requires motorcyclists to have a face shield and safety glasses or goggles in addition to the helmet.
- Interrupting April's conversation with Elena, Rebekah finishes April's sentence with "something wicked this way comes." The Original sister is quoting Shakespeare's *Macbeth* (1606). In act IV, scene 1, the second witch says, "By the pricking of my thumbs, something wicked this way comes." The witch prophesies correctly and, judging by that creepy letter Pastor Young left for his daughter, Rebekah will be right too.

HISTORY LESSON The chalkboard in Alaric's old classroom displays that day's topic of discussion, next to a map of northern Virginia: Sherman's March to the Sea, a.k.a. the Savannah Campaign (November 16–December 21, 1864), conducted by the Union Army's Major General William Tecumseh Sherman and a famous example of a scorched-earth policy. After capturing and setting fire to Atlanta — which Katherine Pierce used as a cover story when she arrived in Mystic Falls in 1864 — Sherman's forces moved toward Savannah, Georgia, destroying much of the South's infrastructure and civilian property along the way. The March ended with the capture of Savannah, one of the South's major port cities.

Behind Stefan and Elena is a poster for "The Great Meeting" in Union Square, New York City, also known as the Great Sumter Rally. After the Confederacy captured Fort Sumter in Charleston, South Carolina, on April, 13, 1861, public gatherings to display Union loyalty were common, the largest taking place in New York City's Union Square on April 20, 1861. In addition to being a decisive show of Union support when Northerners were still actively debating how to treat the rebelling South due to economic interests, the rally attracted more than 100,000 people and was the largest public gathering America had ever seen.

THE RULES Connor explains that only a hunter or potential hunter can see his otherwise invisible tattoo, meaning Jeremy is a potential. Connor quips that he's faster than the average hunter, providing further evidence that he has

supernatural status of some sort. Rebekah is certainly affected after ingesting the werewolf venom (she gets woozy, weak, veiny, and she hallucinates), but she's not in (im)mortal peril. Only the white oak stake can kill her.

PREVIOUSLY ON *THE VAMPIRE DIARIES* In "Before Sunset" (3.21), the boys made a deal: whoever Elena didn't choose to be her #1 love would leave town, a promise that Damon is ready to make good on . . . just as soon as he does a bunch of stuff.

The Mystic Falls students have been using the same American history textbook since their first class with Alaric Saltzman in "History Repeating" (1.09).

Rebekah takes on Elena in this episode after a similar territorial standoff with Caroline in last season's "Smells Like Teen Spirit" (3.06).

Elena tries to use a pencil against Rebekah but the Original sister neatly darts it into Elena's shoulder, ruining her cardigan; Rebekah's big brother Elijah also used a pencil-as-weapon to excellent effect in "Crying Wolf" (2.14).

The last time Jeremy had a meeting with a secret vampire hunter in a MFHS classroom was in "History Repeating," but Alaric dumped the file on Little Gilbert in the trash to give him a clean slate, rather then keeping it like Connor does. But Connor also assigns some extra credit homework: bring him a vampire.

Hayley references the time Tyler spent in the Appalachian Mountains breaking his sire bond after the events of "The Ties That Bind" (3.12).

Just as Stefan talks Elena out of staking Rebekah here, in "162 Candles" (1.08) Elena stops Stefan from killing Damon after Lexi is murdered. Both argue that it's not about protecting the intended target but about saving the would-be killer from what the guilt would do to them.

Elena had a Stefan-turns-into-Damon makeout dream in "Friday Night Bites" (1.03), and she has a similar hallucination here thanks to werewolf venom.

Klaus's hilarious line, "for future reference, one voicemail is just as effective as nine," speaks to Stefan's proclivity for hitting redial, which we first learned about in "Fool Me Once" (1.14) when he left Damon "600 voicemails" after Anna kidnapped Elena.

Caroline refers to her old human self as an "insecure control freak," in a nod to her conversation with Stefan in "Bad Moon Rising" (2.03) where she called her newbie vampire self an "insecure, neurotic control freak on crack."

Damon promised to help Stefan stay away from his ripper tendencies in "1912" (3.16).

OFF CAMERA New wolf in town Hayley is played by Australian actor Phoebe Tonkin, who costarred with Claire Holt in *H2o: Just Add Water* and played fan-favorite Faye on another Kevin Williamson adaptation of an L.J. Smith book series, *The Secret Circle*. Phoebe didn't hesitate to accept the role of Hayley. "I'm so attracted to the supernatural world, the unknown world," she told *The Insider*. "I find that so fascinating. I got into acting to tell stories and be a kid again and use the part of your imagination you can't use as an adult. And I'm such a huge fan of Kevin Williamson, I would do anything for him. To be part of something he created, is so popular, is so well written, and has such a big fan base — there was no question to joining." Claire Holt, who is Tonkin's best friend, was also thrilled. "When I found out she was coming on the show I don't think I squealed more loudly in my life," Holt told *Screen Spy*. "Ever. And I was on set. It's so great." As for the character of Hayley, Tonkin told *TV Line*, "She's a free spirit. She's kind of ballsy. She's different from what I've played before." And Tonkin teased, "She's hiding a secret, and she's trying to find out something very important to her that we're going to [discover] eventually."

While Damon may think he has a new Alaric-style buddy in Dr. Meredith Fell, Torrey DeVitto stressed that Meredith is thinking about work, not being an Alaric replacement. Still, DeVitto likes their dynamic, as she told *Hollywood Life*, "It's cool because he's this erratic character, and she really holds her ground with him and with all the other characters. She's strong-minded and doesn't put up with his bullshit. So deep down, whether he acknowledges it or not, he admires that about her."

FOGGY MOMENTS Why didn't Connor try to kill Tyler after extracting his werewolf venom? Would Stefan (or Caroline or even Elena herself) really let Elena feed on Matt unsupervised? It so obviously and easily could go wrong (and does). April lives alone now? She's an orphan, yes, but she's a minor. It's strange that she could leave her boarding school midway through the year, and not be placed with a family member or the state. Instead she's left to chill out at a rager with a millennium-old vamp.

QUESTIONS

- How did Connor figure out that Tyler was part werewolf? What sort of paralytic did he use on him?
- What happened between Hayley and Tyler, if anything?
- Does werewolf venom have any affect on an average, human, beer-guzzling high schooler?
- Who or what are "the Five"?
- Connor offers to train Jeremy — who trained Connor?
- Now that she's a vampire, how could Elena be useful to Klaus in connection to the Five? Why is Klaus interested in protecting a vampire hunter?
- Will Mystic Falls Hospital name a wing after Damon, assuming he makes his big post-explosion donation?

Klaus: Some secrets are stronger than family.

4.04 *The Five*

Original air date: November 1, 2012
Written by: Brett Matthews and Rebecca Sonnenshine
Directed by: Joshua Butler
Guest cast: Dane Davenport (Jock), Jen Harper (Witch), Michael Lee Kimel (Nate), Jeremy Palko (Frankie), Morgan Pelligrino (Pretty Girl)

Damon, Elena, and Bonnie head to Whitmore College to hunt for coeds and answers, while Klaus schools Stefan on a mysterious group of vampire hunters last seen in 1114.

Taking us the furthest back in time since the flashback of "Ordinary People," "The Five" explores the sibling dynamics of the Originals and the Salvatores, and the formative experiences that shaped the Mikaelsons as young vampires, while Elena learns how to be a newbie vampire in the present day.

Nothing like nearly killing Matt Donovan to help Elena realize something's got to change. In the wake of losing control while feeding, Elena wants Damon to teach her, rejecting the other options of Caroline (too good at self-control) and Stefan (too limited by his ripper past) as potential teachers. As has been established, the brothers act as two paragons of vampirism, each quite different from the other, each with differing philosophies, teaching programs, and ways of handling guilt. Damon believes it's a perk of being a vampire to flip the emotional switch off if the guilt gets to be too much, whereas Stefan fears that state most of all for Elena — that if she is consumed by guilt, she'll turn off her emotions and become lost to the brothers. Where Damon can't be argued with is in his point that vampires are predators; that the feelings and instincts Elena has that are "like Damon" are actually like every other vampire on the show. (Remember Caroline munching chips to sublimate her desire to feed on Elena in "Memory Lane" — "Believe me, it's there"?) It's how you choose to manage those instincts that makes the difference, how close to the edge you dance. For Elena, the trip to Whitmore goes too far, too fast. She's not ready to revel in being a vampire, despite how much pure fun she has and how heady her attraction to Damon can be. Elena is deeply conflicted, thanks to her human moral code and what she wants now that she has bloodlust. So much of her identity stands in opposition to her new instincts and desires. She can't be both Elenas.

Damon's feeding advice is nothing if not practical: see people as a predator does — gauge how receptive they will be to the approach, know who to avoid (stoners, don't want the extra buzz), decide how to do it. But Elena doesn't see people as prey; she sees them as people. That student she approaches has a little sister, and Damon telling her that everyone is a somebody to someone fails to dehumanize the would-be victims. It just makes the whole thing ickier. She still feels for people, and her empathy has only strengthened since her transition, not vanished. What Elena *can* get behind is a little light *Dexter* action: she sees a frat guy roofie the woman he's talking to, and bingo, there's someone who deserves to be punished and stopped from doing the crime he's planning. Damon has to caution Elena to "step away from the ledge" as she feeds without stopping, but with that one bite Elena's ready to dive right into the pleasure/feeding party. She looks happier than perhaps we've ever seen her, and she and Damon are in sync, feeding, compelling, dancing in their own little insular vampire world. It's an experience Elena could never have with Stefan — and one that ends the instant she sees Bonnie and the look of horror on her face. She's brought back to her old human self, the one who would recoil in the same way to see a vampire feeding on an unwilling or compelled victim. As soon as Elena moved on from the roofie guy and started

©Vince Bucci/PictureGroup

compelling and feeding from random partygoers, she lost her vigilante justice excuse; in fact, she's just as bad as the frat boy is.

As Elena takes advice from Damon in present-day, we also see the early days of the Original family's vamping. Elijah cautions Klaus not to cause so much bloodshed that they will be exposed, but Klaus is cocky, welcoming "such infamy," as they watch the original Five kill vampires in the public square. While the vampires the Originals have sired can be killed, Klaus and his siblings cannot — or so they believe — and as a result they lack caution. Klaus and Kol are particularly careless in terms of body count, and in the case of Rebekah, she has no compunction about bedding a man whose sole purpose is to destroy those she and her brothers have created. (A psychiatrist could have a field day with that.) As it happens, the Original siblings are all too trusting when it comes to Alexander and his brethren, and Rebekah falls the hardest — betrayed by her lover for the first time. Klaus mocks Rebekah's romantic failures cruelly, judging her, leeching her happiness and her willingness to love. And that derision stems from the turning point shown in this episode's flashback: once invulnerable, from 1114 on, the Originals know they have a weakness. They can be daggered and left as good as dead. It is from this moment on that the daggers are in Klaus's possession, and (if the timeline can be trusted) not too long from now he uses the first on Finn, keeping the dullest of the Originals locked up and inert for 900 years.

Klaus has consistently viewed love as a weakness — something to be capitalized on in others, and to be trained out of his siblings. In "Klaus," we saw the dynamic between Elijah and Klaus, and the perceived betrayal of Katerina's escape, and here we have a parallel downfall: Rebekah's "foolishness" nearly sees the whole family wiped out. As in past episodes, the sibling-dynamic plotlines complement each other by highlighting the different ways these family members handle fights and forgiveness. Stefan is "over" Damon letting Elena feed on him, but he hasn't forgiven him. Brotherhood trumps betrayal. Klaus, on the other hand, is deliberately obtuse about why he should apologize to Rebekah, justifying his behavior — taking his little sister for granted and patronizing her — as being normal for a big brother. If it weren't for the bloodbath that we witness in the flashback, it would actually be pretty endearing. But the unprecedented rage we see in Klaus during the post-slaughter scene as he harangues his sister reveals how betrayed Klaus was that Rebekah would consider anything more important than family.

Between Elena's learn-how-to-feed road trip and the revelation of Rebekah's past love affair with one of the original Five hunters, there is a common thread of getting so caught up in something that you lose sight of what truly matters to you. Klaus sees total betrayal in Rebekah's choice of love — and the promise of humanity — over loyalty to her brothers, whom she promised to stand beside always and forever. And 900 years later he doesn't seem to be over it, as evidenced by his biting observations about Rebekah's desperate need for love and affection and her "pathetic" trusting nature that leads her into one betrayal after another. That is quite tragic when you consider what we know of Rebekah's history. She's been "killed" by so many people she loves and trusts: her father when he turned his children, her lover Alexander, her brother (multiple times), her mother, even Elena daggered her. And in "The Five," she walks right into Klaus's trap, despite knowing better, despite knowing so well his tricks and manipulations. Klaus uses Stefan, and Stefan uses Rebekah's undying romantic spirit to get from her what they want.

What prevents her character from being a total sap is her ferocity. She is smart, she knows the game that's being played (after all, it has been played for a thousand years), but she refuses to change who she is. She is fundamentally the same as the day her mortal life ended: she loves deeply and desperately and she always will. She has her dibs on Donovan, and it's important to note that she hasn't compelled him. She wants to earn his forgiveness and hopes that he will maybe one day earnestly love her. She won't cheat at something so important. Because as much as Rebekah says she doesn't care about her brother, or the Five, or what people think of her, it's obvious that she cares a lot, perhaps more than most.

Though Rebekah loved Alexander, what made her willing to leave her brothers behind was the promise of a cure. Rebekah sees love as purpose and humanity as desirable. To gain her trust, Alexander tells her what she most wants to hear: that she could be human again, that they would be married, that he loves her. And in the present day, the Cure stands to make other dreams come true. What does Klaus want most? His hybrid army, and the Cure could make that a reality if Elena was made mortal again. What does Stefan want? Elena to be human again. The thing about a story told by a crusading knight who looks like a Disney prince that sounds too good to be true is that it probably is too good to be true. But it's worth a shot.

And Klaus will continue to use people to get what he wants. He's always ahead of the game by a play or two, waiting for others (in this case, Stefan) to catch up. He anticipates how people will react to circumstances or provocation, and he plays them like chess pieces. His strategy is sometimes quite basic: do what I want or you die, as when he kidnaps Jeremy, steals his ring to "incentivize" him, and has him draw the tattoo. It's an effective, if crude, modus operandi. At other times, his tack is more complex and requires an understanding of, if separation from, emotional connection. Klaus has always had a rather gossipy interest in the private lives of the Mystic Falls gang, but there's a practical reason for his snooping: that kind of intel helps him manipulate people. He knows who wants what, who's hurting, and whose happiness could be ripped from under them with a well-targeted threat. He knows how dedicated Stefan is to Elena, and how far he would go to help her: it doesn't take much for Klaus to rope the former ripper into sweet-talking Rebekah into a conciliatory breaking of bread. Though Stefan is forward about the reason he's approaching Rebekah, and Rebekah is wisely cautious — she even tells Stefan that Klaus will "betray you, that's what he does" — both are like rats aware of their experimenter, unable to stop hunting for the cheese in the maze. Stefan demonstrates what he's learned from the master when he offers Rebekah a chance at what she wants in Mystic Falls: a clean slate. He doesn't offer forgiveness because, as with his brother, Stefan doesn't necessarily *forgive* a wrongdoing as much as he moves on from it. Instead, he offers Rebekah a second chance, the opportunity to not be the most-hated immortal teen in town. And when it comes to Matt Donovan, that is a lure Rebekah is attracted to. She wants redemption.

In "The Rager," she tried to apologize, and here she gives Matt a truck to make up for the one he lost in "The Departed." Rebekah is actively working to earn forgiveness from Matt, whereas Klaus is a big believer in bygones: he can act how he pleases, and after the moment of wrongdoing has passed it should be proverbial water under the bridge.

Klaus knows his sister well enough to manipulate her with great precision. When she leaves the dinner pissed, Klaus is unperturbed. It's all part of his master plan. Klaus once again demonstrates his ability to emotionally eviscerate and manipulate Rebekah when he mocks her vulnerability in trusting other men over him, all in an effort to give Stefan a means to get information from her. He deliberately upsets Rebekah and makes her nostalgic about what she lost with Alexander. Basically, he's emotionally primed her to give up the location of the sword to a uniquely positioned informant: her former lover, the endlessly romantic Stefan. Knowing that Stefan won't be able to resist this "deal with the devil," since it means a chance for Elena to become human again, Klaus just sits back and, when the time comes, does the daggering.

But even when she realizes she's been betrayed, Rebekah takes the moment to yell at Klaus, dressing him down the way he did to her. The difference between them is Rebekah is well aware of her "flaws." She knows who she is and she knows the implications of her choices — and they are just as deliberate as his. Where Klaus denies having any need for love, Rebekah admits she would rather give her heart and risk having it trampled than be incapable of loving. She and Stefan believe that, far from being a weakness, love is a strength and it's worth the risk it puts you in.

In the episode where an "ultimate weapon" against vampires is revealed — a cure — and Stefan expresses skepticism that such a thing could exist, we meet Shane, who describes himself as a "true believer" in witchcraft. In Shane's lecture about witches, he calls them the "architects of the supernatural" and Connor's appearance at his office suggests that the professor knows a lot more than the little hints he's doling out to the freshmen in Anthro 101. It's a mysterious introduction of a character: Shane professes to love witches and he knows Bonnie is one, but what is his connection to Connor? And what was his costume for the frat party — killer or victim?

Stefan would be wise to remember that when you make a deal with the devil, you lose more of yourself than you bargained for. It wasn't hard for Klaus to get Stefan back into his clutches, willingly doing his dirty work for him, manipulating and betraying Rebekah. Stefan is already on a slippery slope, showing just how quickly he falls into misdeeds and how far he'll go to fix Elena's identity crisis for her: he's compelled Jeremy, he's allied himself with Klaus, and he's keeping secrets. Though Elena has not blamed him for what happened in "The Departed" (instead she's thanked him for honoring her choice to die so Matt could live), Stefan feels responsible for the suffering she's experiencing. He wants to undo what he did by rescuing Matt, to restore her to the Elena he knows and loves. Interestingly, while Stefan looks for a cure-all, Damon seems to take her crisis personally. To him, it's once again about her choosing between Salvatore brothers — that her disgust after the blood dance is because she doesn't want to be like Damon, she wants to be like Stefan. It's more accurately Elena's own identity crisis about who she used to be, who she now is, and who she will choose to become.

COMPELLING MOMENT Stefan, hilariously annoyed at having to sit through a dinner-table argument between Original brother and sister.

CIRCLE OF KNOWLEDGE
- No Tyler or Caroline.
- In a surprising reference that makes one wonder what Stefan is reading during his downtime, the Salvatore brother comments on Klaus's "red room of pain," a nod to E.L. James's ridiculously popular BDSM erotica novel *Fifty Shades of Grey* (2011).
- The Brotherhood of the Five's symbol (seen on their swords, their hands, and carved on Connor's bullets) appears to be based on the Icelandic magical stave *vegvísir*, which means "guidepost" or "direction sign." Sometimes called the runic compass, the symbol's first recording is in the 17th-century grimoire *Galdrabók*. When drawn on a traveler's forehead in blood, the symbol is said to prevent them from becoming lost. (Fun fact: Icelander Björk has the symbol tattooed on her arm.) The Five's symbol, which begins the map of the hunters' mark, differs slightly from the *vegvísir*: it has six spokes, not eight, and the patterns at each spoke's end vary from it. In keeping with the tradition of last season (where runes were found in the cave in "Ordinary People," 3.08), some kind of angular symbols dot the "branches" of the tattoo (more on those in "Down the Rabbit Hole").
- Damon dresses up as Jack the Ripper for the "Murder House" frat party; the only ripper more famous than Stefan Salvatore, Ripper of Monterey, is the legendary serial killer thought responsible for the Whitechapel Murders of 1888–1891 wherein a number of women were found murdered and mutilated in the London slum. Bonnie and Elena are in costume as two such victims.
- The origin story of the daggers and ash is finally answered . . . in part. Alexander and the other hunters use them against the Original siblings, and Klaus takes possession of the weapons after slaughtering the Brotherhood. This moment marks a key change in the Original sibling dynamics: after 1114, there is a weapon that can neutralize Finn, Kol, Elijah, and Rebekah; Klaus holds that weapon and, as a hybrid, is impervious to it.
- Shane returns Sheila Bennett's first edition copy of Stephen King's *Cujo*, a 1981 horror novel about a good dog gone very, very bad.
- Klaus blames Rebekah for the near death of the family, but the four Original brothers were equally to blame: they knew Alexander and his four brethren were vampire hunters and yet they felt invincible enough

to fall soundly asleep without any protection. Here Klaus makes the same mistake again and underestimates the wiliness of the Five, and Connor escapes.

- San Vittore — the church where Rebekah wanted to marry Alexander, and where she buried him with his sword — is an actual church in Brienno, Italy; its bell tower dates to the 10th century. Standing as it is on the shore of Lake Como, the church would've made quite a picturesque wedding spot.
- In the original pilot script for *TVD*, Damon and Stefan's surname was Whitmore, not Salvatore. The local college gets its name from that abandoned detail.
- Whitmore College must be pretty close to Mystic Falls, considering that Bonnie, Damon, and Elena go there and back in one day; Connor manages to get to Professor Shane's office quickly after his gruesome escape; and Grams used to work there while living in town. Hmmm, any plans for next year, seniors?
- When did the Original siblings leave for the Old World? If Klaus doesn't get his hands on the daggers until 1114, then Finn must have been daggered almost immediately after the events in Italy, since Elijah says in "Bringing Out the Dead" (3.13) that Finn was in a coffin for 900 years. Finn romanced Sage in proto-Mystic Falls (they used to meet up in what became the town square, says Sage in "The Murder of One," 3.18). The way she told the story to Damon, Finn was daggered very shortly after he turned her and, when she related the tale, she was 900 years old. So was Sage also in Italy in 1114?

HISTORY LESSON Klaus tells Stefan that all of the Original siblings followed the Normans to Italy, feeding and turning, as the invaders were conquering southern Europe. The Normans were descendants of Germanic, Norse, and Viking conquerors who settled in a region of northern France called Normandy. The Norman conquest of southern Italy lasted throughout most of the 11th and 12th centuries.

Klaus claims he picked up his torture rack from the Inquisition; though it's unclear which Inquisition he is referring to, the Medieval, Roman, or Spanish Inquisition, all three regularly implemented torture methods in order to suppress opposition to the Catholic Church.

Elijah refers to the Five's mission as "a crusade"; the Crusades were a series of Western European religious military campaigns waged against the Middle East from the 11th to 13th centuries.

THE RULES The Brotherhood of the Five are hunters with supernatural power, created by a witch (just like vampires were). While the original members of the brotherhood had their full tattoos, Connor's grows with each vampire (or hybrid) he kills.

PREVIOUSLY ON *THE VAMPIRE DIARIES* Damon argues to Stefan that Elena needs to learn "snatch, eat, erase" now more than ever, quoting his memorable line from "Haunted" (1.07).

The last time Elena went on a road trip to a college with Damon, Alaric was the third wheel and they headed to Duke back in "Bad Moon Rising" (2.03).

Klaus is a big believer in letting bygones be bygones, at least when it comes to *him* doing horrible things, as he expressed to Stefan in "Homecoming" (3.09) and repeats here to Rebekah at the Grill.

Damon has a "thing" for sorority girls; he brought a gaggle home in "A Few Good Men" (1.15). He also mentioned his college days in "Bloodlines" (1.11), saying he was more into hanging out on campus (with witch Bree in the late '80s) than about attending classes.

In "Haunted," Grams described herself as the "kooky lady who teaches occult at the university," and finally we meet her replacement, Professor Shane, teaching Anthro 113: Introduction to Occult Studies.

Stefan suffered through another dinner party filled with sibling tension at Klaus's mansion back in "Bringing Out the Dead."

Klaus's words to Rebekah about Alexander recall Kol's annoyance with her in "Dangerous Liaisons" (3.14) when she changed her mind about killing Matt: "Don't tell me you like this boy. What did he do? He gave you five seconds of his attention? Don't be so predictable, Rebekah."

Rebekah asks Alexander, "Do you really believe [vampires are] all so evil they must be put down?" in a manner reminiscent of lovestruck Stefan asking his father — another hunter of vampires — if all vampires are evil in "Children of the Damned" (1.13). Both are betrayed by someone they love.

OFF CAMERA Professor Shane, a.k.a. Professor Creepy, is played by Canadian actor David Alpay. Alpay had small roles on *Dollhouse* and *Fairly*

Director Joshua Butler on "The Five"

On his approach to flashback episodes: What I love about *The Vampire Diaries* is that it really does ask a metaphysical question of the viewers: How would you live and love if you had a lifespan of hundreds, thousands, millions of years? Because so many in the show are struggling with the question of immortality, there is a wonderfully fluid sense of time in the series narrative. For that reason, I approach flashbacks exactly as I approach present-day scenes. From a directorial perspective, even though the costumes and locations are evoking a historical time period, the characters are exactly the same. They may be in a different place emotionally in the past, but thanks to the brilliant writing on the show, their struggles are the same as in the present.

On the fiery creation of the Five in the teaser: David Fletcher, the show's brilliant special effects coordinator, protects the actors with flame retardants and then creates that fire on set, always being mindful of the actors' safety. In the opening sequence of "The Five," we were able to safely create the circle of fire and take the flames halfway up the swords. CGI was only needed to augment the fire we shot, and that's what makes the moment feel authentic. It is always more convincing to capture real flames on film if possible, instead of creating fire from scratch in a computer.

On his favorite character moments in "The Five": I absolutely love the relationship between Klaus and his sister, Rebekah. When you put Joseph Morgan and Claire Holt in a scene together, magic just happens. They are so focused and constantly challenging themselves to find new layers in that complex relationship. One of my favorite scenes in "The Five" is when Rebekah wakes up and realizes that Klaus has slaughtered her lover, Alexander. There is something so primal about Joseph's and Claire's performances in that scene. As a director, it was all about allowing them to try different nuances — and in Joseph's case, about finding the right moment for him to lose his temper. In that scene, Julie Plec wanted to see Klaus the most enraged we'd ever seen him in the series thus far, and that was a fun challenge to take on with Joseph.

I am also a member of Team Klefan, as the shippers would say. Klaus and Stefan have such a great chemistry together. I think it is one of the greatest bromances of all time.

On torturing a hunter: Todd Williams was such a trooper. Thankfully, our production designer, Garreth Stover, created a very user-friendly torture rack. Todd could get in and out of that device fairly easily, and we certainly tried to give him as many breaks as possible between camera setups. The rest is Todd's brilliance as an actor. He really sold the torture beautifully, if you will.

On the Damon-Elena bloodlust dance: I really enjoyed working at the Murder House location. Once Garreth Stover transformed the place into a wildly convincing college Halloween party — and director of photography, Dave Perkal, did his magic with strobe lighting effects — I was able to focus on the "blood dance" between Damon and Elena, which was one of the most enjoyable sequences I've ever directed on the show. It showed how erotic a connection would be between two vampires who were physically attracted to each other and also bonding over their bloodlust.

On the major mythology moments: It was such a pleasure to be able to introduce the Cure in "The Five," as well as introducing the character of Professor Shane to the series. David Alpay and I were tasked with making sure the *TVD* audience accepted Shane, liked him, and then suspected him of having a much larger agenda. David is a wonderful actor and a fun guy to be around, so we had a lot of laughs experimenting from take to take with what ultimately took shape as a fully formed character. The same goes for Todd Williams, who made Connor so memorable that he continues to be a fan favorite. I'm so proud of both of them.

One of the most exciting things for me about *TVD* is that no matter what episode I am directing, there are always big stories and big moments. A critic once wrote that every episode of *TVD* feels like a season finale. That commitment to wowing the audience and constantly changing the game is what Kevin Williamson and Julie Plec set out to do from day one. They have made television history in the process, in my opinion.

Legal, but is perhaps best remembered for recurring roles on historical dramas *The Tudors* (as Mark Smeaton, Anne Boleyn's confidante) and *The Borgias* (as Calvino, one of Lucrezia Borgia's suitors). "If I had one word to describe what [Bonnie] feels when she sees Shane, it would be intrigued," Kat Graham told *LA TV Insider Examiner*. "This is a very educated person. And the last person that really knew what they were talking about when it came to anything really about the witch culture and all of that was her grandmother. She's basically had to teach herself Witch 101." In an interview with *Hollywood Life*, Alpay weighed Shane's motives: "The funny thing about this show is that even someone like Klaus, who's seemingly so evil, does the things he does for a reason. I don't even know if Shane is evil, to be honest. It's a little ambiguous; we're not really sure, and I think that's a big credit to the writing, which is getting more sophisticated as the seasons go by. The audience is demanding it. They want something more than just what you might see in a vampire movie."

Alexander, long-dead member of the original Five and Rebekah's erstwhile love interest, is played by Scottish actor Paul Telfer. No stranger to flashback wigs, Telfer has had roles in several period films, TV movies, and miniseries, including *Young Alexander the Great*, *Spartacus*, and *Hercules*. He's also had recurring roles on *NCIS* and British TV series *Hotel Babylon*.

FOGGY MOMENTS Why didn't the 1114 A.D. vampire released into the sun run at vampire-speed into the shade? Poor survival instincts! Don't frat boys live in the frat house, thereby making it a residence a vampire cannot enter without explicit invitation? In "Family Ties" (1.04), the Salvatores needed to be invited into the Lockwood house, even with the party going on.

QUESTIONS
- Elena can't keep anything down but blood from the vein, and she says to Stefan, "Call it the doppelgänger curse or whatever." What about Miss Katherine? She's capable of drinking from a bloodbag, but then she's also proven herself capable of tolerating poisonous vervain. So has she overcome her "doppelgänger curse" . . . or did she never have the problem Elena does? Is Elena clutching at straws?
- Stefan says that Connor can't be compelled — is that because the hunter is on vervain, or is it part of his supernatural skill set as one of the Five?
- What exactly did Klaus do in Italy and Kol do in the East to inspire stories about the Original vampires?
- Who was the witch who created the Five with her "dying breath" (and with fire, magic, and lightning)? How did she choose her five hunters? (What were her criteria other than being totally buff?) Did she forge the daggers? Since someone must have supplied the ash from the white oak and have known the Originals' weaknesses, what or who is the Mystic Falls connection to the dying witch — is it Ayana?
- How did the Five figure out that their marking was a map to a cure for vampirism and how did they learn about the Originals? Why isn't Connor's tattoo fully formed like the original hunters' tattoos were?
- Five hunters and five daggers created for five Original siblings . . . but what about their father, Mikael? Was he involved in commissioning the

daggers and ash or the creation of the hunters? Or did the witch who made the daggers and ash somehow know that weapon would be useless against Klaus thanks to his hybrid nature?

- How does Professor Shane fit into this puzzle? He tells Bonnie he's not a witch but he has alternative ways of practicing, and he holds enough sway over Connor that he follows his order to go to Mystic Falls. Is Professor Shane a member of the Five or perhaps a mastermind behind the brotherhood?
- Have there been active members of the Five for the past 900 years? Is Connor the only hunter or are there four others out there he doesn't know about? Did Connor's military buddy who trained him die, and was it his death that precipitated Connor's hunter mark?
- Is it Jeremy's "true destiny" to become one of the Five? Why Jeremy in particular and why now? How are potential hunters chosen?

Connor: A vampire's like a loaded gun. Eventually it's going to go off.

4.05 *The Killer*

Original air date: November 8, 2012
Written by: Michael Narducci
Directed by: Chris Grismer
Guest cast: Blake Hood (Dean), Michael Lee Kimel (Nate)

Professor Shane starts working his mojo on Bonnie's juju. Connor takes Jeremy, Matt, and April hostage at the Grill. And the Salvatore brothers clash over how to handle the situation . . . until Elena handles it herself.

Some brothers twist each other's arms until they say uncle. Others punch through their brother's rib cage, grip his heart, and force out his deepest secrets. Ah, *The Vampire Diaries.* In "The Killer," the primary questions are who's in charge of this situation and what are the motivations driving their actions? It's clear as mud for the characters, as secret endgames and alliances fuel a violent showdown. Stefan's working with Klaus. Connor's working with Shane, who has some (probably nefarious) plan for Bonnie. Five episodes in, and season four is already proving to be a rare hybrid: a return to some of the themes of early season one — overtly signaled by the "Dear diary" duet and candle-lighting moment in this episode — while exploring much darker, more violent territory, where a philosophy of "by any means necessary" is put to work, and its dangers are revealed.

One thing is clear from top to bottom: Elena is living for her brother, and only wants to protect him. Turning again to her journal after her own death as she did after the death of her parents, Elena's diary voiceover tells us explicitly how far gone she feels, and the visuals reinforce that: she is shown in reflections and in tight spaces with dark frames around her. If it wasn't for Jeremy, she writes, she would give up and end it. It's a serious threat that remains unknown to those around her since she confides the sentiment only to her journal — but that desperation fuels her actions in "The Killer." Elena's and Stefan's states of mind run parallel, as evidenced by their diary-duet voiceovers: both are resolved, despite the hardship that lies ahead, but where Elena feels hopelessness, Stefan feels hope.

Though Elena is keeping her "shame spiral" from Stefan, what he's keeping from her brings them to a crisis of trust. Jeremy's anger at being compelled — again — is instant and palpable, and thankfully, for once, Elena had nothing to do with it. Instead she shares his anger at the betrayal, realizing that she too has been kept in the dark as her brother was made vulnerable to abuse and attack. The bond the Gilberts share is one of the show's foundations, there since the beginning of the series, though not without its tests. Each Gilbert kid is now marked as a killer: one of humans, the other of vampires — a setup for a future supernatural sibling showdown if ever there was one.

With "danger magnets" Matt and April at the Grill as hostages along with vampire-hunter potential Jeremy, the question of how far each character will go in the name of what they value most is explored, each motivated by a tenuous balance of hope and desperation. Stefan must keep the secret of the Cure and keep Connor alive — fighting for his endgame of redemption for Elena. But the newbie vamp is focused on her little brother's safety: being Jer's only family is Elena's defining role, and it's what's keeping her from giving up. It's for her brother that she becomes the titular killer. The danger in adhering so closely to one goal, one mission, is nowhere more apparent than in Connor, who puts his faith in his hunter's mark, believing that if only he completes it, he'll discover the true purpose of a life spent killing vampires — including his best friend. For Connor, the world is clearly delineated:

vampires kill humans, hunters kill vampires; making a deal with Stefan, a vampire, is not an option, no matter how desperately he wants to learn about his mythological history as one of the Brotherhood of the Five.

The competing motivations and guarded secrets lead to an explosive showdown. Like a scene out of a Western, Connor orchestrates a showdown at sunset, drawing the vampires to the Grill with intent to kill them. With the camera low at ground level as Stefan crosses the deserted town square, and Elena peeks through the blinds from the window across, the visual language of a Western comes into play, and it kicks into high gear when bottles explode behind the bar as Connor shoots and Stefan dives for cover in a modern-day equivalent of a saloon shoot-out.

While Shane schools Bonnie, Connor schools Jeremy, teaching him the ropes of being a hunter, simultaneously threatening his life and those of his loved ones. Since he's a former military guy of some description, Connor's used to taking orders and not asking questions, but he wants to "finish his mission" and Shane's keeping Connor in the dark to string him along. Instead of finding answers, Connor ends up in a dank cave far from home with his neck snapped by the "enemy" — a girl who wants to protect her family and her home against a violent attack. So was Connor ultimately wrong to trust Shane? Did he send him, like Klaus did with his hybrid, on a suicide mission to protect his own self-interest?

While Connor wouldn't negotiate with a vampire (or a vampire sympathizer), Stefan has made a pact with Klaus — former enemy #1. But all the secrets, betrayals, and discoveries are powerless, as always, to truly shake the bond between the Salvatore brothers. Damon nearly tears Stefan's heart from his chest in search of the truth, but by episode's end he is signing up for a quest he doesn't believe in to achieve a result he has no personal interest in. Though Klaus suggests at the beginning of the episode that once Damon knows about the Cure he won't be interested in helping because he'd like Elena to stay as is, Damon is frank about the help he offers his brother. It's for Stefan's sake; Damon himself likes Elena either way. It is an on-point question that Damon asks of his brother: can Stefan love Elena as a vampire? Their relationship grew from Stefan's admiration of her humanity, and it's been clear from the past five episodes that he is desperate for her to hold on to it. Where does Stefan's motivation to cure Elena of vampirism truly lie?

The question that goes unasked is what will Elena want for herself: Stefan sees in her suffering a clear indication that she'll want the Cure, but he makes an assumption there, and he dismisses the immediate necessity of protecting Jeremy, which is Elena's only priority. While the episode ends with only Damon in the loop and not Elena, the betrayal Elena already feels is stark.

Both brothers boss Elena around throughout this hostage scenario, but it's the first time since she has turned vampire that she decides to take things into her own hands. She's been training; she wants to rescue her brother and destroy Connor. And she shows Damon that he is underestimating her. Besides being a nice recall of the "way to a vampire's heart" moment from last season, Elena proves to Damon she can tackle him like a pro, and he responds by just slightly adjusting her aim, so she would hit the heart. It's a moment that is later echoed when Elena goes up against Connor in the caves and he misses his target, leaving him susceptible to a little neck-snapperoo. She is a new vampire, with less experience and strength than either Salvatore, but it's nice to see her in an active role now that she has supernatural skills. Double-edged sword, of course: if you want to be on the battlefield, you have to wage battle. And Elena does. When her pleas don't work, she springs into action, and ultimately is the one to kill Connor.

On a show where the kill count is so high, it was refreshingly honest to see Elena so destroyed by the fact that she killed someone. Despite the fact that it was an awesome death scene — her "You missed" was such an action movie line — the aftermath shows how human and how sane Elena still is. That's the way you should feel after snapping a man's neck: horrified and like you've betrayed who you are. *TVD* has shown us again and again that if you put a character in terrible circumstances, they will do terrible things, and after three seasons it's Elena's turn to prove how dangerous she can be. However much it was an act of self-defense, and done in protection of her little brother, Elena is gutted.

Another thread to this episode relates to the resistance the characters have to being told they *have* to do something. Damon's "I don't want to. I don't have to. Not gonna" perfectly encapsulates the general attitude of willfulness, and it's echoed by Caroline who kicks back with a "You don't tell me what I *have* to do" in her anger over the Tyler-Hayley situation. But in a more fundamental way, free will is exactly what Tyler and Hayley are after: thanks to the sire bond, Klaus has the power to force his hybrids to do his bidding — even when it means walking into certain death — and they plan on freeing them from that fate.

© Chris Hatcher/PRPhotos.com

Thanks to the help of the ambiguous Professor Shane, Bonnie earns her own freedom, declaring that she doesn't have to be afraid of the spirits anymore. Though she doesn't mean it at first, as she repeats the mantra its meaning sinks in and liberates her from that fear. While Matt never stops trying to get April safely out of the Grill, he and Jeremy truly liberate April when they give her the vervain bracelet in the aftermath of the showdown. Jer knows all too well what it's like to be manipulated and confused, to feel like you've lost a part of yourself to compulsion, and he safeguards April from that fate.

COMPELLING MOMENT The conversation between Stefan and Damon in Stefan's room at the end of the episode — adversarial but full of brotherly love, funny but getting to the heart of the tension between them, and of course punctuated by sips from bourbon-filled tumblers.

CIRCLE OF KNOWLEDGE
- Bonnie is flipping through Professor Shane's book, which is entitled *Book of the Occult*. One of his *three* books.
- Shane tells Bonnie that Aborigine spirit guides turned him on to the magic herbs he encourages her to drink as tea. Though "aborigine" is a general term for people, plants, and animals that are native to a country or region, the term is more commonly associated with the indigenous people of the Australian continent. Traditional Australian Aboriginal spiritual beliefs, called The Dreaming, are based on the worldview that everything in nature (animals, plants, minerals) possesses a spiritual essence.
- Shane uses a kind of hypnosis therapy on Bonnie. Developed in the 19th century and often dismissed as "playacting," hypnotherapy sees a subject put into a state where their sensory perception is dulled (Shane uses the repetitive sound of a metronome and some mind-altering herbal tea on Bonnie). Rather than being unconscious, the subject under hypnosis has very focused attention, and the hypnotist can make suggestions or elicit information. Modern hypnotherapy is used for things like helping a patient quit smoking by reducing his or her anxiety around the change in habit. In this witchy-world, it's used to reduce Bonnie's fear of using magic again. The hypnotized state is not dissimilar to that of someone in meditation (which Bonnie says she can't do, despite sitting still for seven hours). In meditation, a person mindfully focuses and maintains a

stillness, blocking out sensory stimuli and changing the level of thinking from the mundane to the divine, the mystical, the present, or nothing at all. Though Bonnie is skeptical, Shane proves able to un-block her in one very long session, and she lights the candles in the room with her mind.

- Hayley gets a nice little meta-line with her quip to Caroline, "Yeah, I don't do teen drama"; this is actress Phoebe Tonkin's second supernatural teen drama on The CW (the other being *The Secret Circle*), and *TVD* is, of course, created by the teen-drama-loving masterminds Kevin Williamson and Julie Plec.
- Damon refers to Klaus's hybrids as the Lollipop Guild, the tough-looking but confection-bearing trio of singing Munchkins from the 1939 film *The Wizard of Oz*.
- The manner in which new hunters are activated is similar to the slayer mythology on *Buffy the Vampire Slayer* where would-be vampire hunters, all female, are "potentials," unaware of their supernatural destiny until the active slayer is killed. Then one of the potentials gains her power and becomes *the* slayer.

HISTORY LESSON Mystic Falls' vast tunnel structure dates as far back as 1000 CE, when we see Rebekah and Klaus committing Original vandalism on a cave wall in "Ordinary People" (3.08). Elena states that the tunnels beneath the Mystic Grill and the Lockwood mansion were part of the Underground Railroad, a network of secret routes and safe houses for smuggling slaves out of the South and into the Northern free states and Canada. Despite its name and the use of said tunnels, the movement was neither a railroad nor underground; it was a decentralized organization run by abolitionists and allies that began in the early 19th century and was at its height in the 1850s. This raises interesting questions about which Mystic Falls families were part of the Railroad, either as "agents" (those who helped slaves find the Railroad), "conductors" (guides along the route), "station masters" (those who hid slaves in their homes), or "stockholders" (financiers). When Tyler found out about the old Lockwood mansion's "freaky underground cellar" in "Bad Moon Rising" (2.03), Carol clearly implied that the Lockwoods were slave owners in the 1860s, so it seems unlikely the family knew what the tunnels were being used for at the time.

THE RULES Bonnie tells Shane that witches have a natural resistance to manipulation, but he's able to make her remove her earring with the power of suggestion, hypnotize her, and help her regain confidence in using magic. After a hunter dies, the beginning of a mark, invisible to others, appears on a potential hunter's hand (which must be very confusing for those newbies who've not encountered another of the Five).

PREVIOUSLY ON *THE VAMPIRE DIARIES* Elena and Stefan dust off their respective journals in this episode, and we hear their parallel entries in voiceover, harkening back to early season one. Damon also sneaks a peek at his baby bro's diary here, just as he liked to do back in the good old days.

Damon isn't getting an answer from Stefan's phone and so he gets Elena to try calling him, just like he did in "Let the Right One In" (1.17); thankfully, this time Stefan's just being a sketchy (if well-intentioned) liar, and isn't being tortured by angry tomb vampires.

Jeremy is visibly pissed when he finds out he's been compelled again: Damon compelled him in "Haunted" (1.07) after he witnessed vamp Vicki being killed, and Damon messed with his mind again in "The New Deal" (3.10) when Elena decided she needed to send him to family friends in Denver for his own safety. This is the first time he's been compelled by Stefan.

This episode marks the second time Jeremy is shot at the Grill by someone intending to hit a vampire: in the season two finale, "As I Lay Dying" (2.22), Sheriff Forbes accidentally kills Jeremy after werewolf-bite-crazy Damon darts out of the way.

In Shane's office, Bonnie fails to light the one candle she wants to, but all the rest in the room are alight; this is much like the party at the Lockwood mansion in "Family Ties" (1.04) when she unwittingly lit every candle in the dining room.

Jeremy gives April the bracelet he got from his sister, which Stefan gave to Elena for him in "Unpleasantville" (1.12).

Damon maintains a solid skepticism about the existence of a cure for vampirism, just as he did about Elijah's elixir that would protect Elena from dying (permanently) during Klaus's hybrid-activating sacrifice in "The Last Day" (2.20).

OFF CAMERA New York City native Todd Williams had several recurring guest turns on television shows (*Tilt*, *Third Watch*, *In Plain Sight*) before landing the role of the formidable vampire hunter Connor Jordan. "When I initially got the audition, there wasn't much of a breakdown of the character,"

Williams told *Entertainment Weekly*. "All it showed was that he was formerly a Navy SEAL and that he was intense. I didn't know what I was going to be doing on the show until I actually got to Atlanta." While Chris Grismer and Julie Plec gave him more backstory when he arrived, the character was still being developed. "So each episode, I'd find out more information about him, and each time, it just made me more excited because I've never done a character like this before. I remember the first week, I'm getting yanked out of the truck by Ian [Somerhalder], and we're sitting there on the ground, and I'm shooting him, and I felt like an action star. I was like, 'This is so fun.' I was having such a blast."

During a press screening for the episode, writer Michael Narducci explained the importance of Elena's choices, via *LA TV Insider Examiner*: "I've been on the show a while, and something I feel like I've always wanted is for Elena to do more — to not always be the damsel in distress [but] to go out and protect her brother. If Jeremy's in jeopardy, it's very important that we have Matt, the high school sweetheart, in jeopardy, what's Elena going to do? Is she going to wait for all of these other people to get involved to save them or is she going to get involved and do something?"

FOGGY MOMENTS When Connor and Shane talk in his office, Shane seems to know that killing a hybrid would be difficult, and he infers from "lore" that removing the head or heart should do the job. Considering that Klaus is the first hybrid, made active only a very short time ago, how could there be lore on killing hybrids? Is the lore just fiction that happened to get it right? Or does Professor Creepy sometimes just make stuff up?

QUESTIONS
- Is Tyler telling the truth about his plan with Hayley?
- Are there more active hunters out there? Have there been for centuries? How does one find a hunter?
- Will Jeremy keep his mark a secret?
- What is Shane's master plan and how does it involve Bonnie?
- Are Elena's hallucinations fueled by guilt or is an outside force at play?

"Katherine": Maybe it was worth it when you were worth it,
but you're nothing now. You're a monster, Elena. You deserve to die.

4.06 *We All Go a Little Mad Sometimes*

Original air date: November 15, 2012
Written by: Evan Bleiweiss and Julie Plec
Directed by: Wendey Stanzler
Guest cast: Erin Beute (Miranda Gilbert), Ser'Darius Blain (Chris)

Elena is terrorized by the Hunter's Curse, and the creepy professor brings his
occult exhibit (and a lot of useful exposition) to Mystic Falls High.

Though the Salvatores literally lose Elena twice, it's Elena nearly losing her sense of self that's at the heart of this episode. To understate the situation, she's had a rough go of it so far this season, losing a grip on who she wants to be and believing she's a monster undeserving of the love and loyalty that surrounds her. Thanks to the supernatural-strength anxiety attack that is the Hunter's Curse, Elena battles with a very real (if extremely heightened) problem: her worst anxieties threaten to overwhelm her, as she hears the voices of those she's wronged (Connor), those who hate her (Katherine), and those whom she feels she's disappointed (her mother). Elena is racked with self-doubt and self-disgust; her passing mention of suicide in "The Killer" becomes her actual plan as Connor's spirit needles her relentlessly. Thanks to her friends' willingness to do anything for her (more on that below), Elena is saved in the nick of time, and so her journey in this episode is not a tragic one but a necessary one. She is forced to deal with her demons, and when the sun rises over Wickery Bridge, Elena seems more at peace, having waged that battle and nearly lost herself in it. Seems the third time she goes over that bridge really is the charm, and instead of the dawn consuming her, it once again acts as a symbol of a new era — one she begins with Damon.

But what is sacrificed in the name of saving Elena? "We All Go a Little Mad Sometimes" shines a spotlight on the moral failings of our heroes, with Elena at its center, facing the consequence of committing murder for the first time in her life. But it is the solution to that problem — Jeremy killing Chris to free Elena from the Hunter's Curse — and Tyler's furious reaction that really brings to light how far astray the "good guys" have gone. Stefan, Damon, Caroline, Bonnie, and Jeremy frankly conspire to kill someone and then do it. And in the process, they do a favor for the Big Bad by handling Klaus's wet work for him (hybrid Chris had betrayed his boss and broken his sire bond).

Think back on season one's Tyler Lockwood — forcing himself on Vicki Donovan, scrapping with Jeremy, being a dick to his best friend, making out with his friend's mom. Who knew *that guy* would be the one to help strangers, to call baloney on the excuses made to justify actions, to believe that the team he's a part of extends beyond the Mystic Falls born-and-bred, to risk his life to help other "monsters" who have been robbed of free will. Slowly and painfully, Tyler has developed a clear-eyed moral authority, and he knows that the show's red shirts — whose necks have been so easily snapped or hearts ripped out by our two leading men — are just like him, hybrids forced through their sire bond to Klaus to betray their own sense of right and wrong. Why are their lives discarded but the core gang's are preserved? (Beyond, of course, the fact that this is a television show, and cast members tend to stick around a little longer than the silent-on-camera performers.)

As Elena hears a chorus of "you deserve to die" under the torment of the Hunter's Curse, the other side of the question arises: who deserves to live. Even without the excuse of a sire bond, our gang has done some pretty terrible things when forced into a corner (see: Bonnie Bennett, always between a rock and a hard place). What is interesting about "We All Go a Little Mad Sometimes" is Tyler questioning whether survival by any means necessary is really an acceptable strategy. Caroline brushes off Chris's death because he was a stranger to her, but he was a friend to Hayley and to Tyler. As Damon pointed out to Elena in "The Rager," *everyone* is someone's sister or aunt or lover or brother. The dead Connor tells Elena that he had a family himself — a brother and parents who've now lost him, thanks to her. In the *TVD* world, even a serial killer who's brutally murdered countless people is loved and cherished and would be mourned . . . right, Stefan?

One of this series' refrains is that there is always a choice. (In this case, for example, they could have locked up Elena safely in the old vampire jail cell, and waited for Jeremy to make his first kill under less morally shady circumstances. Of course, that would have made for a pretty boring season.) But the poor characters are very deliberately put under time constraints by plot constructs in order to prevent exactly that kind of moral thoughtfulness — those dastardly writers! From the tick-tock of the gym clock, to tight deadlines on supernatural transitions, to villains with zero patience, *The Vampire Diaries* often showcases a frenzy of questionable (or flat-out bad) decisions. Here we have Stefan's willingness to turn a stranger for no other purpose than to sacrifice him (as he texted to Caroline) and Jeremy's decision to behead a hybrid, more or less making him a murderer. All for Elena. The relentless time-crunch is what makes *The Vampire Diaries* famous for its pacing and its ability to blaze through story at three times the speed of other TV shows. But it also makes for some shady, shady choices and some fascinatingly ambiguous characters who are positioned as the show's good guys.

The frenetic pacing and lack of deliberation finds its perfect counterpart in the quiet break-up scene on the porch at the end of "We All Go a Little Mad Sometimes." The gradual breakdown in Stefan and Elena's relationship this season inevitably led to this moment where both are being as honest and grown-up about their feelings as they know how. It's no easy task to admit that what they had hoped for in their forever together hasn't panned out. That dying and becoming a vampire has changed Elena and pulled her away from Stefan — just as his return to being a ripper did last season. They have lied to each other and trust has broken down between them, and the connectedness they once shared has been disrupted. Thanks to the werewolf venom in "The Rager" and the Hunter's Curse here, we've seen what's been haunting Elena when it comes to Stefan: she feels unlike him as a vampire, and the human Elena he loves is gone. It's a sad, beautiful, tragic scene thanks to how in control of their characters Paul Wesley and Nina Dobrev are. A subtle look expresses the complicated reality of their feelings for each other, and hers for Damon, as they sit on the Gilbert porch that has been the site of so many important scenes, facing away from one another.

Whatever the fallout from that breakup will be, it will play out in concert with their uncomfortable alliance with Klaus. He acts in Elena's "best interest" — trying to protect her from the consequence of killing a hunter by locking her up — and, while this cure for vampirism is in play, his endgame aligns with hers. But as much as he wants her alive for future hybrid-making if she becomes human again, there seems to be something personal to Klaus's treatment of Elena in this episode. He "felt time" for those 52 years, 4 months, and 9 days of being psychologically tormented by the five hunters he killed. Is that what makes Klaus so . . . *Klaus*? Suffering from the Hunter's Curse for just one day becomes a turning point in Elena's life, so imagine what it would do to a person over that great span of time. It is within this period that he daggers Finn, which means that the first time he put a sibling in an extended time-out he was under the constant barrage of five hunters, able to take any form (like that of Esther or Mikael or little Henrik) to make Klaus feel unworthy of his existence. Did this experience change Klaus from an impulsive, violently inclined Original to the as-evil-as-it-gets mastermind we know today? This revelation gives us another glimpse of his troubled humanity — like on Caroline's birthday, when he admitted he's thought about ending it once or twice — and it's coupled with his twisted but gallant declaration to Caroline that if he held power over Tyler still, he'd never have let him hurt her.

Klaus further embroils himself in the lives and futures of our beloved Mystic Falls kids, this time with Jeremy, the "next Chosen One." Jer's now a crucial part of Klaus's plot to uncover the Cure, and so he's under Klaus's watch. What the Original hybrid will want, presumably, is for Little Gilbert to kill as many vampires as he can to complete his tattoo, which puts Jeremy on dangerous ground. Sure, the Cure would help undo his sister's vampirism, but becoming a killing machine would require a massive change of attitude in the Jeremy we know. He'd have to dehumanize his "targets" and convince himself they're not worthy of living. In the past, Jeremy has tried on the role of hunter: in "Brave New World," he halfheartedly whittled a stake, vervained Damon's bourbon, and lurked in the Salvatore house ready to attack, but he couldn't go through with it. He's a firm believer that vampires are not evil monsters who deserve final death, as he tried to explain to Connor in "The Killer." Knowing Vicki and Anna, and seeing his sister's experiences with her own undead paramours, has shaped Jeremy into a Gilbert at odds with his family's anti-vampire legacy. He's loved and mourned and fought alongside vampires. With Elena going loco in this episode, Bonnie is the only one who steps up to make sure Jeremy at least has *some* context for his choice: she gives him Shane's file of info on the Five, saying, "You need to know what you're getting yourself into" (by killing a vampire and becoming one of the Five). It's a critical choice that Jeremy makes: his new identity as a hunter, spelled by witches to have extra power and singular purpose, is in conflict with who Jeremy has very consciously decided to be. How can he complete his mark without losing his moral compass? Which vampires or hybrids are fair game in a world where even those who have killed a multitude are forgiven or made into allies?

And to make things ever more complicated, Professor Shane drops the mother lode of mythological exposition during his stop at Mystic Falls High with his traveling occult show (because that's a thing): a guy named Silas

Caroline Dries on Her Fellow Writers

In *Love You to Death — Season 3,* Julie Plec had this to say about co-executive producer and writer Caroline Dries: "[She] has the voice of the show better than anyone I've seen — sometimes better than Kev and me." We asked Dries about the particular aptitudes of some of her fellow *TVD* writers.

- **Brian Young** ("The Rager," "Catch Me If You Can," "Because the Night," "The Walking Dead") has been on the show from the pilot, so he's good at knowing the tone of the show. What works/what doesn't. He has a really good Damon voice. He also tries to make every single sentence into a pun. Usually they're really dumb, but every once in a while it's hilarious.
- **Rebecca Sonnenshine** ("The Five," "A View to a Kill," "She's Come Undone") is really good at details. She's good at tracking things. There are a lot of changes to track and my mind gets overwhelmed, so she's good at managing it all.
- **Brett Matthews** ("The Five," "After School Special") is good at boy stuff — like weapons and hijinks. He also thinks of great one-liners.
- **Elisabeth Finch** ("My Brother's Keeper," "Bring It On") is good at finding little human moments between two characters.
- **Michael Narducci** ("The Killer," "Catch Me If You Can," "Bring It On," "She's Come Undone") is great at the Originals' voices and finding clever turns of phrase. He's great at Damon's voice, too. And he's like a walking Shakespeare, Greek mythos wiki.
- **Julie Plec** ("Memorial," "We All Go a Little Mad Sometimes," "O Come, All Ye Faithful," "Stand By Me," "The Originals," "Graduation") is good at everything — writing, pitching, editing, producing. It's annoying.

was buried alive and left "powerless, immortal, and alone" by a betrayed witch named Qetsiyah. How will this tale tie into the uncovered connections between Shane and Pastor Young (thanks, P.I. Matty Donovan!) and Shane and Connor, not to mention Shane's interest in Bonnie Bennett, and his seemingly limitless knowledge of all things creepy?

"We All Go a Little Mad Sometimes" marks that delightful moment in a season of *The Vampire Diaries* when the disparate plot pieces click together into one super storyline, and push on to the cusp of *something big* before the winter break.

COMPELLING MOMENT The porch break-up. Perfectly, quietly heartbreaking.

CIRCLE OF KNOWLEDGE

- The title of this episode comes from the famous scene in Alfred Hitchcock's *Psycho* (1960), when Norman Bates (Anthony Perkins) sits with on-the-lam Marion Crane (Janet Leigh) in the parlor of the Bates Motel. Of his mother, Norman says, "She's not a raving thing. She just goes a little mad sometimes. We all go a little mad sometimes. Haven't you?" Norman has lost his grip on reality, just as Elena is unable to distinguish between the living and dead, the real from the imagined, under the Hunter's Curse. And for an episode that features a bloody shower scene, a nod to *Psycho* is apt.

- Professor Shane's first name (which he doesn't seem overly fond of) is Atticus, a curious choice for a character who seems to be up to no good. The name Atticus means "man of Attica," a historical region of Greece that includes Athens. In 315 CE, a soldier named Atticus was one of 40 Christian martyrs who were first brought to near death by exposure (left naked on a frozen lake) and then burned at the stake. But the best known is Atticus Finch, the iconic character from Harper Lee's novel *To Kill a Mockingbird* (1960), who has stood as a paragon of morality, integrity, and justice, and (as portrayed by Gregory Peck in the 1962 film adaptation) was voted by the American Film Institute as the greatest hero in American film.

- Shane claims that Silas's tombstone, which he handles very casually for a priceless artifact, is the world's *first* tombstone. So how old is Silas? Mentions of tombstones date back to biblical times (Jacob was said to have placed one at the grave of Rachel back in 1553 BCE), and the burial of the dead in tombs dates back to the Neolithic era.

- In his tale of Silas and the witch he betrayed, Shane says, "Hell hath no fury like a woman scorned," a phrase drawn from William Congreve's 1697 play *The Mourning Bride*: "Heaven has no rage like love to hatred turned, Nor hell a fury like a woman scorned."

- The name Silas traces its origins to Latin and is a shortened form of the Greek name "Silvanus," which means "of the forest." In the New Testament, Acts of the Apostles, Silas is a Christian missionary companion of Paul the Apostle. Silas and Paul were imprisoned together in Phillipi until an earthquake broke their chains and freed them. He is observed as a saint by the Roman Catholic, Lutheran, and Anglican churches, and is often depicted holding broken chains. Qetsiyah is of

Hebrew origin and translates to "cassia," a cinnamon-like tree bark. The name also has biblical origins: the second daughter of Job was named Qetsiyah.

- Damon introduces himself to Shane as someone interested in the "origin of a species"; while Charles Darwin (1809–1882) published his theory of evolution in 1859, *On the Origin of Species*, Damon is interested in a less scientific, more magical origin story — that of the hunters.
- Damon calls Jeremy "Van Helsing," a nickname Stefan also bestowed on Alaric when he first discovered his hobby in "Children of the Damned" (1.13). Van Helsing, the famous vampire hunter from Bram Stoker's *Dracula* (1897), is the first slayer of note in vampire fiction and now battles for top slayer spot with Ms. Buffy Summers. For a fascinating rundown of the slayer in folklore and fiction, check out Liisa Ladouceur's book *How to Kill a Vampire*.
- After Elena is back to herself, Hunter's Curse broken, Damon quips, "Teenage suicide. Don't do it," in a reference to the twisted and awesome movie *Heathers*. In the 1988 film starring Winona Ryder and Christian Slater, a string of (supposed) teen suicides inspire the fictional pop group Big Fun to record the insta-hit "Teenage Suicide (Don't Do It)."
- This is the fourth episode in a row to feature a magic-ring snafu: Rebekah steals Elena's in "The Rager," Klaus takes Jeremy's in "The Five," Stefan absconds with Damon's in "The Killer," and Elena plunks hers over Wickery Bridge in "We All Go a Little Mad Sometimes."
- Damon jokes that vampires hate to swim, but a vampire's aversion to water is a long-standing aspect of folklore, which L.J. Smith included in the original book series. In *The Struggle*, Stefan explains that running water is a barrier to vampires whose Powers are strong. The TV show's vampires don't have that restriction and, personal preferences aside, are able to swim.

THE RULES Thanks to the Five's magical origins, if a hunter is killed by a vampire he can "haunt" him or her; as Shane says, "Legend says that if a hunter is killed by that which it hunts, then that person will be cursed to walk the earth in torment." The implication is that if a human should kill a hunter, they would not be susceptible to the curse. A "potential" hunter is activated by killing a vampire (or vampire-werewolf hybrid) and the tattoo on his hand extends up his arm with the kill.

© Andrew Evans/PRPhotos.com

HISTORY LESSON According to the chalkboard — with its charming illustration of a rocket and propulsion equations — history class has moved on from the Civil War to the *Apollo 11* moon landing. On July 20, 1969, American astronauts Buzz Aldrin, Michael Collins, and Neil Armstrong became the first to land a lunar module and, subsequently, Aldrin and Armstrong became the first humans to step foot on the moon's surface. And just as Damon is intensely skeptical about the Cure, there are conspiracy theorists who believe the lunar landing was a vast government hoax, propagated in order to gain traction in the Space Race between the U.S. and Soviet Union.

PREVIOUSLY ON *THE VAMPIRE DIARIES* The knives of the Gilbert kitchen get more bloody action in this episode, when Elena jams one into her brother's neck (temporarily) killing him. In the past, we've seen Elena cut herself while chopping garlic causing Stefan to vamp out ("You're Undead to Me," 1.05); Jeremy slice his hand open to tempt Anna ("There Goes the Neighborhood," 1.16); Katherine chop off John's fingers ("Founder's Day," 1.22); Elena wield one against Katherine ("The Return," 2.01); Jenna stab herself while under compulsion ("Plan B," 2.06); AlariKlaus threaten Jenna ("Klaus," 2.19); Jeremy decapitate a hybrid with the cleaver ("The New Deal," 3.10); Elena stab Alaric to death, at Alaric's request so he'll Gilbert ring–resurrect ("Bringing Out the Dead," 3.13); and Alaric's evil alter ego get stabby with Meredith ("Break On Through," 3.17).

Caroline says the charm bracelet Tyler gave her is in the box of things she's returning; he gave it to her for her birthday in "Our Town" (3.11).

Also in "Our Town," Klaus mentions to Caroline in his beautiful speech on the nature of an eternal existence that he's contemplated ending it "once or twice over the centuries, truth be told." Seems as though at least one of those occasions was during the terror of the Hunter's Curse.

As Elena walks to Wickery Bridge, she has flashes from "Growing Pains," "The Departed" (3.22), "The Five," and "The Killer." In addition to twice going off the bridge in a car (shown in "The Departed"), Elena had a funereal moment here in "Our Town" with Matt when she said goodbye to the girl who nearly died in the car crash with her parents.

Elena is not the first daylight-ring-wearing vampire to remove it when contemplating suicide by sunlight. Stefan took his off in "Blood Brothers" (1.20), Damon in "As I Lay Dying" (2.22), and Isobel died (thanks to Klaus's compulsion) in "Know Thy Enemy" (2.17).

Chris is not Jeremy's first kill: he axed a hybrid on the Gilbert porch in "The New Deal."

OFF CAMERA The difficulty in filming this episode, explains Pascal Verschooris, was the scene on Wickery Bridge that takes place at dawn, as the Hunter's Curse drives Elena to attempt suicide. "How do you shoot dawn? How do you make dawn last for three hours? We had a long scene taking place just prior [to] sunrise between Elena and Damon and we wanted to see the sky moving into a blue/gray color. The problem is that in real life this lasts a few minutes. On feature films, they shoot these scenes over several nights. We did not have that luxury, so we built our bridge on a high platform at the top of a small, hilly road and set up a dozen very powerful lights at the very far end, with trees, smoke, and screen, and it worked. But to come to that [required] several brains [and] conversations. From the 'no can do' to 'yes we can'!"

FOGGY MOMENTS Where was Carol Lockwood while hybrids were getting hammered in her house? Slumbering it with Liz? Klaus knows how powerful the Hunter's Curse is, yet he leaves Elena locked in a room with lots of things a resourceful vampire could use to kill herself (like wooden legs of furniture). Seems reckless, even as a temporary solution.

QUESTIONS
- How does the Hunter's Curse work? Does the dead hunter have corporeal form in the land of the living? Do witches assist the hunter so he has intimate knowledge of the victim's psyche, insecurities, and weaknesses? Or are they all hallucinations driven by the vamp's subconscious mind?
- Klaus's Hunter's Curse (to the power of five) must have ended when five new hunters had each made their first vampire kill and were activated. Have there been five active hunters since 1166–1167? Did they ever know about each other, or have they been operating in isolation, like Connor was?
- Since Jer beheaded a guy in the Lockwood foyer, is Tyler and Jeremy's friendship over?
- How is Professor Shane connected to Pastor Young?
- Ever-resourceful Klaus had not heard a "whisper" about the Five after the slaughter of 1114 until Connor turned up. So how does Shane know so much about the hunters? How does Shane know "everything about everything," as Bonnie says?

Elena: My brother wants to kill me.
Damon: Welcome to the club.

4.07 My Brother's Keeper

Original air date: November 29, 2012
Written by: Caroline Dries and Elisabeth R. Finch
Directed by: Jeffrey Hunt
Guest cast: Gabrielle Douglas (Girl), Maurice Johnson (Police Officer), Joshua Mikel (Patient)

A Miss Mystic Falls competition isn't complete without a murderous rampage, and this year Jeremy the awakened hunter brings the bloodshed to the pageantry.

As Caroline warns Stefan in the opening scene, there's a fine line between sublimating his urge to go tear someone's throat out and going insane. And as Stefan focuses on Jeremy's hunter mark, he quickly takes a turn for the nutty. While he doesn't go on a ripper binge, his dedication to finding the Cure takes him to the dark twisted places in himself that he tries to deny. On the surface he's doing this for Elena, to "fix" her, but he follows Klaus's command to get Jeremy to develop his mark like a dutiful henchman: killing the hospitalized murderer (as if Mystic Falls has *regular* murderers to contend with as well as supernatural ones), force-feeding him Jeremy's blood to turn him, and then riling up Jeremy so his hunter instincts take over. It's awful and amazing and, thanks to Paul Wesley knowing exactly how to make this fascinating, it's all tinged with a deep sadness. While Stefan is seemingly in control of himself, Elena's death and resurrection as a vampire has shaken him to the point that he is focused only on the glimmer of hope of turning Elena back to her old (and by implication "real") self. He tells Jeremy that Elena isn't "supposed to be" a vampire. It's significant that while Stefan immediately starts working on completing Jeremy's tattoo, Damon is the one trying to find another way, the one who leaves Jeremy out of it. And there's a very real and sudden consequence to Stefan's actions: Jeremy nearly kills Elena.

In the aftermath of that, Stefan seems to finally understand what he's fighting for, and against, when Elena tells him, "You don't have to love me like this" and that "his" Elena is dead, and that for her some things — like Jeremy losing his humanity so she can have hers back — are simply not worth it. She *has* changed since she woke up in transition, and watching her come to terms with that has already been a long process this season. But after the Hunter's Curse, she's closer than ever, standing up for her new identity, even when it means being at odds with those closest to her. And if she doesn't want the Cure if the cost is losing her brother, then why is he trying to get it for her? That moment leads into the impossibly sad situation Stefan finds himself in back at his house: he leaves so Damon and Elena can have some privacy. But just as he begins to consider letting go of Elena, and giving up on the dream of getting her back to her old self, Caroline gives him a good reason not to give up on her just yet.

Assuming Caroline's theory is bang-on, this sire bond means that Elena's actions this season have, in part, been compelled by Damon's wishes. But viewers know it doesn't mean that *all* of her romantic feelings for him stem from the sire bond. And here, the two exchange significant glances while watching the new court do the "Intimacy of the Near Touch" waltz. The reminder of their epic moment in "Miss Mystic Falls" way back in season one was deliberate, as is their slow dance reprise by the fire. A sire bond doesn't negate all the Damon-Elena chemistry we've seen over the series, but it does massively complicate things. This show is at its best when there are *so many layers* to the emotional narrative, and "My Brother's Keeper" gives us that in spades: in the midst of a super-hot, long-anticipated sex scene, we get a mythology twist that has intense consequences for all involved.

It's a pretty diabolical twist that makes every side of this triangle all the more tragic: Stefan, on the verge of finding a little peace in an Elena-is-a-vampire world; Elena, finally coming to terms with who she is now and trying to do things on her own terms; and Damon, who will soon discover the best day of his life was tainted. Back in "Bloodlines," Damon wanted his road-trip good times with Elena to be real; he didn't compel her, because what he wanted was a true connection. All he has ever wanted from her (or from Katherine in the past) is that ever-elusive reciprocated love, for someone to love him back. And now he gets the girl, and it turns out her choice may not have been entirely her own.

Since season one, Jeremy has been subjected to compulsion again and again, the poor kid, but now he's incapable of being compelled. While it feels

© Bob Mahoney/The CW/Landov

like a victory for him — and certainly that moment with Stefan was *awesome* — the same thing that frees him comes with a price. His dream of killing Elena — and dissociating her from the idea of his "real" sister — shows us just how serious the hunter change is. The magic that makes him able to lift two kegs with ease (he's going to be employee of the month at the Grill, for sure) has also given him certain impulses that could lead to highly regrettable actions, like staking his own sister in the neck at a town event. Just as that sister has new vampire tastes, and a sire bond that draws her to Damon, Jeremy is navigating new territory: he knows who he wants to be, but has powerful urges that make him act in opposition to that goal.

Each of the Gilbert siblings needs a guide through this mixed-up mess, and they each get one, though it doesn't turn out to be the person they'd expect. Jeremy can't lean on his sister anymore, but Matt steps up, as he always does — taking care of both Gilberts without a moment's hesitation. Matt won't let Jeremy keep his hunter status a secret. He brings Elena into the loop, and talks Jeremy down when he's attacking her. He steps up to act like a big brother when Elena decides it's best for Jer if she moves out of the house. Elena has found solace with Damon, leaving Stefan and Caroline, who are on the same wavelength with each other, to argue with Elena over what's best for her.

Seeing Caroline in Caroline-mode, bossing around the pageant volunteers, is always good fun, but more interesting is the different dynamics between her and Elena, and her and Klaus. On the one hand, she warns Elena away from falling for Damon, and based on how Damon treated Caroline in season one, it's understandable that Caroline would be seriously concerned for her best friend's welfare. (She seems to discount the seriousness of Stefan's serial killing and lying tendencies when she evaluates him as a "soul mate," but nobody's perfect.) But while Caroline is concerned for Elena, she can't help but be charmed by Klaus, no matter how resistant she is at first or how their date is really part of a ploy that helps his hybrids free themselves of his control. Klaus prevents a scene between Elena and Caroline at the pageant. He's interested in her and playful and ridiculously charming, but he can also be introspective and observant — and we see these moments of humanity almost only when he is with her. Caroline quite obviously has a nice time with Klaus (a fact that Tyler doesn't fail to notice, even as he has his own chummy relationship with Hayley). His touching tale of the frailty of human life is somehow both profound and disturbing, given how readily he's extinguished life in his 1,000 years of being the biggest, baddest vampire around. Though Caroline and Stefan butt heads with Elena about how she is supposed to act, and who she is supposed to love, the reality is, in these complicated, messy dynamics, what's "best" isn't necessarily what's right. Letting go of your fixed ideas about what "should" happen may be the only way to truly sublimate your darker instincts.

COMPELLING MOMENT Damon and Elena finally get down, as Caroline finally gets it — Elena is sired to Damon. Well played, *TVD*!

CIRCLE OF KNOWLEDGE
- No Bonnie in this episode.
- The phrase "my brother's keeper" comes from the biblical story of the brothers Cain and Abel. After Cain has killed Abel, God asks Cain where

his brother is, to which Cain (rather sassily) replies, "I know not; am I my brother's keeper?" God then curses Cain to be a fugitive and vagabond. The sibling rivalry and violence make the Cain-Abel story an apt backdrop for *The Vampire Diaries*: Jeremy is intent on killing Elena (and Elena accidentally killed Jeremy in the previous episode), and let's face it, Stefan and Damon are always at odds. But the answer to Cain's question seems to be yes, you are your brother's keeper — whether it's literally family (as with the Gilberts and Salvatores) or a friend (Matt steps up for Jeremy). Whether we are at each other's throats or at peace, *TVD* argues in this episode and elsewhere that we're responsible for protecting and caring for family.

- Stefan's blood addiction is often talked about in Alcoholics Anonymous terms, as Caroline does in this episode, calling herself his sober sponsor. An alcoholic's sponsor is the go-to person for support, friendship, and counsel in times of crisis.

THE RULES We learned about the rarity of vampires being sired last season when Damon figured out that Tyler was sired to Klaus, but here we get a little refresher on why hybrids feel bound to Klaus. With Jer's mark activated, he experiences vampire-killing dreams, the overwhelming urge to kill vampires (akin to a newbie vamp's wild thirst for blood), and his instincts change. As a hunter, he's super strong and full of energy, and he cannot be compelled. Professor Shane says that the hunter's map leads to the secret location of the Cure, which is somehow contained and can only be accessed after a Bennett witch performs a spell.

PREVIOUSLY ON *THE VAMPIRE DIARIES* Stefan tries to sublimate his ripper rage by working out in the forest, similar to his attempt to distract himself from his bloodlust by working out in "Under Control" (1.18).

Damon suggests a little brother bonding with some Tri Delts, which is what Stefan called the women Damon fed on in "A Few Good Men" (1.15).

The Miss Mystic Falls competition has lots of callbacks to the episode "Miss Mystic Falls" (1.19). In addition to being the end of Caroline's reign, we have the "weird dance thing" (as Matt describes it), a missing escort and a last-minute replacement, and a replica of the Elena-comes-down-the-stairs moment with Damon waiting for her. Klaus reads Caroline's Miss Mystic application, and the impressive list of accomplishments is an echo of her rhyming them off in front of the judges in the season one episode. In a subtler callback, Stefan's first-season line to Amber Bradley, "I'm not sad; I'm freaking hungry," is revisited when he says to Caroline on the phone, "Oh, I'm not depressed. I just want to rip into someone's artery and feed until I can't breathe anymore."

Caroline expressed some strong pro-Stefan feelings back in "Do Not Go Gentle" (3.20), telling Elena, "Stefan is your epic love. And I'm not going down without a fight."

Jeremy first attempted whittling in "Brave New World" (2.02), when he was so determined to kill Damon that he made his own stake. He admits that it's "a lot harder than it looks."

Klaus's interest in Caroline's Miss Mystic Falls application recalls their conversation at the ball in "Dangerous Liaisons" (3.14). After Klaus compliments Caroline's dancing skills, she says, "Well, I've had training. I happen to be Miss Mystic Falls," to which Klaus replies, "I know."

OFF CAMERA 2012 Olympic gymnastics gold medalist Gabby Douglas makes a cameo appearance as one of Caroline's Miss Mystic Falls event helpers. Douglas is a huge fan of *The Vampire Diaries*, so, following her Olympic win, the *TVD* cast recorded a special congratulations video and Julie Plec offered her a walk-on role.

Caroline Dries loves "the moment when Klaus is reading Caroline's Miss Mystic Falls application. I thought that made him so lovable and charming."

FOGGY MOMENTS Tyler tells Hayley that Caroline has bought them more time because Klaus is attending the pageant with her. How did that buy them more time? Is Klaus capable of only holding one thought in his mind at any given time? Would he not notice that his hybrids are AWOL? And what happened to the animosity between Caroline and Tyler after she and her pals killed Chris the Hybrid at the end of the previous episode? Why did Tyler think that Kim the Hybrid had broken her sire bond to Klaus? She looks exhausted and says to him she doesn't know how much more of it she can take, but we've been told that only when turning is no longer painful is the sire bond broken. So shouldn't she be able to change forms like a champ and be a touch peppier about it if the bond was broken?

QUESTIONS

- Lots of questions about the prof-turned-pageant judge. Shane manages to appear no-nonsense and forthcoming but he only shares the information that will help him, you know, not get killed by Damon. He doesn't answer Damon's question about his connection to the pastor. What are Professor Shane and Hayley up to? When did Hayley join forces with Shane — before or after Tyler met her?

- Hayley's boating accident story sounds like a big old fib. If it is, who did she actually kill and who are/were her parents? Why is Hayley so invested in the hybrids breaking their sire bonds?

- Shane says only a Bennett witch can do the spell for the Cure — was Ayana involved in the original magic that created the hunters and/or the Cure? Why does Shane want the hybrids to be free of the sire bond? Was Shane telling the truth about other hunters being hard to find?

- The hybrid sire bond is borne of gratitude for being freed from the pain of turning every month, as we were reminded in this episode. What is the vampire equivalent? What does Elena feel innately grateful to Damon for? Is there a cure for being a sired vampire?

- Is Stefan going to continue to "crash elsewhere" or will the sire news bring him back to the Salvatore manse to protect Elena from her sire-bond instincts?

- Caroline asks the question of Klaus but doesn't answer it herself: would she take the Cure and become mortal again?

© Frank Micelotta/PictureGroup

Caroline: How can you trust him?
Stefan: Because I think that he loves her as much as I do.
He can't be selfish with her. Not anymore.

4.08 *We'll Always Have Bourbon Street*

Original air date: December 6, 2012
Written by: Charlie Charbonneau and Jose Molina
Directed by: Jesse Warn
Guest cast: Takara Clark (Valerie), Micah Parker (Adrian), Adina Porter (Nandi), Madeline Zima (Charlotte)

Stefan and Damon travel to New Orleans to learn more about the sire bond, which dredges up memories of their time there during World War II. Tyler and Hayley assert control over the rebelling hybrids.

Poor Elena and Damon don't even get through their one secret, selfish day together before the whole thing blows up in their faces. With the question of the sire bond at the forefront, "We'll Always Have Bourbon Street" pushes characters to take a position, make judgments, and decide what is, for them, the right course of action.

In the process, characters misjudge each other, misjudge their situations, and create a discord, which is the episode's greatest strength. Problematic can be good: just as the Salvatore brothers are at odds with each other, sometimes the audience *should* be at odds with the characters and their choices. It's more challenging, more fun, and, definitely, more frustrating that way. At the heart of the episode is a debate about the ethics of forcing people's behavior in the name of what's "right," reminding us that being judgmental often speaks more about the person doing the judging than anything else, and that the line between selfless and selfish is sometimes razor-thin.

Though they are far from being the only ones, Stefan and Caroline both have a judgmental streak, and when it comes to Damon, they find it difficult to bite their tongue or give him the benefit of the doubt. The flashback to the last time the brothers Salvatore were in New Orleans, in the 1940s, shows us one reason why Stefan believes Damon is selfish: as "penance" for his ripper days, Stefan plans to ship off to Egypt to be a frontline ambulance driver; Damon promises to join him, but never shows. Judgments are often based on incomplete evidence, and that's what has happened here. For the past 70 years, what Stefan didn't know was that Damon didn't flake on him just so he could stay in NOLA and party with Charlotte. His no-show is a direct response to Lexi's condemnation of his character. Lexi is just as critical of Damon as are Caroline and Stefan, and she blames him for Stefan's ripper turn in 1912, despite the fact that she counseled Stefan not to do just that. At her assertion that Damon would only damage his brother, as he did in 1912, by joining him at war, Damon puts aside his own desire to have the company of his little brother in deference to Stefan's rehabilitation. Similarly, in the present day, though he first scoffs at the idea of the sire bond, Damon immediately tests the bond and then works to break it.

Initially, Stefan doubts Damon's ability to do the "right" thing, the self-less thing, in this situation: to put his desire for Elena aside and break the bond. In a classic brother moment, Damon spits it back at Stefan: how self-less is Stefan's motivation? Is his only and true interest to protect Elena's right to free will and self-determination or is he after a "Team Stefan" version of her? The situation is a tangled knot of moral implications, romantic feelings, bruised egos, and 160 years of history between the Salvatores. The brothers still don't know each other as well as they think, as Damon proves in his sepia-toned flashback. It sucks for them, but man does it make for compelling TV.

In 1942, Damon killed a dozen people in the (misguided) hope that it would fuel a witch's spell to break Charlotte's sire bond. While Stefan passes judgment on Damon's past massacre, it has been only one day since he killed a man in the name of finding the Cure for Elena, and he was also willing to do it in "We All Go a Little Mad Sometimes." For Damon, the chance at a clean slate with Elena is motivation enough to resort to "extreme measures" again. The question of how far the brothers would go for Elena arises again and again this season.

At the Salvatore house, Caroline has a hard time "laying off the hate" (to be fair, she is drunk on Dom and high on spirit tea), and it's not long before she's judging Damon's promiscuity while in the same breath excusing Stefan's recent string of bloody murders. Caroline ignores the capacity for evil in Stefan because of what he's done for her — his friendship when she was transitioning, his kindness, his understanding — just as she ignores the capacity for good in Damon because of what he did to her. When she tells Elena about the sire bond and immediately assures her that it's not her fault, that Damon took advantage of her, she could just as easily be speaking to

"I loved writing Damon and Stefan in the present day, and I loved writing the boys with Lexi back in the day, but figuring out that story was a nightmare. Very little actually happens in the episode, and I tend to have a very plot-minded brain, so I was a bit at a loss because I felt the episode was treading water. At one point, I remember saying to my cowriter, Charlie Charbonneau, 'If we just didn't do this episode, would anyone miss it?' To this day, I don't know!"

— Jose Molina

her pre-vampire, season-one self. That Caroline was Damon's "lapdog," at his beck and call, used by him as he terrorized her, his brother, and Mystic Falls. These are the darkest corners of the characters on *TVD*: both Salvatores have behaved reprehensibly, unforgivably. So, as much as it's a bad example for the kids at home when Caroline uses sex-shaming insults (which she does here for Damon, and did last season for Rebekah), and sad to see her lose her open-hearted attitude ("Boy likes girl. Girl likes boy. Sex."), it does make sense. What she was put through should never be diminished, nor should its impact on her character be underestimated. The series itself tends to do both, and here, Elena does as well. She knows that Damon used compulsion on Caroline and abused her (remember her indignation in "Family Ties" — where has that Elena gone?), but Elena shows no empathy here for her friend's position, only her endless capacity to forgive the Salvatores of their sins. Caroline's opinion on the issue of Elena's bond is also shaped by her experience with Tyler and his sire bond from last season. He changed, defected and joined Team Klaus, he became unable to control his actions toward her or his friends, and his moral decisions were clouded by loyalty.

What does the sire bond mean for Elena's future? Enter Charlotte, a warning of just how much power that bond has. In a refreshing change from last season's overreliance on magical escape routes for sticky plots, Nandi the NOLA Witch says there is no vampire equivalent to a hybrid's gratitude at being freed from the lunar change. And, assuming she knows her stuff, the bond is derived from strong human feelings between sire and sired — feelings that are heightened to the extreme during the transition to vampire.

We've heard again and again (and again) about how "heightened" a vampire's feelings are, and those emotional extremes are considered just as legitimate and real as a human's feelings. That Damon and Stefan love Elena is not up for debate. We accept those heightened vamp feelings as valid. So, are Elena's heightened feelings for Damon negated by the fact that she is sired to him? Or are they legitimate and to be honored? In the cliffhanger final scene, she argues the latter. Elena alone knows what she felt for Damon before the change — feelings she never articulated, that she hid from those around her (as best she could). Elena is the only one who can evaluate whether what she feels now is markedly different than what she felt then.

But, as a sired vampire, she has also become a puppet unaware of her strings (until now). Damon has unwittingly manipulated her actions — most notably her inability to consume blood from any source but a living human — and she was clueless. The restraints she is so happy to be free from, as she sips on a blood bag with her girlfriends, were artificial to begin with; she has suffered since she turned because of Damon's philosophy that newbie vamps should feed from the vein, not from the bag or the bunny. In a sexual relationship, if one partner is a doting servant sired to the other, there are *huge* implications, which is why the opening scene is careful to show reciprocated attention (ahem) between Damon and Elena. It is very clearly not a twisted sex-slave scenario, which was a clear subtext to Stefan's presumption that Damon took "full advantage of" his sire bond with Charlotte. But the question remains: is Elena's happiness a reflection of Damon's? Or is it her own? Is the bond deluding her? Or is Tyler's suggestion that the sire bond has no effect on emotions, just on actions, true for Elena? How can she ever know for sure? And can Damon be trusted with that power over her, if that distinction between action and feeling is true?

Elena isn't the only one with puppet strings she is unaware of. As Tyler fights to free his people from the evil overlord that is Klaus, he's completely trusting of Hayley — who's manipulating him for her own gain and who is herself being strung along by Professor Creepy. Kim, such a rebellious hybrid, points out to taskmasters Tyler and Hayley that the point of breaking the sire bond is to have free will, not to be told by new bosses what they "have" to do (especially when it's torturously painful). But even without the bond, these half-werewolves have a pack mentality that Hayley encourages Tyler to capitalize on. Her motivation is self-interested, but his is to do the right thing and break free from Klaus permanently. There's a nice comparison to be made between Tyler and Klaus as hybrid leaders. Klaus dictates his will to those who are powerless to object, while Tyler responds to a challenge

Caroline Dries on the Sire Bond

We obviously knew Elena was going to be a vampire. We tried to shape the premiere into a "Will she turn or will Bonnie find a way to keep her a human," but I think the audience figured she'd go vampire. We also knew we were going to have her sired to Damon. A *lot* of people who didn't like our sire bond twist still tweet me their rage — as if I was at home writing the Damon/Elena sex scene and it just popped in my head that Elena should be sired to Damon and I just scripted it on the fly. The fact is, that story decision was calculated from the very beginning — her inability to drink blood from the bag, her pull toward Damon, her decision to kill Connor — we laid the clues in advance knowing this was where we were going to go.

Hey, I wanted to see [the long-awaited Damon and Elena hook-up] too, so it was like writing fan fiction. I didn't feel any pressure, except as a writer I'm always looking for new ways to write the words "kissing" and "making out." I knew once it was being shot that it was going to be incredibly hot and sexy and deliver on our expectations. It didn't occur to me until after I saw the cut [of "My Brother's Keeper"] how much the fans would hate Elisabeth [Finch, cowriter] and me for the sire bond thing.

from Kim by asserting his dominance and the justice of his cause. His alpha leader moment is inspired not by self-interest; he uses his power for the group's benefit and protection (from the bully Klaus). Tyler has become the anti-bully, and he's willing to put his own desires aside to accomplish that. He's become sober, adult, and benevolent, for the most part. Again, looking back to season one, it's an unexpected but believable character development, which has more than a little to do with the wonderful side effects of loving Caroline.

But what do sire bonds or free-will debates really amount to when there's an apocalypse on the horizon! Nandi tells Damon and Stefan that Expression, the form of magic in which Shane is schooling Bonnie, is incredibly dangerous: "Channeling the power of human sacrifice calls on darkness that can't exist on this plane *without swallowing it whole*." In his ongoing commitment to combine handsomeness with creepiness, Professor Shane assures Hayley that the fact her birth parents are dead isn't an obstacle to her having a little face time with them. With 12 council members dead, and 12 hybrids being rounded up for some nefarious purpose, and 12 innocents sacrificed for an Expression spell back in 1942, the refrain that "We are the beginning" (first heard from the pastor in the season premiere) is only getting more End of Days–y. What kind of overthrow-the-order-of-the-universe plan does Shane have? What is *his* motivation?

COMPELLING MOMENT Stefan's layered reaction upon discovering just how powerful Charlotte's sire bond is to Damon, after Damon accused him of wanting Elena returned to "original factory Team Stefan settings." Paul Wesley lets us know the wealth of implications this has for Elena, Damon, and Stefan in the briefest of reactions, and he plays snarky so very, very well. "*Literally* every brick."

CIRCLE OF KNOWLEDGE
- No Matt or Jeremy in this episode.
- "We'll Always Have Bourbon Street" is a reference to a famous line from *Casablanca*, "We'll always have Paris." The classic American film from 1942 is set during World War II and follows Rick Blaine (Humphrey Bogart) who is torn between his duty to help fight the Nazis and his reignited love for Ilsa Lund (Ingrid Bergman), now married. At the end of the film, Rick, who describes himself as "no good at being noble," makes a selfless choice, sending away the woman he loves with her husband, Victor Laszlo, to protect them from the Nazi threat, and staying behind himself. She doesn't want to leave him, but he insists, arguing that she belongs with Victor and if she stayed, she'd regret it: "Maybe not today, maybe not tomorrow, but soon and for the rest of your life." Ilsa doesn't want to break her vow to never leave Rick, but she's assuaged by his suggestion that she never will truly leave him, as they'll "always have Paris" — the memory of the time they spent together in love. Here, Damon is cast in the role parallel to Rick Blaine, forced to make a difficult and selfless choice. His sire-bonded lady love from 1942 is easier to say goodbye to (and they'll always have Bourbon Street) than Elena. In a non-romantic context, Damon makes a Rick-like choice in the flashback sequence, following Lexi's advice and staying behind in New Orleans (as Rick does in Casablanca) while Stefan sets off for the war, safer without Damon's blood-drinking ways to influence or corrupt him.
- Damon says that Charlotte went all *Fatal Attraction* on him. He must be a fan of the 1987 Michael Douglas/Glenn Close film as he also referred to it last season when he suspected Meredith of being the killer on the loose in Mystic Falls ("The Ties That Bind," 3.12).

- The Salvatores return to the French Quarter of New Orleans, name-dropping famous streets like Bourbon, Dauphine, and Dumaine. The witch Valerie says her Nandi's grimoires were destroyed in Katrina, but she may be lying about that, as well as her age. The French Quarter was relatively unharmed in the devastating August 2005 hurricane that killed close to 2,000 people in the United States and saw the levees break in New Orleans, causing stunning amounts of damage.
- Bonnie says that Shane's stash of herbs "opens up your *qi* or whatever." Qi (also spelled *chi* or *ch'i*) is the Chinese term for life force or energy, which permeates and connects all things. While Bonnie, Caroline, and Elena seem to have more of a recreational-drug party time — perhaps thanks to pairing it with bottles and bottles of Dom Pérignon — people who do *qigong*, the practice of cultivating and balancing *qi*, combine breathing, movement, and mindfulness with various herbal remedies.

HISTORY LESSON The North African campaign of World War II was waged in Egypt, Libya, Algeria, Tunisia, and Morocco beginning in June 1940. After officially entering the war, the U.S. provided military assistance to Allied forces in North Africa in May 1942. That campaign ended in May 1943 in an Allied victory, with Axis forces (Germany, Italy) retreating to Italy. It's worth noting that American author Ernest Hemingway volunteered as an ambulance driver during World War I and it's entirely possible that Stefan read about, and was inspired by, Hemingway's experience and volunteered to serve as an ambulance driver himself in Egypt.

THE RULES A vampire sire bond is markedly different from a hybrid's: it is based on strong feelings the sire felt for the vampire before transformation. Werewolf packs in the *TVD* universe have alphas, challengers, and dramatic reassertions of who's boss, following in the longstanding tradition of wolf packs depicted in other supernatural stories. Shane is teaching Bonnie "Expression," a different form of magic unconnected to the spirit world, which Nandi describes as worse than dark magic.

PREVIOUSLY ON *THE VAMPIRE DIARIES* Now that we know Damon had personal experience with a vampire sire bond (Charlotte in 1942), his ability to figure out what was going on with Tyler in "Smells Like Teen Spirit" (3.06) makes a lot of sense.

By 1942, Stefan was not yet "feeling himself," according to those diary entries from "The End of the Affair" (3.03).

Stefan gives Damon grief for not joining the war effort (unaware of his actual motivation), calling to mind Giuseppe Salvatore calling Damon a deserter for leaving the Civil War in "Children of the Damned" (1.13).

Caroline "jumped into bed" (as Elena puts it) with Damon back in "The Night of the Comet" (1.02).

Valerie uses magic to slow the aging process, just as Chicago witch Gloria did in "The End of the Affair" (3.03).

A guy wipes out an entire village *one time* . . . and no one lets him forget it. Lexi refers to Stefan as the "Ripper of Monterey," which he became after the events of "1912" (3.16).

Damon expressed his need to do right by Elena in "Rose" (2.08), when he declared he couldn't be selfish with her and confessed his love before compelling her to forget it.

OFF CAMERA American actor Madeline Zima brought the hopelessly sired Charlotte to life. Zima has acted since she was seven years old, spending six years on Fran Drescher's sitcom *The Nanny*. More recently she's had recurring roles on *Heroes* and *Californication*.

FOGGY MOMENTS Not to be cruel to Charlotte, but why would Damon bother seeking out a witch and killing a dozen people when he could just kill Charlotte if the sire-bond situation was making him crazy? It also seems like a pretty ludicrous idea to send a vampire who freaks out at the sight of human blood to the front lines of World War II so he can see "death and blood as part of life." Um, Lexi, do you remember the Civil War and all that blood, all the wounded, all those corpses? Not exactly temptation-free times. Damon's guilt-free attitude would be the least of Stefan's problems.

QUESTIONS
- How did Lexi find out that Damon had killed a dozen people?
- Why is Shane uniquely positioned to find out about Hayley's biological parents? (Did she already try Binging them? Worked to find Isobel.)
- Sire bonds in vampires are rare, and yet Damon has had two sired to him. Does Damon have particularly strong wooing powers? Something in his blood?

- Have we seen witches use Expression before, or only spirit magic and dark magic?
- Is it a coincidence that in 1942 Valerie tricked Damon into sacrificing 12 humans so she could use that energy for Expression and that Shane is connected to the deaths of 12 humans and is teaching Bonnie how to use Expression?
- Shane repeats the phrase Pastor Young used in "Growing Pains": "We are the beginning." Of what?
- Will Caroline be able to keep Elena's hook-up with Damon a secret from Stefan?
- How many bricks *are* in New Orleans?

Carol: Klaus, please. Don't hurt him. He's my son. He's all I have.
Klaus: And you're all he has. There's a beautiful symmetry to that, don't you think?

4.09 *O Come, All Ye Faithful*

Original air date: December 13, 2012
Written by: Michael J. Cinquemani and Julie Plec
Directed by: Pascal Verschooris
Guest cast: Micah Parker (Adrian)

At the lakehouse, Jeremy tries to overcome his homicidal urges toward Elena. A plan to take out Klaus ends in a Winter Wonderland of bloody horror.

The Vampire Diaries' first foray into holiday fare is far from your average Christmassy programming, and what a beautiful, poignant, and *bloody* episode it is. "O Come, All Ye Faithful" hits a melancholic but hopeful tone — fitting for the holiday — as it explores the existential loneliness that plagues immortals (and mortals alike), emphasizes how important trust and family are, and illustrates the challenges we face in seeking purpose and peace.

To pick up on Caroline's *A Christmas Carol* reference, Klaus serves as a sort of Ebenezer Scrooge (but one who doesn't need ghostly visitors to reach self-understanding, thanks to the wisdom of his thousand years). His fate is a cautionary tale for the other characters, his isolation and crimes a sort of high-water mark to measure themselves against. And yet Klaus is much more than a foil to our heroes; he's a compelling, heart-wrenching (literally and figuratively) character in his own right, one who engenders sympathy in spite of his villainy. Like Caroline and Stefan feeling guilty about their part in plotting Klaus's downfall, we are led to feel for this guy as he murders his hybrids for their betrayal, feeling his loss even as heads and hearts fly.

His speech to Stefan about why he keeps the victims' letters resonates because it hits on the anxiety that he and Stefan both face, which is a very human fear: that of being utterly and infinitely alone. We see the effect of that isolation, or the fear of it, across storylines and characters in "O Come, All Ye Faithful," and Klaus is correct. There is a "beautiful symmetry" in it. Stefan observes that what sets everyone else apart from Klaus is their relationships, their trust, their family, and in Klaus we see his failed attempts to build those things. With Caroline, he knows her kindness comes not from pure good-heartedness but from an ulterior motive, and her flip reply that they "don't have a *thing*" (however innocuous) speaks to the emptiness of the relationship that Klaus keeps trying to establish with her. And with his former buddy Stefan, Klaus has been trying a very different tactic from last season: instead of holding him hostage, he's treating him as an equal (as far as Klaus can manage). He confides secrets of great import, he answers questions, he shows him the sword, he doesn't punish Stefan for spreading the secret of the Cure. But Stefan doesn't trust him, doesn't confide in him; instead, he acts as Klaus has in the past. Stefan uses Klaus and then discards him (albeit with a heavier conscience). Klaus's attempt to treat Stefan with respect has failed to earn him any. And on the other side of the spectrum, his utter disrespect for his hybrids has engendered rebellion.

That moment when we see both the ferocity and the pain of Klaus betrayed is just so genius. He's misty-eyed at the thought of what he's about to do: kill the hybrids he created as a replacement family, kill those whose loyalty he could not maintain even though it was magically enforced. No one is on his side. While Klaus acts as a touchstone for Stefan, who compares himself and his own wrongdoings to the "bad guy" and finds they're not so different, he also serves as a point of comparison for Damon during this sire-bond schmozzle. The difference between how Klaus and Damon treat their sires is stark: Klaus gets free labor from his hybrids and abuses his power, which leads to rebellion and slaughter. Damon, on the other hand,

© Andrew Evans/PRPhotos.com

fears misusing his power even one iota. He hates the idea of it, resents the fact of it, and is wild to rid himself of it, while his sired loves and adores him, and she doesn't mind the bond's existence. She trusts him to do right by her. But ultimately both Klaus and Damon set out on a course for a future without their sires (Klaus's first step being far more drastic and permanent than Damon's).

Though Klaus knows the isolation of eternity better than any of the other characters, that central theme pops up across the other storylines too — most hauntingly in the legend of Silas that Shane tells to Elena and Damon. Each element of the tale resonates with the modern-day vampires: a great love that cannot be, jealousy, betrayal of trust, the end of a friendship, revenge, and unending isolation — unending, buried-alive isolation. (Even that detail parallels with the plan to encase Klaus in concrete.) Shane tells Elena he has lost his wife and son, and that he lives with the pain of having lost what he loves the most, while Hayley proves willing to do evil in order to find a connection with family, to stave off her own isolation. She's not the only drifter without ties: April Young, orphan, may have been crowned Miss Mystic Falls, but she's alone in a terrifying new reality.

While the Salvatore brothers find themselves apart — Stefan's feeling of awkwardness about Damon's sire bond with Elena escalates into jealousy and betrayal by the end of the episode — the Gilbert siblings are able to reestablish their bond, thanks to the emotional touchstone that is Bonnie Bennett. It's heartbreaking to hear the hunter in Jeremy dehumanize Elena and devalue his relationship with her, and then see sweet, strong-arms Jer snap back to himself, hopeful that the hypnosis worked. With the Gilberts and Bonnie putting their trust in the shady professor, Shane is able to actually help — despite his other, less-than-standup plan. With some "intuitive" help from Damon, he hypnotizes Jeremy into finding another way to be: instead of only wanting to kill vampires, including his sister, he's able to channel the love and protective feelings he has for Bonnie into a "detour." While Bonnie and Jeremy have always maintained their connection, to see their bond put at the forefront like this is a warm and fuzzy moment. As Stefan says to Caroline at the end of the episode, it is those bonds, that trust, that gives each person's life meaning and value. The trust that Jeremy has in Bonnie now envelops Elena, and the siblings are able to be family again — an important moment since they are each the only family the other has. And no one likes to be alone on the holidays.

At odds with his brother again, Damon sees Elena and Jer together and being nostalgic, and he feels the absence of that in his life. Ironically, the sire bond makes Damon more isolated and distant from Elena, uncomfortable with her affection, and feeling their every interaction is tainted by his unfulfilled promise to his brother.

It's painful to watch the breakdown in trust between the Salvatore brothers over the course of the episode; Stefan believes Damon's already done the right thing and pushed away Elena, when the truth of the matter is he hasn't — but he hasn't been as dastardly as Caroline believes, either. The time spent between Elena and Damon in the 22 or so hours since they talked about the bond has been innocent — it's the secret, selfish day they didn't get to enjoy, and still don't get to, really. But when Caroline reveals what she does know — and her report completely lacks the nuance of the situation — Stefan's trust in his brother is broken, and he lashes out, upset and hurt that they slept together, that Damon hasn't lived up to his end of the bargain. Caroline is in the middle of a balancing act of loyalties that gets messy here not only with Elena and the Salvatores, but with the unsired hybrids' interests coming into conflict with those searching for the Cure. As she divulges information, it shows just how hard it is to be an ally to everyone and to be on everyone's side with only their best, if conflicting, interests at heart.

Betrayals abound in "O Come, All Ye Faithful." Stefan betrays Klaus's trust, and breaks their alliance, in his attempt to steal the sword and let Klaus walk off to the "slaughter" with the hybrids. Caroline is torn between alliances: though Klaus knows what she thinks of him, they *do* have a "thing," and it will hurt him to know her part in the events of the day. But more critically for her, Caroline is torn between Stefan's hunt for the Cure — which she's after too, perhaps more for Elena's sake than her own — and Tyler's freeing of the hybrids. Tyler wants her "support" but he doesn't show any understanding of why the Cure is important to her personally; he only brushes it off as valueless to hybrids because they'd go back to monthly suffering.

Klaus knows all too well that he is without an emotional touchstone — no one will say to him "I love you even when I hate you," as Caroline does to Tyler — and to punish Tyler for helping the hybrids break their sire bonds, he takes from him his last family member. (You just know things are not going to end well for Carol after that heart-to-heart with her son.) Tyler is willing to make a great sacrifice, to let his body be Klaus's prison cell, encased in concrete — missing out on his senior year, on graduation, and putting himself at great risk should the plan go awry. But instead of Tyler sacrificing himself for others, he is left the sole survivor. Tyler took hybrids from Klaus, so Klaus kills them all and Tyler's mother for good measure. His only family now gone, Tyler will suffer more knowing his mother paid for his choices. It's an incredibly cruel, and effective, retaliation.

"O Come, All Ye Faithful" is fittingly concerned with sacrifice and

Director Pascal Verschooris on "O Come, All Ye Faithful"
During prep, I had "Carmina Burana" [a cantata by composer Carl Orff, and a Hollywood staple for epic battles and other dramatic sequences] in my head the entire time. I discussed with our stunt coordinator, John Copeman, that I wanted to create a sort of stunt opera. It was choreographed that way. How do you kill so many people without a rhythm? The cut gave it that classic orientation I was looking for. John Copeman did an amazing job, as well as Joseph Morgan, and the result is there. I also think that because we were emotionally engaged with these characters, their deaths were more meaningful and made all of the opera that much more powerful.

I did not realize until later that it was, in fact, the first "holiday" episode. It was a lot of fun to bring candy canes to the screen but more so (and this is gonna sound creepy), it was really cool to kill the mayor with Christmas in the background. In prep, I was thinking about *Die Hard* and thought it would be cool to finish on such a high note.

It was bittersweet because I always enjoyed working with Susan Walters, so killing her character was hard emotionally, but it was definitely incredible to finish the story with a snowflake, a dead body, and a Christmas song.

martyrdom; after all, it's a Christmas episode. From the soundtrack to that fake snow falling on the town square to that stunning slaughter scene, this is an exceptionally well-constructed hour of television, and what better gift for the *TVD* family than that?

COMPELLING MOMENT The brutal and balletic hybrid slaughter.

CIRCLE OF KNOWLEDGE
- "O Come, All Ye Faithful" is the English translation (written by Catholic priest Frederick Oakley) of the hymn "Adeste Fideles," most likely composed by John Francis Wade. The popular Christmas song celebrates the arrival of Christ. Besides kicking off the episode with Christmas holiday spirit for the Mystic Falls Winter Wonderland, the name rather playfully points out the fates of the unwillingly faithful (those bonded to their sires). And we sure have a vengeful god in Klaus who punishes his faithless hybrids, with something a lot worse than a lump of coal in their stockings, as that much more beloved Saint Nick is wont to do.

- Postmodern art is a movement that emerged in the 1970s as artists reacted to or rejected the experimental nature of Modern art. It encompasses a wide variety of media, styles, and past influences, and blurs the lines between high and pop art. So when Stefan comments snidely on Klaus's "postmodern snowflakes," it's possible he's not being very complimentary.
- Seeing Klaus at the Grill, Caroline quips, "Here to steal Tiny Tim's crutches?" casting Klaus as Ebenezer Scrooge in Charles Dickens's *A Christmas Carol* (1843). Like the mean old grump from the Christmas classic, Klaus is plagued by loneliness, having driven away his real family, his created family (the hybrids), and behaved in ways that prevent Caroline from acknowledging they even have a "thing," like drinking champagne together.
- "Dickens was a dark man. You would've liked him." To chat up Caroline, Klaus shamelessly name-drops the 18th-century English author whose own impoverished childhood led him to become one of the foremost social critics of his time. Dickens campaigned for children's rights in particular, which makes the idea of Klaus being friends with Dickens, or at least acquainted with him, more than a little amusing. Klaus is also implying that Caroline likes "dark" men — like Klaus himself.
- Damon busts out a "Survey says . . . ," perhaps feeling the wholesome game-show spirit at the lakehouse; *Family Feud* has been on and off the air since 1976, and reached a ratings high with host Steve Harvey.
- Among the letters Stefan finds in Klaus's chest of killer keepsakes is one written in French (*My love, the days pass too slowly being so far from you*), a postcard sent to Michigan, and a passionate letter from "your forever man" Alphonso whose train journeys are only tolerable because he knows his beloved awaits him and whose life before "was only a shadow of an existence." One hopes Alphonso and his love were able to "meet again standing on the beach with the gentle waves lapping at our feet" before Klaus killed him (or, more likely, both of them).
- A massacre mystery is unraveled with the events of "O Come, All Ye Faithful": in the season premiere, the vampires were captured but not killed because Shane ordered it so. He wanted Connor to be the one to kill the vampires so he would complete more of his mark, which in turn would get Shane closer to the spell that will release Silas. The unsiring of the 12 hybrids seems to also be part of Shane's master plan: he was goading Klaus into committing a massacre for him.

- R.I.P. Carol Lockwood. We will remember you for your poise, your compassion for a post-turn Tyler, and your ability to organize and execute innumerable Mystic Falls events. The fact you were murdered at one of those events . . . Well, there's a beautiful symmetry to that, don't you think? We raise our martinis in your memory.

HISTORY LESSON Stefan can't help but be his best snarky self when he's around Klaus, so he reminds the Original, "Abraham Lincoln freed the slaves, you know." In addition to being a callback to Stefan's dismissal of Klaus's failed hybrids as a "master race" in "The Hybrid" (3.02), it's also a neat reminder that Stefan was around when the 13th Amendment to the United States Constitution was adopted in 1865, which outlawed slavery.

THE RULES Using hypnosis, Shane is able to access Jeremy's subconscious instincts as a hunter — to kill vampires, even Elena — and give him a choice. Instead of just following his conditioned response, he can now choose between the kill response or the detour option, which is guided by his instinct to protect Bonnie, now extended to Elena and other vampires he doesn't consciously want to kill. Though they don't get to test it out, Bonnie thinks Caroline's idea of using the body-jump spell to put Klaus into Rebekah's inert daggered corpse should work. (File that away under ideas to use later.)

PREVIOUSLY ON *THE VAMPIRE DIARIES* Elena remembers being deeply in love with Stefan the last time she was at the lakehouse; in "Crying Wolf" (2.14), she stood at the end of the dock, wrapped in the same blanket she is here, with Stefan.

Klaus reminds Stefan about his own form of keeping mementoes: in "The End of the Affair" (3.03), Klaus takes Stefan back to his old 1920s apartment where he kept a list of names of all those he'd killed on the wall in a closet.

References to Klaus's artistic talents began in his very first appearance in "Klaus" (2.19), when Elijah told Elena that he and Klaus had planted fake Curse of the Sun and Moon drawings throughout various cultures. In "Dangerous Liaisons" (3.14), Klaus shows Caroline his paintings and drawings in his studio, during the Mikaelson ball. And then there's that horse drawing.

OFF CAMERA "It really was a Winter Wonderland," Candice Accola told *Entertainment Weekly* about filming *TVD*'s first holiday episode. "It was just cool enough in Georgia that you could be sipping on your hot tea, coffee, or latte sitting outside, and they've got fake snow and all these beautiful lights and they're playing Christmas music. It was a cool week to go to work."

As much as Joseph Morgan loved filming Klaus's bloody vengeance, he admitted to *Zap2It* that he also loved playing the Klaus and Caroline dynamic. "Working with Candice [Accola] is wonderful, obviously, and I love exploring the great range that the writers have given Klaus this season," he said, adding, "[Klaus is] quite captivated by Caroline. She's really gotten under his skin at this point. She brings out a more playful side to him, which I think he loves, though still with a certain sociopathic glint in his eye." In an interview with *TV Guide*, Michael Trevino insisted Caroline is only acting with Klaus, but admitted, "At the end of the day, emotions come out. Klaus is a charismatic immortal!"

Julie Plec told *TV Line* that the loss of his fellow hybrids would hit Tyler hard. "It's a setback in that his confidence came from this feeling that he had a place and he had people that were looking to him," she said. "As his mom said, 'You're a leader of people like your father was.' He was really growing into that, and to feel like they all paid the price for that confidence will definitely set him back a bit. The question is, how will he rebound from that?"

Discussing Caroline and Stefan's friendship in the wake of Stefan and Elena's break-up, Candice Accola told *TV Line*, "I don't necessarily see Caroline bringing out a fun and frivolous side to him at this point just because, right now, [there are] so many weighty things going on within both of their lives. They're going to find a comfort with each other and a comfort within their friendship because they both are in the difficult situation of wanting to support the ones that they love even if they don't agree with what they're choosing to do."

FOGGY MOMENTS Adrian takes Klaus's painting to the Grill unframed, but it's in a gilt frame when Caroline is looking at it.

Acknowledged as an error by Julie Plec on Twitter: when Stefan and Elena came to the lakehouse in "Crying Wolf," Elena said it was her first time back since her parents had died, but here she says that Jenna made them come back at Christmastime following their May deaths, which would have been before "A Few Good Men" (1.15).

When Caroline calls Stefan, he says he has new info from Klaus about the sword — but didn't Stefan already know that the sword was the way to read the map of the tattoo? In "The Five," Alexander tells Rebekah what it does, and Klaus and Rebekah relate all that info about the Five to Stefan. The location of the sword is what he tricks Rebekah into telling him, willing to betray her because he knows the object's significance to finding the Cure.

Was Hayley always planning on admitting to Tyler that she'd betrayed him? Was that her way to save him from the slaughter? Because Tyler was planning on going to the Lockwood cellar to meet the witch (who didn't actually exist) and the unsired hybrids, and he would have been ambushed by Klaus as the other hybrids were.

QUESTIONS

- Will Hayley get the info on her birth parents from Shane?
- Why did Klaus use the hunter's sword in his slaughter of the hybrids? Was it a significant choice? Did he bring it with him because he didn't trust Stefan, or because he already knew he'd have to kill a dozen defectors that day? The sword was part of the initiation spell the witch used to create the Five. Is there a purpose for the sword besides reading the map of the tattoo? (Did the other hunters have swords and if so where did those end up?)
- After this full-scale hybrid revolt, will Klaus still be interested in building another hybrid army? Will he still want to turn Elena human again so he can use her blood, or will this sour him on his whole master plan? Does Klaus consider himself even with Tyler, now that he's killed Carol and left him without family, or does Tyler still have a target on his back?
- Where will Damon and Jeremy find the vampires to kill in order to complete the mark? Will they turn people, like Stefan did in "My Brother's Keeper"? How many vamps does Jeremy have to kill to complete the mark?
- How does Shane know where Silas is buried?
- Who is the link between Silas and the hunters? Was the "dying witch" who created the hunters the one who buried him alive over a century earlier (and thus could have created a map, sword, and counterspell to free him)? If Silas *invented* the immortality spell he used on himself, does that mean he is also a super-vamp like the Originals? Does he pre-date Esther (was she using his spell?) or were two immortality spells independently created?
- April, doesn't that dagger look like it wants to come out of Rebekah's chest?

Rebekah (to Stefan and Elena): Why are my least favorite people always the most durable?

4.10 *After School Special*

Original air date: January 17, 2013
Written by: Brett Matthews
Directed by: David Von Ancken
Guest cast: Erin A. Smith (Pizza Delivery Girl)

Rebekah grills Caroline, Elena, and Stefan in the Mystic Falls High library; Klaus takes Jeremy's training into his own hands; and Bonnie gets a dad after 75 episodes.

The drama of a regular high school pales in comparison to that at Mystic Falls High. "After School Special" lives up to its name, but instead of dealing with teen pregnancy or the dangers of drugs (you'll jump off the school roof!), it's a lesson in truth, lies, and the power of both to hurt. Substitute teacher from hell Rebekah compels her would-be pupils into revealing whatever she wants them to. And there's a lot of fun to be had both on campus and at the lakehouse where Damon acts as coach to his two teen charges. Elements like Matt and Jer wrestling, Klaus's little counting game, and Rebekah's sharp tongue bring levity to counterbalance the otherwise heavy revelations between Stefan and Elena.

April Young seems almost obsessed with the fact that those she thought were her friends were actually *lying* to her, more disturbed by that than the supernatural truths Rebekah revealed to her. But as Rebekah's compulsion-fueled game of Truth or More Truth plays out, it's clear that sometimes *not* telling the truth is the humane thing to do. In the intensely awkward library scene, Caroline acts as the audience stand-in, begging Rebekah to stop making Elena and Stefan spill more than they already have and cause even greater misery and pain. But, as the saying goes, the truth will out.

Rebekah wants revenge: on Stefan for his part in her latest daggering and on her brother Klaus for his millennium of betrayal. But as much as Rebekah hates Klaus, she's adopted his strategy here. When Tyler betrayed

Klaus and led the hybrids to rise against him, Klaus decided to not physically punish Tyler but to hurt him back by killing his mother. Similarly Rebekah doesn't go for physical torture in order to get even, she goes for the emotional torture. Both want to hurt others the way they've been hurt — they know how truly miserable an eternity alone is and do their best to inflict that pain on others. (A well-adjusted lot, those Mikaelsons.) Rebekah's attempt to have wolf-Tyler kill Stefan, Elena, and Caroline is halfhearted; she could easily kill them herself, but she'd rather witness their turmoil, content in the knowledge that, even if they survive this no-vamp-running in the hallways scare, they have a lifetime of pain ahead of them — which in a twisted way means she will not be alone with hers.

An unintended consequence to Rebekah's brand of mayhem is that it helps Tyler more than it hurts him, ultimately. Instead of continuing to bottle his anger and grief as he does at the memorial assembly (or by taking it out on his cell phone), Rebekah forces him to give the beast inside him the reins. Happily he doesn't kill his girlfriend or friends in the process, but the end result of Tyler losing control is him letting in his grief. As he accepts comfort from Caroline, he expresses his guilt and feeling of responsibility for his mother's murder. A heartbreaking moment.

Also in the running for the greatest pain, misery, and suffering in "After School Special" is Mr. Stefan Salvatore — forced to hear his "epic love" Elena say she's in love with his brother. Not only did she sleep with Damon, she's in *love* with him and she's not in love with Stefan anymore. The poor guy has been fearing this exact thing for ages, and there it is: his fear realized. Though he still tries to protect her from Rebekah, his manner toward Elena markedly changes — and it's never more apparent than in that desolate walk down the empty hallway away from her, not stopping, not turning back, not indulging her need to talk it out and (let's be honest) help Elena feel less guilty about it. And, of course, there's the unbelievable choice that precipitates that moment: Stefan says that he wants to forget, to lose all the good memories to erase the suffering, the scar tissue that is Elena Gilbert as Rebekah puts it. He feels the opposite of what Elena felt back in season one's "Haunted." When Damon first compelled Jeremy to forget about Vicki's vamp turn and death, Elena told Stefan she didn't want to be compelled to forget the pain she felt and the horror she had witnessed because that would mean losing what she felt for Stefan. Here Stefan, devastated as he is, asks for a reprieve from the pain. But Rebekah, for her own reasons, denies him the easy way out.

"The biggest challenge for us [on a season-to-season basis] is having high-stakes jeopardy while staying grounded in reality as much as possible. Never getting too bored or too sci-fi/fantasy. Every episode requires us to put a bunch of people who have a high tolerance for pain and death in life-threatening situations. That is hard enough, but we also need that over-arching season jeopardy — like opening the doors to hell on earth, but making it feel tonally like our show. And then making that feel fresh."

— Caroline Dries

And so to avoid a lifetime of wondering how much influence that pesky sire bond has over Elena's heart, the race for the Cure is on with various motivations driving the hunt. Elena wants to be human again; Rebekah says she wants to force Klaus to take it so he's left powerless; Stefan and Damon want Elena to take it so she's cured of the sire bond, as well as vampirism; Klaus wants to breed more hybrids with a renewed supply of doppelgänger blood; and Shane wants to raise Silas — and all those who died in his name.

While Stefan's terrible day goes from Damon-style day-drinking at the Grill to even greater heartbreak, Damon experiences a joy he's been waiting his whole life to experience. After Elena tells him she loves him, that expression on his face speaks volumes — namely that he's been waiting to hear that (from one doppelgänger or another) for 150 years. A perfect touch to a solid Damon episode. From him bossing around Matt and Jer to his sassy repartee with Klaus to his broody voicemail-on-repeat listens, Damon shone in all his Damon-y goodness in "After School Special." He is not scared of Klaus — and shooting him for Carol Lockwood was well-deserved vengeance — but Klaus sees through the "bad" Salvatore's good behavior and recognizes the darker side that's being denied there. Klaus's presence and desire to cut to the chase (or massacre, as it were) brings out that same logic in Damon: "His idea was better." The best plan really is to turn innocents and then slaughter them — assuming you've set all your moral compunctions aside. How will Elena react to this slaughter, committed partly in her name? Will Jeremy do as he's told and start staking the bar patrons?

Though ultimately Damon decides on a Klausian course of action, his instinct is to protect Jeremy — not to let him go hunting before he's ready

© Andrew Evans/PRPhotos.com

— and that theme of protection runs through "After School Special," beginning in its opening scene where the only two remaining parents in Mystic Falls (or so it seems) hold a mandatory assembly at the school. With Carol Lockwood's departure, another parent fills the void: Bonnie's dad, about whom we've heard very little over the last three and a half seasons, is making up for lost time, as he tries to impose a little law and order in Mystic Falls as interim mayor (after six other people said no thanks to the position — hilarious). Rudy makes it clear to Liz that he's taking the thankless job to protect his daughter, who in turn gets fired up at the idea of him trying to boss her around. Bonnie's pretty much had free rein since her Grams died, and she's proven that while she always has the best of intentions, she could use some guidance and supervision. Ironically, the protection spell she does on Shane results in near death for April, as Bonnie unwittingly ties the orphan's lifeforce to the tortured prof's. And in a strange turn, the willful Kol returns to town, last seen in Denver in "Heart of Darkness," and declares that the apocalyptic, hellish doom that Silas will bring with him is not worth the Cure: in effect, *Kol* of all people acts as protector of the entire world when he kills Shane. Too bad for the planet, Shane ain't properly dead — thanks to his gifted pupil who thinks she just protected the righteous side.

COMPELLING MOMENT Klaus and Damon's fireside hangout — there could be another Mikaelson-Salvatore bromance in the works . . .

CIRCLE OF KNOWLEDGE
- No Matt in this episode.
- *After School Specials* began in 1972 on ABC with made-for-TV movies broadcast (you guessed it) after school. Running until the mid-1990s, the most memorable after school specials were heavy-handed morality plays for teens about hot topics like drug use, pregnancy, alcoholism, and abuse. Whatever the worst possible outcome, that's what befell the poor lead character. Kinda like at Mystic Falls High, but without the supernatural hijinks.
- "After School Special" calls to mind a classic *Dawson's Creek* episode ("Detention") where the gang had Saturday detention (in a plot line nod to the John Hughes film *The Breakfast Club*) and troublemaker Abby Morgan weaseled secrets out of Joey, Dawson, Pacey, and Jen in the high school library.

- There may be an ever-shrinking student population at MFHS, but that doesn't stop them from having a beekeeper society: a poster advertising the club can be seen behind Elena when she exits the mandatory assembly. The chalkboard in the biology classroom (which Stefan peers into looking for Rebekah) still has the same notes about frog dissections that were visible in "We'll Always Have Bourbon Street," when Damon asked Elena to try blood-bag blood again.
- Rudy Hopkins says to Liz of Carol, "She did not go gently, did she?" using a turn of phrase from the famous Dylan Thomas poem about a dying parent, also used as a title for the season three episode "Do Not Go Gentle."
- Damon's surprising (and endearing) familiarity with children's literature continues when he calls Jeremy the "Little Hunter That Could," a play on *The Little Engine That Could* (1930) about a train engine that repeats "I think I can" as it chug-chug-chugs its way through a difficult task, just like Little Gilbert.
- In his second Darwinian reference of the season, Damon suggests that Jeremy learning to protect himself before attacking a vampire nest (the first time "nest" has been used in that context on this show) is a solid "survival of the fittest" strategy. And certainly, someone as fit as Jer should survive.
- Compulsion doesn't work on Shane; "A little trick I picked up in Tibet," he tells Kol. He's not the first human able to circumvent vampire compulsion: Bill Forbes trained himself to resist it, but Professor Shane seems more likely to have gone the route of mysticism, meditation, and Buddhism.

HISTORY LESSON If Silas and Qetsiyah lived 2,000 years ago, that means they predate the Original family by 1,000 years, and that puts them firmly in biblical times (late 1st century BCE/early 1st century CE), contemporaries of Jesus Christ and the first emperor of Rome, Augustus Caesar. Despite the heavy biblical connections, it is unclear *where* Silas and Qetsiyah lived.

THE RULES Bonnie's protection spell accidentally links Shane to April, and April experiences his injuries (and presumably he is saved when she is healed by Stefan's blood?). The magic Bonnie used is called Expression, which is separate from the nature and spirit world and is neither good or bad — it's neutral and limitless, defined only by its user. (Or so says Mr. Massacres-Are-No-Biggie Shane.)

PREVIOUSLY ON *THE VAMPIRE DIARIES* Grams and Bonnie talk about her dad in "162 Candles" (1.08); he didn't like Bonnie staying with Grams too much, because Grams will "fill [Bonnie's] head with witchy juju." The two also agreed that Rudy Hopkins "lacks imagination" and "is always right."

Bonnie recognizes Kol too late when she passes him in the hallway outside Shane's office because they've never really interacted: they barely cross paths in "All My Children" (3.15) when Bonnie helped Esther with her spell to make her children human again and Kol showed up with his brothers.

Klaus gives Damon some unsolicited whittling advice, and he snarks back, "I know how to whittle." Maybe not: Stefan gave him a hard time about his ability to whittle in "The Murder of One" (3.18) when they were making stakes from white oak.

Caroline covers a naked Tyler and holds him, like after his first transformation in "By the Light of the Moon" (2.11).

Stefan wants Rebekah to make him forget like Klaus made him forget in "The End of the Affair" (3.03).

OFF CAMERA New Mystic Falls mayor and Bonnie's always-out-of-town father, Rudy Hopkins, is played by veteran American actor Rick Worthy. Worthy has had several memorable roles in genre shows like *Heroes* (as Matt Parkman's partner in the LAPD), *Supernatural* (as the Alpha vampire), and *Battlestar Galactica* (as Cylon Number Four, a.k.a. Simon), but he's perhaps best known for playing several different characters throughout the Star Trek franchise, including *Deep Space Nine*, *Voyager*, and *Enterprise*. He also costarred in the ABC Family miniseries *Fallen* with Paul Wesley. "It's a good gig," Worthy told *Supernatural Radio* of his work on *TVD*. "*The Vampire Diaries* is awesome [and] there are a lot of *Supernatural* fans who also watch." Kat Graham revealed to *ET Online* that fans had written her, Julie Plec, and CW Network president, Mark Pedowitz, about Bonnie's father, well before the role was cast. "They are not shy with their opinions and they've always wanted to see Bonnie's dad."

FOGGY MOMENTS Caroline and Stefan might be more successful at sneak attacks if they stopped staring at their phones and texting each other. And it looked pretty and all, but who left all those candles burning unattended on the wooden gym bleachers in the deserted school?

QUESTIONS
- How do Kol and Rebekah know about Silas? Does Silas want to raise *all* the dead or just those who died for him? How does Shane know what Silas will do once freed? Why does Shane want to free Silas?
- Did the power of Bonnie's protection spell have to do with the lovely human-bone pendant she was using to connect to Shane? How did Shane get the human-bone pendant considering it came from the 2,000-year-old witch Qetsiyah?
- Is Jeremy ready to kill all those vampires at once?

> *Professor Shane: You're accusing me of orchestrating a mass murder.*
> *Do you know how ridiculous that sounds?*
> *Sheriff Forbes: It's Mystic Falls. It's actually one of the*
> *least ridiculous things I've heard.*

4.11 Catch Me If You Can

Original air date: January 24, 2013
Written by: Brian Young and Michael Narducci
Directed by: John Dahl
Guest cast: David Ryan Shipman (Mystery Man)

Kol sics a compelled Damon on Jeremy, while Stefan and Rebekah engage in team-building exercises as they join the race for the Cure.

Things get a little more out of control than usual in Mystic Falls in "Catch Me If You Can" (which is to say: a lot) as characters are thrust into situations where their ids go totally unchecked. Whether under duress, compulsion, some mystical force, or on a misguided mission, these characters just don't recognize their behavior as being *that* bad, and it's wildly entertaining. They're not crazy — just passionate!

Stefan, hanging with his new ally Rebekah, isn't the only one who has a little devil whispering in his ear telling him to just let go: Jeremy is thrown into hunter overdrive thanks to Klaus and Damon's plan, but he knows he's on the edge and it's all he can do to keep his "detour" strategy active and not shoot to kill. Compelled by Kol, Damon cannot stop his hunt to kill Jeremy, which would have the net effect of losing the map and keeping Elena a vampire forever, sire bond intact. Though Kol did threaten to rip off Jer's arms (very creative work-around to the Hunter's Curse!), his clear perspective on the larger picture is kind of important: raising Silas could mean the *end of time*. Of course, he's not motivated by general do-goodery to stop a group of self-obsessed vampires from ending the world in order to see if a girl really loves one guy or the other. Kol has his own selfish motivation: he's immortal and he'd rather not spend his very long life living in hell on earth.

Kol's determination that that will never happen (going as far as to raise the white oak stake against his sister) is counterbalanced by Shane's fanatical devotion to seeing that it does. To do that, he needs Bonnie under his thumb. She is being toyed with by Shane (who in turn is being harassed by the cops thanks to Rebekah and her minion April), and he goads her into unleashing her new and limitless power . . . only to rein her back in with his hypnotic mantra that *she's* in control. Shane continues to be weirdly compelling; even Bonnie's dad's insight into Shane's character doesn't protect him from being hoodwinked, just like everyone else. Bonnie's right to not trust Shane, but, as with so many other uneasy alliances between characters (see: Elena asking Klaus for help), she needs his guidance to prevent her from becoming a power-obsessed "time bomb." He's created a monster in Bonnie and then rather cynically positioned himself as her only access to self-control.

And then there's Ms. Sire Bond: the usually self-aware Elena is clueless to the fact that she hasn't been making the same choices old Elena would. Elena is beginning to change from the empathetic heroine to an object of derision and frustration, as she is in this episode. Matt tells her that the old Elena wouldn't trust Damon with Jeremy after he sided with Klaus's plan to kill all those people. Jeremy reiterates that Damon does not care about *him* as anything more than a means to an end — as a tattoo to be revealed. (Though it's not true, as evidenced by Damon's willingness to die rather than kill Jer, it's a reasonable assumption for Jeremy to make.) And when Elena repeatedly says she doesn't want to hurt innocent people or have her loved ones do horrible things, but then fails to make decisions that prevent that, Elena comes off as a hypocrite — or, as Rebekah puts it, a child who only thinks of herself. The problem is, of course, she has limited self-determination, thanks to the sire bond. Each time she starts to object to Damon's modus operandi, his reassurances work on her in a way that they wouldn't on a free-willed, fully rational person.

It's her delusion of having self-control that makes Elena frustrating to the other characters. This season has been peppered with acts of compulsion and with overwhelming mythological urges, and, like Damon under Kol's compulsion, most of the targets realize that they are being manipulated. The hybrids broke their curse. Damon does his best to right the course he's on by warning Jeremy and by urging Jeremy to kill him. In contrast, Elena hasn't fought her sire bond at all, in fact she doesn't feel fettered by it or that she has betrayed herself. For however long it lasts, Elena being cut off from both Salvatores (Stefan wanting her out of the house, and Damon imprisoned to protect Jeremy) seems to be the best thing for her. She's at her brother's side, putting his welfare first. And clever vamp that she is, it doesn't take her more than a minute to come up with a diabolical master plan: kill Kol, and thereby erase his entire line of vampires. Jeremy won't have to spend his lifetime killing vampire after vampire, Damon's compulsion will break, and . . . countless anonymous vampires will drop dead. Who are the vampires in Kol's line? Are they the less murderous Caroline and Lexi types, or are they repeat offenders — like Stefan or Damon? The problem with loving vampires who've done their fair share of bad, bad things is that when you set out to kill some nameless vampire, you're aware that you're murdering *someone*. It's an arguably unavoidable result of the basic premise of this show, but it's one that creates a strange immorality in the characters we have grown to love.

Rebekah advises Stefan to stop caring and just have fun. Nothing like keeping a character bottled up for seasons (save for a ripper vacation or two) and then letting him smoke some witchy weed and get down with an ex-girlfriend for some double-the-crazy sex. Fun is, in fact, possible, especially for viewers watching Stefan let go, stop caring (as much as he can . . . he's still *Stefan*), take some pleasure in snapping his brother's neck and bleeding him out to weaken him, and have a legitimate reason to keep him under lock and key. It was a nice throwback to the season one animosity between the brothers, but instead of Stefan feeling conflicted about it, he displays a devil-may-care attitude that is quite entertaining. And after Elena's (compelled) brutal honesty in "After School Special," there was something satisfying and painfully honest in Stefan's moment of retaliation, particularly the heart-stopper of a line "You don't know what I look like when I'm not in love with

Tyler Cook on Editing "Catch Me If You Can"

This episode holds a special place in my heart for a few reasons. If you look back on the year as a whole, I doubt that many people would single this one out as being anything special but I think that is why I'm partial to it. "Catch Me If You Can" was just 42 minutes of nonstop, balls-to-the-wall fun. We open up on a wild chase through the forest as Matt is being hunted by these newly formed vampires. Klaus is at his most devilish throughout the episode. Damon being compelled by Kol into hunting down and killing Jeremy is a fun twist. I also love seeing the Stefan/Rebekah relationship play out a little bit. We only got to see their relationship very briefly in "The End of the Affair" [3.03] and it was fun to explore why they are so attracted to each other (bonus points to see Stefan going after someone other than Elena).

The Act 6 scene between Stefan and Elena ["You don't know what I look like when I'm not in love with you"] is particularly devastating. Everything about that scene, the way it was written, performed, and directed was just painfully honest. I took a long time to cut it because I wanted to get the tone and emotion of it just right and I just remember connecting a lot to the scene. We all have break-ups and go through hard things and I just remember needing a really strong drink after I finished cutting that scene.

Another reason I liked the episode is that I was able to use some of my own personal favorite music. The xx, Zola Jesus, Phantogram, Sallie Ford, and the Sound Outside, these are bands I love that I got to feature in a really cool way.

And lastly I got to work with John Dahl who is a director I admire tremendously. He is very economical in the way he directs, and it's so easy as an editor to see his plan and execute it and have it turn out really well. There is one scene in the beginning of the episode, when Damon and Jeremy walk into the bar and find out that Kol has killed all of the vampires, that I think is a master class in how to direct tension/suspense in a really cool way.

you." He calls her out on her hypocrisy: yes, Rebekah has tried to kill Elena (and others), but hasn't Damon done terrible things too? After being unable to truly have fun with Elena at the beginning of this season, Stefan is finally able to let go and enjoy himself with Rebekah.

And what a welcome change of pace it is to finally see Rebekah in a power position. She's leading her own Race for the Cure team, easily seduces the last man she loved, is wise about protecting the tombstone from him, stands up to both of her brothers (with mixed results, admittedly), and shows off her appreciation for other cultures while she's at it. She's something of an

© Emiley Schweich/PRPhotos.com

underdog among the Originals and, while no one believes for a minute that she's given up on love, it's a pleasure to watch her pretend.

COMPELLING MOMENT Rebekah inspiring *Stefan* to say this: "Crazy sex is always good." And then to have some.

CIRCLE OF KNOWLEDGE
- No Tyler or Caroline.
- Beyond its long-standing use as a playground taunt, *Catch Me If You Can* is the title of Frank Abagnale Jr.'s autobiography published in 1980 and turned into a feature film starring Leonardo DiCaprio and Tom Hanks in 2002. Abagnale was an incredibly successful con man who posed as a Pan Am pilot and cashed bad checks to the tune of $2.8 million in the 1960s. Between the race for the Cure, Kol compelling Damon to kill Jeremy, and all the newbie vampires compelled to kill Matt, it's an episode chock-full of high-stake pursuits, like the caper it shares a title with.
- When Stefan and Rebekah start poking around Shane's office at Whitmore College, Rebekah declares the professor has "a bit of an afterlife fetish." Objects in Shane's office include: Hopi prayer feathers, traditionally tied around the forehead of the deceased before burial; a Han Dynasty soul vase, thought to be vessels that were filled with fruit to accompany the deceased to the afterlife or containers intended to house the soul; and the so-called Polynesian sacrificial knife, which, despite Rebekah's assertion that it's a "brutal way to die, but at least you appease the gods," couldn't be Polynesian, as it's made of metal and it was in Polynesia's Stone Age, four centuries ago, that human sacrifices took place.

THE RULES We get a refresher on the subtleties of compulsion: only the vampire who compelled you can "de-compel" you. If you take vervain after being compelled to do something (like bite off your own tongue), the vervain only prevents further compulsion, it doesn't erase previous commands. Kol, like Klaus before him, tests that Damon is vervain-free and susceptible to compulsion by making him stab himself. If an Original is daggered, their compulsion over someone ends.

PREVIOUSLY ON *THE VAMPIRE DIARIES* Rebekah wistfully recollects the days when Stefan was fun, which we glimpsed in "The End of the Affair" (3.03).

Kol's carefully worded promise to Klaus — that *he* won't hurt Jeremy — is a trick that Elijah trotted out in his first appearance in the series in "Rose" (2.08).

When Elena pleads with him to resist the compulsion to kill Jeremy, Damon says he's not Stefan, who resisted Klaus's compulsion to feed on Elena (for as long as he could) in "The Reckoning" (3.05).

As Stefan points out, this is not the first time Damon has gone after Jeremy: Damon snapped his neck in "The Return" (2.01).

To prevent him from killing Jeremy (again), Stefan locks his brother in the handy-dandy Salvatore cell, where Damon has spent time before ("You're Undead to Me," 1.05).

OFF CAMERA Kat Graham spent most of her early season four episodes working closely with David Alpay and she was highly complimentary of her costar. "When I find out I have scenes with him, I get really excited," she told *Hollywood Life.* "He's one of the most professional, brilliant actors I've ever worked with. He's so focused, he always knows his lines, he's always early. He's such a great guy to work with, and we just have this natural chemistry."

Editor Tyler Cook found cutting the teaser especially fun: "It was just great to do this giant chase through the forest with Matt and Jeremy being hunted by all of these newly formed vampires."

QUESTIONS
- How many people has Kol turned in his 900 years? (He only spent from 1910 'til last season daggered.) Just how large a vampire genocide would Jeremy be committing if he could get his hands on the white oak stake and kill Kol?
- Why does Kol hate Damon so much?
- Who was the Mystery Man? Is there another team looking for the Cure?
- Does Bonnie have her magic under control?

Damon (to Klaus): If you're gonna be bad, be bad with purpose.
Otherwise you're just not worth forgiving.

4.12 *A View to a Kill*

Original air date: January 31, 2013
Written by: Rebecca Sonnenshine
Directed by: Brad Turner
Guest cast: Persia White (Abby Bennett)

Mayor Hopkins cancels the Decade Dance but that doesn't stop Stefan from giving Rebekah a tour of the greatest hits of the '80s. Elena plans a hit of her own.

A great '80s-themed episode, "A View to a Kill" plays to all the strengths of *The Vampire Diaries* (and, no, those are not limited to Steven R. McQueen's pectorals): it was fun and funny, scary and violent, full of excellent reusable turns of phrases (e.g., revenge-sex handbook; villain bonding time; dysfunctional, bickering lunatics . . .), and packs an emotional punch thanks to the balance of out-there supernatural situations and relatable moments. From the (perfectly soundtracked) Stefan sneak-out the morning after getting down with Rebekah to the boys glued to their video game and the sink full of dirty dishes, to the actual parenting crackdown on Bonnie (parents! parenting! in Mystic Falls!), "A View to a Kill" blended reality with OTT insanity. This show does that like no other when it's at its best.

Mayor Rudy Hopkins takes an entirely different approach than the event-happy Carol Lockwood did: putting vervain in the water, sizzling the town's vampires without warning, instituting a curfew, and cutting out extraneous fun. It's like he has noticed that vampires tend to pounce at a town-wide event. As hilarious as it is when Bonnie tries to argue that she was doing aegreat job of protecting the town (she tries, but . . .), the conflict between her and her suddenly omnipresent father — not to mention her AWOL vampire mother popping back into town for a family meeting — plays out like a proper teen TV moment. Except here, Bonnie's not "acting out" by doing drugs or hanging with the wrong crowd; she's messing with potentially earth-ending witchcraft. And she's powerful enough to win the battle against Rudy and Abby and declare herself emancipated from the spirits.

As Bonnie's parents work together to control their daughter, over at the Gilbert household it's time for the sibling duo to team up. That home is at first the only safe place for Jeremy — since Kol has not yet been invited in — but by episode's end it's been turned into a site of violence and then a prison for Klaus. Elena and Jer work together to defend their house, their future, and their family against Kol's unrelenting and vicious attack, and their success against him comes down to how well they fight side by side, each willing to die for the other. Next to the Christmas massacre of "O Come, All Ye Faithful," this knock-down-drag-out fight scene is a highlight of the season's action sequences.

The bonds of family are, of course, not limited to the Gilberts, and, as Stefan warns Elena when she tells him her plan, the Originals may bicker and dagger, but they are *family* always and forever. By killing Kol — and Klaus rather unfortunately witnesses his baby bro burned to death — the comfortable alliance they've had with Klaus comes to an abrupt end, and the wrath of Klaus tends to be mighty. What consequences will such an irrevocable action bear for the Gilberts, their allies, and the remaining Originals?

And how does it tie in to the captivating villain bonding between Klaus and Damon? Do bad things for good reasons, says expert Damon, if you want a chance at forgiveness. Is there honor in revenging one's sibling? Certainly Mr. Honorable Himself, Elijah, thought so back at the end of season two, when he plotted to kill Klaus for destroying the family. In Klaus's wonderful scene with Damon in the Salvatore holding cell and then later when he sees Kol murdered, Joseph Morgan gives us that perfect amount of emotional connection with his character — Klaus is still formidable and fearsome but his longing for forgiveness from Caroline and then his pain at losing his brother is palpable. In his fury trapped on the other side of the threshold to the Gilbert house, Klaus reveals his true motivation in chasing down the Cure. It's not about creating more hybrids; it seems he's learned his lesson there. He wants to destroy the Cure, to prevent anyone from trying to eradicate him with that "ultimate weapon."

Add Rebekah to the list of Originals who make you feel for them. In "A View to a Kill," she owns her healthy skepticism and, instead of being duped and daggered as she was in "The Five," she's in charge. She knows what Stefan will do, but it turns out she also knows the way *not* to be betrayed by Stefan. She's honest. From her straightforward reaction to their hook-up (and the potential for more) to calling him out on his would-be trickery with the dagger, Rebekah is as self-possessed and confident as she's ever been. When she opens up to Stefan, she's in different company than with her brothers, who mock her for her sentimentality; Stefan's a kindred spirit (as his adoration for the earnestness of '80s flicks demonstrates). Her burning desire to go to a high school dance is not about boredom, it's about getting what she most wishes for: the average experiences a 17-year-old girl might take for granted. And like her big brother revealing his true motivation for chasing the Cure, Rebekah says that she is not interested in it as a way to punish Klaus (which, funnily enough, is what he's trying to prevent), but because she wants nothing more than to be human again — to have a second chance, a fresh start. An opportunity to make and keep friends, to love and be loved, to have fun, to grow up and maybe have a family. Stefan sees his own wishes reflected in hers and so he can't betray her. She doesn't "deserve" to be daggered any more than the rest of them deserve that kind of treatment.

He understands that they have a lot more in common than is visible at first blush, and he makes a true ally out of her — despite knowing that his choice upsets Elena's master plan to "kill" two Originals with one stone (or one dagger plus a body-jump spell, to be more precise). In a twist on Damon's advice to Klaus, Stefan is "good with purpose" and he will likely be forgiven because his deviation from the plot was motivated by something noble.

Elena and Jeremy, on the other hand, have acted in the spirit of being bad with purpose, killing Kol and the countless vampires that he's sired in the past 900 years. Will finding the Cure prove worth it?

COMPELLING MOMENT Staked to the wall by a railing post, unable to pull it out, Elena decides to drag it all the way through her, so she can save her brother from losing his Hulk-arms to Kol. Gruesome and fierce. Both Gilberts are certified badasses.

CIRCLE OF KNOWLEDGE
- No Tyler or Caroline.
- The 14th James Bond film, *A View to a Kill* (1985) is the last to star Roger Moore as British MI6 agent 007. And what a spectacle to go out on: the opening sequence features Bond on a makeshift snowboard escaping down a mountain while the Beach Boys' "California Girls" plays and Russians pursue him. Toss in Grace Jones, Christopher Walken, a horse race, a jump off the Eiffel Tower, the threat of "microchip technology," the Cold War, and a title sequence featuring women in neon bodypaint

Dave Perkal on *TVD*'s Cinematography

On the joy of cinematography: I enjoy creating an image that resonates. If I could hang that image on the wall and it would live on its own, then I've done my job. Sometimes there is a serendipitous moment that creates a fortuitous synergy, and those are things that keep you coming back for more.

On creating the *TVD* look: I use the notion of a painterly gothic frame and work from that. How far I push that idea and how dark I go depends on the characters and the emphasis of the particular scene. While the individual scenes vary, the episodes as a whole are visually similar to maintain the look of the series. I like the flashback scenes the best. It's my opportunity to create a different look within the world of *Vampire Diaries*.

On shooting in the dark: It does create its own challenges. Is a glint in the eye enough or do I need to show just a little bit more? Contrary to popular belief, dark lighting actually requires *more* lighting, because you have a lot of little lights rather than one big light.

On the camera department: Cinematographers are always the final word on composition and framing and I have fantastic camera operators that act as a second set of eyes. The opportunity to collaborate with operators who will elevate my ideas is invaluable. This show is particularly challenging for the camera department. The shots are complicated and difficult, but the greater the challenge the more they rise to the occasion. One thing we always do is remember to make our job fun. The crew is like family, and because of the long hours many of us spend more time together than we do with our actual families.

gyrating to the theme song by quintessential '80s pop group Duran Duran, and you've got a cheesefest extraordinaire. Like every Bond film, *TVD*'s "A View to a Kill" features a major villain, a secret plot to take him out, and an action-packed fight.

- Kol asks Elena if she's killed anyone or if she's a "Mary Sue vampire." The term "Mary Sue" originated in *Star Trek* fan fiction and came to be shorthand for an idealized, unrealistic female character who acted as the author's wish-fulfilling proxy in the story. Kol may be taking a dig at the Twilight Saga's Bella Swan, often labeled a Mary Sue vampire.

- Eighties fashion, defined by acid washed denim, neon colors, Lycra, Spandex, and shoulder pads, might indeed have been "tragic," as Rebekah declares, and worse than 17th-century Puritan smocks (think plain, somber, and no peek-a-boo skin showing). While Rebekah's outfit is topped off with the clip-on koala bear, Stefan rocks a *Top Gun* style jacket.

- In his role as dance DJ, Stefan rather hilariously puts on a song by The Cure ("Lovesong"), a fitting choice for these Cure-obsessed immortals. While it was a pain for Bonnie to inflate them all, Caroline's 99 red balloons homage to Nena's 1983 hit song "99 Luftballons" looks pretty freaking awesome.

- Stefan explains the appeal of '80s films to Rebekah, saying it's an era of "love, friendship, the possibility of anything happening" as in Rob Reiner's 1987 adaptation of William Goldman's *The Princess Bride*, a romantic comedy-fantasy that is now considered a cult classic, and Cameron Crowe's 1989 romantic comedy-drama *Say Anything*, starring John Cusack as Lloyd Dobler, who memorably stands in his love interest's yard with a boom box over his head, blasting Peter Gabriel's "In Your Eyes." John Hughes's 1985 comedy-drama *The Breakfast Club*, about five high schoolers ("a brain, a beauty, a jock, a rebel, and a recluse") who spend Saturday detention together and transcend their stereotypes, gets more play when Stefan tries to teach Rebekah the "slide" that the gang does as they run through the empty hallways attempting to escape the notice of Principal "Mess with the bull you get the horns" Vernon.

- Kol tells Elena that he's run with witches in 14th-century Africa, 17th-century Haiti, and 1900s New Orleans. What vaguely connects these groups of witches is Voodoo, specifically West African Vodun, Haitian Vodou, and New Orleans (or Louisiana) Voodoo. Many Africans who were transported to Haiti in the 17th century were forbidden from practicing their religion and were forced to observe Catholic beliefs; practitioners would disguise their deities and spirits as Catholic saints, thus leading to the development of Haitian Vodou. A similar incarnation happened in Louisiana, whose African American population combined aspects of African religious beliefs with Catholicism and French-speaking culture. While they are related, Haitian Vodou and New Orleans Voodoo are not interchangeable terms or belief systems. New Orleans Voodoo, in particular, has a more pronounced folk magic aspect.

- Damon makes a joke about busting out of the cell "like the Hulk" — a little foreshadowing for Jeremy's major shirt-ripping, biceps-bulging, Hulk-out moment at the end.

THE RULES The hunter's mark becomes visible to non-hunters once it's complete.

PREVIOUSLY ON *THE VAMPIRE DIARIES* Stefan's assessment of the Original family as "dysfunctional, bickering lunatics" that "stick together no matter what" is a snarkier perspective on the sibling's motto "always and forever," first heard in "Ordinary People" (3.08).

Damon declares that Stefan (who slept with Rebekah) has taken a page out of his own "revenge-sex handbook": feeling slighted by Elena, Damon hooked up with the Original sister in "Dangerous Liaisons" (3.14).

Damon and Klaus log some good villain-bonding time here, calling to mind Stefan and Klaus's solid chats in season three, one of which took place in the very same cell in "Heart of Darkness" (3.19).

Kol makes a reference to the batting cages of Denver, which is where Damon and Elena found Jeremy had unwittingly befriended an Original brother in "Heart of Darkness."

Rebekah's luck with high school dances has been pretty miserable: after 1,000 years of not going to one, she was daggered by Elena on homecoming ("Homecoming," 3.09), possessed by her mother before the 1920s Decade Dance ("Heart of Darkness"), and has this '80s dance canceled on her.

Kol confirms he was daggered by Klaus in New Orleans which pinpoints where Kol's century-long coffin confinement began, which Elijah first mentioned in "Bringing Out the Dead" (3.13). Still don't know the why.

With his super-vamp reflexes, Kol gets good at the Xbox game quickly, just as Damon did when he played with Jeremy in "Children of the Damned" (1.13).

Abby Bennett uses the same magic powder to knock out her daughter that she used in "The Ties That Bind" (3.12), but it's less effective this time on super-Expression-powered Bonnie.

Stefan rocks out to a little Bon Jovi and reminisces about his BFF Lexi, and their time with the band, which we first heard about in "162 Candles" (1.08).

Rebekah knows that Stefan is attempting to manipulate her for the dagger: her uncanny ability to tell when Stefan is lying was first displayed in "Disturbing Behavior" (3.04) — though it failed her in "The Five."

OFF CAMERA Kat Graham told *TV Guide*, "This is the first scene that Bonnie and Kol have had together and it's honestly one of the most intense scenes I've had with one other person since I don't know when." Claire Holt thinks Stefan and Rebekah bring out good things in each other. "Listen, I love working with Paul Wesley," she told *ET Online*. "He's such a fine actor and such a fine human, so any time our characters get to interact, I'm happy."

QUESTIONS
- Klaus mentions that Kol has stolen his daggers. With Kol R.I.P., where will the daggers end up? Back in Klaus's possession? Lost forever?
- What did Kol do to get daggered by Klaus 100 years ago? He's *really* touchy about it.
- What are Mayor Hopkins's "resources" for acquiring enough vervain to affect the town's entire water supply?
- Just how many vampires did Jeremy kill by staking Kol? How extensive was his sire line?
- What sort of revenge will Klaus take on the Gilbert kids?

Stefan: Every single moment of the last 146 years has been ruled by the pain of being a vampire. And this Cure ends that. It ends the guilt. And it ends the suffering.

4.13 *Into the Wild*

Original air date: February 7, 2013
Written by: Caroline Dries
Directed by: Michael Allowitz
Guest cast: Camille Guaty (Caitlin Shane), Alejandro Livinalli (Man), John Gabriel Rodriguez (Massak)

Shane leads the gang to an island off the coast of Nova Scotia in search of Silas and the Cure. Even trapped in the Gilbert living room, Klaus manages to turn the tables on Tyler and Caroline.

With a witch, a tombstone, a completed hunter's mark, and the location of Silas's tomb known to Shane, "Into the Wild" takes us from Mystic Falls to Mystic Island where season-long questions about second chances, clean slates, and the difference between having hope and being manipulated come to a head.

Back in "The Five," when we first met Professor Atticus Shane, he described himself to Bonnie as a "true believer," and here when we hear his story, it's clear how accurate a label that is. Shane *believes* because he is desperate to have his wife and child back. He knows magic is real because his wife, Caitlin, was a powerful witch who died trying to perform necromancy to raise their son — and a year ago he chose to believe in the apparition who appeared to him in the form of Caitlin. His desperation to get his old life back is strong enough to transform this man, who wouldn't serve a meat dish at his wedding, into someone who orchestrates massacres and kidnappings. We've known that Shane has an "afterlife fetish" and that his dedication to the cause of raising Silas is fanatical (sorry, *passionate*), but the heart of his quest hadn't been revealed until now.

His story of losing his family clearly tugs on Elena's heartstrings. But as earnest as he may seem, Shane has also proven himself to be quite the mastermind schemer. He's trained Bonnie in Expression and given her access to great power and then made himself integral to her safety, using that power as an insurance policy for himself. It comes in handy when just-in-the-nick-of-time Elena stops Damon from killing him. Shane's carefully doled out information about Silas, the Cure, what Expression can do, and his personal story in order to lead Bonnie and company down a path he desperately needs them to follow. In the character of Shane, the dueling forces of optimism and manipulation are made manifest: he's neither a sucker nor a con artist — he's both.

And Shane's not alone in wanting a second chance at a lost paradise of a life. Just as he wants to reclaim the life he had with Caitlin and his infant son, Sam, Rebekah wants a do-over at being a human, Elena wants to go back to having that imagined future she talked about in "The Last Day," and Stefan wants a reprieve from the guilt and shame of being a ripper. Back at home, the quest for second chances is just as active, if confined to the Gilbert living room rather than an island that keeps the adventurers going in circles. Klaus is trapped and *pissed off*, but his attitude shifts from needing to show Tyler who's in control to grasping at the possibility of a sliver of a chance that Caroline might one day (maybe) forgive him his sins. Klaus displays the extremes of his personality: his #1 villain side in sassing Tyler like a champ (the drowning recommendation? shivers) or luring Caroline into staking range to regain the upper hand, and, by episode's end, his shining-eyes wish for redemption from Caroline. What she thinks of Klaus matters to him. Through Caroline, we've seen glimpses of his humanity — he goes into villain overdrive because he's hurt (not because he's bored or purely evil). As she fades away from the werewolf toxin, she says that anyone capable of loving is capable of being saved, but unless he saves her, they'll never know if he's redeemable. Caroline gives him the hope of being "saved," and so despite the fact that it is a "weak" move, he reverses the damage he's done to Caroline and feeds her his blood. As much as she remembers all the horrible things he's done, Caroline gets Klaus, and that understanding might just give him a second chance.

The same could be said of the quest for the Cure. It seems everyone has hopes and dreams, imagined outcomes, and fantasy futures relying on the Cure, the pot of gold at the end of the rainbow, and while they are risking a great deal in this quest, if they don't follow it to its conclusion, they'll always be left wondering. They'll never know if the sire bond is what made Elena want Damon over Stefan, if being human again will give them the emotional fulfillment they lack in their vampire lives, or if Silas really can raise the beloved dead.

Everyone's blind optimistic belief in the Cure as a fix-all to their problems is nicely balanced by Damon the Skeptic. He doesn't "like to speculate"; what he gleans from Shane's dead-wife-vision story is "don't eat the poisonous flowers." Elena is convinced she understands the sire bond, her true feelings, and how the Cure will change everything she wants it to change while leaving intact everything that she wants to stay the same, but Damon knows that none of them has a clue of what will *actually* happen. (It's like Tyler's speculation about what will or won't happen to Klaus's bloodline if he took the Cure. It's just that, speculation. There's no way for Tyler to know that, he just *wants* it to be the case.)

Damon's skeptical attitude is, from Elena's point of view, another example of Damon doing what he always does: sabotaging something because he doesn't think he deserves it. What rings true in this pained discussion of Elena's dream of a human life with a human Salvatore is Damon's comment, "That's not me, Elena. That's Stefan." Without doubting the earnestness of Elena's feelings for Damon (which could not be any more earnest), Damon must, at times like this, feel like a Stefan substitute, trudging the path that Elena imagined herself on with Stefan. So, no, Damon doesn't want the Cure for Elena, and he doesn't want the Cure for himself. Though he once stood in the middle of a near empty road and confessed to a stranger that his one true secret was his desire to just be human again ("The Descent"), here Damon says he's over it: that there's nothing more miserable on earth. Does he mean that, or has a season's worth of people telling him the Cure is the worst thing for his relationship with Elena finally sunk in? Has something fundamentally changed in him between then and now? Is he the only one who accepts his lot in life and doesn't want that tantalizing second chance?

Just as Shane is a fascinating study in contradictions, so is Rebekah. Rebekah doesn't think of herself as "evil"; she is guided by the same motivation as Elena — to protect her loved ones — and she rightly argues that there isn't much difference between the two of them. Their dynamic has been one of betrayal again and again, and when the tombstone is missing, Rebekah is instantly suspicious and on the edge of tears, "Was any of this real?" But it has been, definitely from Stefan's side, and even from Elena's, particularly after Rebekah saved her life from that super-stake booby trap. By giving her the white oak stake, Elena gives the three of them a second chance — maybe not at being *friends*, but as allies in pursuit of the thing they want most in the world. That Cure.

COMPELLING MOMENT Caroline convincing Klaus to save her.

CIRCLE OF KNOWLEDGE
- No Matt.
- *Into the Wild* is American writer Jon Krakauer's 1996 nonfiction account of college graduate Chris McCandless, who hitchhiked to Alaska after donating his college fund to charity and abandoning his possessions, and walked alone into the wilderness. Four months later, he was found dead. Adapted into a film by the same name in 2007, McCandless's story is often cited as an example of idealism turned tragic. This optimism gone tragically wrong parallels Shane's unrelenting belief that the ends will justify the means if he can resurrect Silas and be reunited with his son, Sam, who was killed in a car accident, and with his wife, Caitlin, a witch who died using Expression in an attempt to bring back Sam.
- "The world's most obscure, desolate island" is supposedly 200 miles off the coast of Nova Scotia, the Canadian province that is made up of a peninsula surrounded by the Atlantic Ocean and two islands. The farthest of

which, Sable Island, is only 110 miles from the mainland (population: 5) and looks nothing like the (fictional) Silas island.

- According to Shane, there are legends about Silas island, starting with a group of miners who were excavating a well, went mad, and bled themselves dry. In the opening flashback, we see Shane enter a mine shaft where names — "John Moredock" and "Melanie" among others — are scrawled on the rock wall in what appears to be blood. It's possible some of the slides he showed in his occult exhibit ("We All Go a Little Mad Sometimes") were photographs of the mine-shaft walls. While the island has attracted explorers, including Shane, it also has its own booby-trap-loving inhabitants who don't seem to want anyone going in the Silas well.
- Jeremy's tattoo consists of two distinct parts. The circle of runes and swords on his upper left chest is the map to the Cure. The part that extends down his right arm is the story of Qetsiyah and Silas. Qetsiyah's descendant (a.k.a. Bonnie's ancestor) is responsible for creating the Five over a millennia after Silas was entombed, and the hunters' mission is to find Silas, force him to take the Cure, and then, when he is human again, kill him.

HISTORY LESSON There is a loose connection between the heritage of the Haitian and Louisianan witches who warned Kol of the hell-on-earth Silas would wreak ("A View to a Kill") and the history of Nova Scotia. In the 18th century, the British exiled large numbers of Acadians (who were mostly French speaking) from present-day Nova Scotia and the other Atlantic territories in *Le Grand Dérangement* (or "Great Upheaval"). Many of the displaced ended up in Louisiana and Haiti. The Cajun people descend from those Acadian exiles, and the name Cajun itself is derived from the word "Acadian."

THE RULES Massak, Shane's islander helper witch, is able to fudge Bonnie's locator spell so that she can't retrace the path she's taken, and he seems to disorient Stefan and Rebekah so that they go in circles while searching for Jeremy.

PREVIOUSLY ON *THE VAMPIRE DIARIES* Rebekah wishes someone thought to bring s'mores, the tasty campfire treat she first had in "Smells Like Teen Spirit" (3.06) when Damon was faux-seducing her.

Rebekah and Elena bicker over their mutual betrayals: Elena daggered

© Bob Mahoney/The CW/Landov

Rebekah in "Homecoming" (3.09) and Rebekah caused Elena's death in "The Departed" (3.22). Rebekah later points out that Elena has been instrumental in plotting two of her brothers' deaths — Finn in "The Murder of One" (3.18) and Kol in "A View to a Kill" — and that when she caused the accident in "The Departed" she was protecting herself and her brothers as Evil Vampire Alaric tried to wipe out her family (and killing Elena was the only way to do that).

After Klaus had compelled Tyler to bite Caroline in "Our Town" (3.11), he later told Caroline the attack on her wasn't "personal," and here as Caroline lies dying from his werewolf venom, he says, "Nothing personal, love."

Damon tells Elena that he used to want to be human, a callback to his existential crisis in the middle of road in "The Descent" (2.12).

Elena offers Rebekah the white oak stake as a peace offering, in the same way she offered Elijah the dagger in "Klaus" (2.19) to show she was trustworthy.

OFF CAMERA When promotional stills featuring Damon standing on a beach surfaced, it was hard not to recall a certain island-centric television series Ian Somerhalder once appeared in; Damon even jokes with Shane, "Couldn't they have hidden this Cure in Hawaii?" where *Lost* filmed. "Basically, I missed *Lost*, and I asked to relive my glory on *Lost* and do a *Lost* episode," Ian Somerhalder joked to *Zap2It* when asked about filming outdoors in the middle of winter. "We were actually lucky, it was a bit of a warm spell in Atlanta, so it wasn't too brutal." What *was* brutal in the episode was Damon's "no more Mr. Nice Guy" confrontation with Shane. "Look, this Shane guy has a lot of shit going on, excuse my language," he told *TV Line*. "He's got a lot of stuff he's hiding. He's a master manipulator, and that's really why I like him. He and Damon, they're not too far off. Again, he has ill intentions, but they're for righteous reasons." He also had praise for the actor portraying Shane. "I love Dave Alpay," he told *Zap2It*. "He's brought so much life to Shane, man. Not only is he handsome as hell, but he just brings it, he brings it every time."

Concerning whether Caroline's appeal to Klaus's good side was a ploy or honesty, Joseph Morgan told *Zap2It* that he believed Candice Accola played it as genuine: "I also think it's more interesting if she was — it sort of adds a level of complexity to her character, rather than, 'Oh, we're playing another thing on Klaus.' It's more if it comes from a genuine place. As an actor and a character, I bought into it."

FOGGY MOMENTS Why did Elena bring water on the hike? Old human habits die hard? When Shane went down into the well a year ago and injured himself, losing two liters of blood, how did he get out and escape the island without being killed by the guy who was chasing him? Or is that when he made an ally of Massak? Isn't Bonnie in danger from Expression, and therefore reliant on Shane to guide her, only *if* she uses it? If she doesn't use the magic, then wouldn't she be safe as houses?

QUESTIONS
- In response to Tyler's threat that he'll force Klaus to take the Cure, Klaus argues it just might cure his entire sire line; Tyler scoffs at that. Neither of them actually knows. What *would* happen if an Original took the Cure?
- If the line of Bennett witches can be traced directly back to Qetsiyah, does that mean she and Silas both lived in or near Mystic Falls over

2,000 years ago? How was the witch who created the Five related to Ayana, the Bennett ancestor who lived over a hundred years before 1110 and knew Esther and the Original vampires in Mystic Falls?

- Why was the man (Massak?) chasing Shane in the opening flashback? Why didn't he follow him into the pit? In the opening scene, Shane says, "Congratulations. We made it." Who is he talking to? His ally Massak, ghosty Caitlin, or someone else?
- Is the "island lore" about a group of teens found drained of blood after a spring break gone wrong true — and if so, who killed them? Or did they kill themselves in attempts to speak to their loved ones?
- How did Shane originally get his hands on Silas's tombstone? His story about it being donated to Whitmore College seems more and more like a big old lie.
- What will Massacre #3 be? Did Shane originally intend on having the third massacre complete before coming to the island or does it matter if they're done before or after raising Silas?
- Who saved Jeremy's life from the hatchet attack? The hunter who jumps Damon at the end?
- What is the hunter's mark purpose in raising Silas if it doesn't actually contain a spell, or is it just a map?

Stefan (to Shane): You know what it's like to have hope,
and now you know what it feels like to lose it.

4.14 Down the Rabbit Hole

Original air date: February 14, 2013
Written by: Jose Molina
Directed by: Chris Grismer
Guest cast: Camille Guaty (Caitlin Shane), John Gabriel Rodriguez (Massak)

The Cure is found — and lost.

"Guess that's what happens when you're dumb enough to hold out hope," Stefan says in "Down the Rabbit Hole," and the idea of sacrificing and failing, of placing faith in something that turns out to be false, is central to this episode, as the gang learns there's only one dose of the Cure. One dose that ends up in the hands of Katherine Pierce. In an action-packed adventure of an episode, with shirtless spells and cave-in-causing witchery, the quest to get the Cure ends with a cliffhanger that delivers the unforeseen cost of never giving up.

The promise of the Cure has driven much of this season's action: not only could it be a way to defuse Klaus, but a cure for immortality means restored humanity. "Down the Rabbit Hole" sees several nuanced discussions of the Cure, and we learn who wants to take it and who doesn't. In Stefan and Elena's first post–break-up "friends" talk, he admits that his desire to be human predates her, because in the long run "even the good parts [of being a vampire] kind of suck too." It's an interesting turn for Stefan who has been so outwardly focused on Elena's situation this season (and, well, since he returned to Mystic Falls). After finding out that there's just the one dose, Elena regrets that so much effort has gone into getting the Cure for her, but Stefan's point lands home, that it hasn't just been for her. Each of them has their own personal motivation for trudging around that crazy island.

Pack of selfless vampires that they are, Elena wouldn't take that sole dose even if she could get her hands on it. She believes she doesn't deserve it any more than anyone else, and that instead of fighting who she's become since her death, it's time to accept it. The concept of their humanity being restored as a cure-all was always, Elena realizes, false: she changed when she died on Wickery Bridge, and becoming human again wouldn't reverse the past, her actions, or how her identity has changed into who she is now. The conversation that Stefan and Elena have at the top of the cliff about being vampires contrasts that between Caroline and Klaus. When Caroline says, "We all want the Cure," she seems to mean that she wants it for her friends, not for herself. Though we only hear it from Klaus, his words ring true: "You prefer who you are now to the girl you once were." Caroline does seem to prefer herself now — the heightened strength, the agelessness and fearlessness — and the growth she's experienced in her short time as a vampire. Hers is a self-possession that most other vampires lack.

While Stefan is among those who long for humanity again, he would put his own happiness aside for Elena's, and he doesn't bother denying Rebekah's guess that he'd give the one dose to Elena if given the chance. Rebekah later acknowledges that Damon has done something selfless in allowing Stefan and Elena this final sprint for the Cure together, and Damon's not alone in being selfless in "Down the Rabbit Hole." Bonnie and Jeremy have nothing to gain personally from finding the Cure, and everything to lose. But instead of sitting it out, both are driven by the desire to help their loved ones and they're willing to endanger themselves in the process. Expression killed Shane's wife, and yet Bonnie fearlessly goes forward. But just when success seems certain, their quest ends in failure.

Similarly, Vaughn's purpose-driven life goes unfulfilled. From the first moment the hunter arrived onscreen, attacking Damon at the end of "Into the Wild," he's been focused on what he needs to do, and hasn't deviated from that plan. Where Connor didn't know what the endgame of the tattoo was, Vaughn is in on the Silas of it all, and knows who that one dose of the Cure is intended for: Silas. As single-minded as Shane is to resurrect Silas, so is Vaughn to kill Silas — and both make the same error of relying on a connection between Damon Salvatore and Bonnie Bennett. (Do they see something between those two that Damon and Bonnie don't?) Equipped with just as many ingenious weapons as Connor had (these hunters are creative), Vaughn pushes forward to the "wishing well," as he calls it, and upon finding Jeremy there doesn't waste time trying to convince his fellow hunter of the justness of his cause. He'll battle his own kind in the pursuit of his one goal.

Klaus has a tendency to be single-minded and immovable, and though he spends nearly all of "Down the Rabbit Hole" trapped in the Gilbert living room, he's still able to best Tyler and keep the gang under his thumb. He's annoyingly clever and multilingual, which comes in handy as Caroline and Tyler try to decipher the sword's markings. But even upon his release from the spell binding him to the living room, Klaus's actions are not quite as starkly evil or revenge-y as they once were: he seems to be *trying* to redeem himself in Caroline's eyes. It's clear from his conversation with Caroline that his desire, or ability, to show compassion and mercy is relative. For a Big Bad like him, granting a head start to Tyler seems benevolent. For Caroline, Klaus's "kindness" is devastating. On the Porch of Epic Moments, Tyler and Caroline bid each other a tearful goodbye, refusing to give up hope that they can one day be together.

As the gang realizes there was more to the story than any of them knew — and more teams in the running — their hope and illusion of control is shattered. It's Damon who feels it most profoundly, deciding to just lie on the ground by the well for a bit, having a siesta; he tells Rebekah that he's come to peace with the fact that no matter how hard he tries, he can't control everything.

As for Shane, as well prepared as he was, in the end, he too is deluded. The Caitlin he sees is not really his wife's spirit, but Silas. Vaughn doesn't manage to kill Silas, and no one on the expedition manages to snag the Cure. The doppelgänger strikes again. And Jeremy lies on the crypt floor, frighteningly still . . .

COMPELLING MOMENT Bonnie and Jeremy together, determined, trusting each other, and willing to sacrifice themselves to find the Cure for their loved ones.

CIRCLE OF KNOWLEDGE
- Matt Donovan is safely offscreen for this episode.
- "Down the Rabbit-Hole" is the title of the first chapter in Lewis Carroll's 1865 novel *Alice's Adventures in Wonderland*, but the parallels between this episode and Carroll's book extend beyond that particular phrase. Driven by curiosity, Alice follows the white rabbit down a rabbit hole, "never once considering how in the world she was to get out again"; Alice thinks of the hole itself as "a very deep well" and at the bottom of it is a long passage. Alice finds a tiny door and sees a beautiful but unreachable garden on the other side of it. Alice decides to drink the contents of a bottle labeled "Drink me" and her size changes, shrinking so much that she fears "it might end . . . in my going out altogether." Alas, the key needed to open the door to the garden is now impossible for her to reach. Crying with frustration, Alice scolds herself saying there's no use in it and advises herself "to leave off this minute!" The chapter ends with Alice having cake labeled "Eat me" and expecting other "out-of-the-way things to happen." Just as Alice's adventures continue to take her into a strange fantasy world that overlaps and confuses with reality, *The Vampire Diaries* characters also go on an adventure that begins with a rather impulsive descent through a very deep well and into tunnels with, for broken-legged Shane, no plan to get back out again. While Alice is chasing the rabbit, the gang is chasing the Cure — the magic potion labeled "Drink me" that promises to grant them access to the fantasy land of "unicorns and rainbows" (as Damon called it). But ultimately it is as unreachable as the beautiful garden Alice glimpses on the other side

The Five & Their Wonderful Toys

Have you discovered a strange tattoo on your hand? Overcome with the sudden need to kill vampires? Let Connor, Vaughn, Alexander, and Jeremy — certified members of the Five — give you pointers on nasty weapons and clever maimings for every occasion.

- **Vervain: It does a hunter good.** Connor perfected the sly handshake trick: steep a fingerless glove in vervain, offer your hand for a polite shake, and if you hear a sizzle, shoot that sizzling thing like the undead plague it is. If you're Vaughn, you take it a step further: Keep a captured vampire compliant by tying him up with a rope soaked in vervain or incapacitate him by shooting a vervain-laced fishing line weighted at both ends and introduce your target's neck to the nearest wooden post. The truly lucky hunter (ahem, Little Gilbert) will have access to a kitchen sink, a spray hose, and a vervain-tainted water supply.

- **But what about werewolf venom?** Connor introduced a potential game-changer: *Werewolf venom.* Brutal but extremely dangerous to acquire, unless your venom supplier is faux-bedridden in a hospital, then you can waltz right in and shove a needle into his fangs, easy peasy. Once you've done that, weaponizing the venom is just a matter of playing *Breaking Wolf* for a few hours with that impressive chemistry set you keep in your RV.

- **It's a trap!** Make sure to booby trap your RV, your home, your bed, your island — just anywhere you're going to be ... for the rest of your life. And if we're honest, that won't be very long.

- **Cultivate an appreciation for the classics.** While it's fine to use that "Find a Vampire" app on your smartphone, never underestimate the deep satisfaction that accompanies driving a wooden stake that you whittled yourself into that cold and squishy vampire center they call a heart. Stakes are also good for newbie hunters because they are versatile and easy to hide on your person especially if, like Jeremy, you can distract your intended victim with arms like Jurassic-era redwood trees and the stunning breadth of your chest. Also handy if you lose your gun or run out of bullets — right, Connor?

- **Always remember that sun-time is fun-time.** Don't make your job more difficult than it needs to be. Sure, Alexander can attest that wrangling a vampire into a crate is no simple feat, but once daylight rolls around? You have an instant presentation on your hands, with dramatic flare to spare. Nothing warns the masses to the demonic creatures in their midst quite like spontaneous combustion by sunlight. Be sure to keep your flowing locks away from the flames, and go shirtless to ensure an even tan.

- **No weapons? No sweat.** Your *body* is a weapon; that extra strength you have isn't just for lifting kegs. Take a cue from Connor: if your intended victim has a fondness for body jewelry, wait for them to get close and then bite that handy piece of metal right off. Once you've picked free of your chains — congratulations! Those heavy metal links can now be used to choke a hybrid and, with a little elbow grease and a can-do attitude, you have one righteous beheading on your chain-filled hands. It'll be tough-going at first, so put your shoulders into it, and be shirtless if at all possible.
- **Who's the Boom King? You're the Boom King.** Throughout your hunter career you will have opportunities to devise, test, and employ a range of Van Helsing cocktails guaranteed to put the ammo in your witch-appointed whammo. Feeling artistic? Copy Connor's meticulous eye for detail and engrave special Five-y symbols on your wooden bullets for maximum impact and discomfort. Why settle for a regular grenade when you can pull a Vaughn and rig that sucker with wooden spikes that explode outward, penetrate the chest cavity, go through the heart, and lodge in the spine?
- **There's no such thing as an innocent bystander.** Fulfilling your destiny justifies a by-any-means-necessary approach. Try gut-stabbing a teenage girl to use her flowing blood, terrorizing bus boys and holding a town's bourbon supply hostage, or even setting aside your loathing of vampires long enough to seduce your way to that ultimate ash-and-dagger climax. Your Qetsiyah-blessed mission to find Silas and shove the Cure down his 2,000-year-old desiccated throat absolves you of any obligation to people who get in your way. And you get a pretty awesome tattoo to boot.

of the teeny door. And just as Alice reprimands herself for bemoaning her lot, Elena declares her "pity party" over and she trudges onward on her own trip through a wonderland full of "curiouser and curiouser" out-of-the-way things. The chapter that follows "Down the Rabbit-Hole" in *Alice's Adventures in Wonderland* is titled "The Pool of Tears," and considering Jeremy's death at the end of this episode, it's quite possible Elena will find herself, like Alice, shedding gallons of tears.

- Shane says the tombstone — chock-full of Qetsiyah's calcified blood — is more valuable than the Hope Diamond to those in the supernatural know. The large, bluish diamond, which is housed at the Smithsonian Natural History Museum, has an estimated value of $250 million.

"There was very little pressure [in terms of writing the death of a major character] because we knew it was the right thing to do. I had no doubt of that, so all I had to do was execute the plan. I pushed for the plot point when we first mapped out the season, so I was happy that I was the one who got to pull the trigger. Of course, when the time comes to film the scene you feel bad for the actor, but McQueen couldn't have been nicer or sweeter (as he always is). Here he is, on the day before Christmas hiatus — covered in blood, lying on the ground for hours, and facing an uncertain future for his character — and he was actually the last one on set because he wanted to make sure to say goodbye to everyone."

— Jose Molina

- Caroline says the sword contains a "cryptex," citing the 2006 film adaptation of Dan Brown's monster bestseller *The Da Vinci Code* (2003) as her source. The word "cryptex" is an invention of Brown for the device that "used the science of *cryptology* to protect information written on the contained scroll or *codex*." The sword is actually more of a cipher than a "cryptex" (sorry, Caroline). Klaus called the hilt of the hunter's sword a cipher in "O Come, All Ye Faithful" when he told Stefan about it. (So, sorry Tyler, but your big "discovery" of it isn't exactly news.)
- "Don't worry, love. You know I'd never hurt you," says Klaus to Caroline. Um, except for the time yesterday when he stabbed her, bit her, and nearly let her die.

HISTORY LESSON The writing on the sword and in the tattoo is Aramaic. While modern Aramaic is still spoken, the language that Qetsiyah and Silas may have spoken 2,000 years ago would be Middle Aramaic (which roughly dates from 200 BCE to 200 CE) while the witch who created the hunters would be contemporary to Late Aramaic, both "dead" languages. With a millennium to study all manner of things, Klaus happens to be fluent in just the exact Aramaic required. The symbols in the hunter's tattoo are from the Aramaic alphabet, which bears a resemblance to the modern Hebrew alphabet.

THE RULES Vaughn's tattoo (and presumably those of any other active hunters) completed when Jeremy's did, and it disappears as Jeremy's does. Elena makes an unbelievably long jump from the cliff-top, much more impressive than jumping off the Salvatore boarding house roof.

PREVIOUSLY ON *THE VAMPIRE DIARIES* Damon's hilarious quip about his flawless skin and lack of tattoo knowledge is a bit of a fib: Ian Somerhalder's *hic et nunc* arm tattoo has been shown onscreen, when he was lying in bed with Lexi in "162 Candles" (1.08).

Damon tells Vaughn, "You want to know something, just ask," echoing Shane's offer to him at the Miss Mystic Falls pageant in "My Brother's Keeper."

Rebekah tells Klaus, "Fool me once, shame on you. Fool me a hundred times . . ." — a recurring sentiment on *The Vampire Diaries* and title of the season one episode "Fool Me Once" (1.14).

Caroline asks Tyler how many times they will have to say goodbye. Tyler has a habit of leaving Mystic Falls on a moment's notice: he left town after the werewolf debacle of "Crying Wolf" (2.14) and again after attacking Caroline's dad in an attempt to break his sire bond to Klaus in "The Ties That Bind" (3.12). He was supposed to leave after the council found out about his supernatural status in "The Departed" (3.22), but he did a little body-jumping spell with Klaus instead.

With the appearance of Katherine in Silas's crypt, it's evident that Stefan was right about there being another team hunting the Cure back in "Catch Me If You Can." The guy who tried to steal the tombstone from Shane's office was compelled to bite off his own tongue and kill himself, much like Isobel's minion offed himself in "A Few Good Men" (1.15). Isobel, of course, learned all her tricks from Katherine.

OFF CAMERA Hunter Galen Vaughn is played by English actor Charlie Bewley, best known for his role as Demetri, one of the Volturi vampires, in the Twilight Saga films. "Vaughn poses a pretty substantial threat," Ian Somerhalder told *TV Guide*. "He's a formidable adversary." And he praised Bewley to *TV Line*, saying, "Charlie, the actor who plays Vaughn, is awesome. He brings a lot to the role."

FOGGY MOMENTS Klaus has been in the Gilbert living room for three days, with only one bite of Caroline to sustain him. Should he not be a little weakened or look a little desiccated?

Why would Qetsiyah's witch descendant use Aramaic (which Klaus theorizes is Qetsiyah's native language) in the swords and tattoos she created and spelled for the Five in 1110? Why not choose something a little more contemporary to her time? Or did she also speak Aramaic but a later variant of it? If Qetsiyah buried Silas near present-day Nova Scotia, was she native to the North American continent but somehow spoke Aramaic, which originates from the Middle East? Or as a super-powerful witch was Qetsiyah able to cross the Atlantic about 1,000 years before the Vikings and 1,500 years before Columbus?

How does Vaughn know that there is only one dose of the Cure? He says, "So it is written," but his full tattoo only appeared when Jeremy completed his own, so he hasn't exactly had the opportunity to translate the Aramaic.

If Shane was only interested in bringing back his dead wife, had no "evil" intention, and convinced Pastor Young that he could see his own dead wife again if he sacrificed the council in the name of Silas, what was the "great evil" that Pastor Young wrote about in his letter to April? Why did Shane say Silas's intent was to "wreak havoc on the world" in "We All Go a Little Mad Sometimes"?

How did Jeremy know that Vaughn was a hunter? Vaughn doesn't explicitly tell him (he just says they are on the "same team") and his tattoo is gone by then.

QUESTIONS
- How long has Vaughn been spying on the Mystic Falls crew?
- Will Silas suffer from the Hunter's Curse?
- Did Katherine kill Massak and take the tombstone? What does she want with the Cure? Is she planning on killing Klaus or negotiating for her freedom?
- Will Shane survive?
- Is Jeremy really dead?

Elena: How? How are you going to help me?

4.15 *Stand By Me*

Original air date: February 21, 2013
Written by: Julie Plec
Directed by: Lance Anderson

With her friends by her side, Elena comes to accept that Jeremy is dead.

In an unexpected and short scene, Stefan and Meredith find common ground in how they experience others' grief: how each death is hard, no matter how many you see, because watching someone on a collision course with the pain of realizing that their loved one is gone never stops being a special kind of torture. And we the viewers experience just that, as we watch Elena come home with her brother's body, refusing to accept he is dead. When Stefan tells his brother that Jeremy's ring won't bring him back, Damon says, "She won't survive this" and that question of how Elena will manage to keep living in the wake of her brother's death is the subject of this honest, gut-wrenching episode about loss. Julie Plec has written in "Stand By Me" an achingly honest, nuanced, and unflinching portrait of raw grief.

Upon finding her brother killed by Silas, Elena turns immediately to reassurances, as she's done so many times before: *It's fine. You'll be okay.* She sees that ring, and cradles her dead brother, reassuring him, and herself, that he'll come back to life. That's what Elena has always done: to get through the hell thrown her way, she believes that *somehow* things will work out for the best and she stays strong for her little brother. And she's not wrong when she tells Stefan and Caroline that there is a sliver of a chance that the Gilbert ring will bring her brother back to her. But at what point is that hope so remote that it's time to let it go? Elena struggles to even entertain the possibility of Jeremy being truly gone, let alone accept it. She can barely say the words "my brother's dead" even when preceded by "There's absolutely no way . . ."

The confrontation between Meredith and Elena is a powerfully realistic scene, with Meredith giving Elena the medical facts of decomposition, trying to break through her denial. The rituals surrounding death that we go through are grounded in immediate necessities: funerals happen quickly for a reason. The realities of losing a family member are made starkly real in "Stand By Me," and Elena, who was presumably sheltered by Jenna and John after her parents died, can't handle it — not yet. Instead she lashes out, arguing that their world is not governed by science, but by magic. The girl who wrote in her diary that she wasn't a believer in "You're Undead to Me" here denies the reality in front of her — so terrifying an idea it is.

But Elena's argument, though incredibly heartbreaking, is not irrational — we're not operating in a world that only follows the rules of science; magic applies here. It would be hard to accept the reality of death when you've just come from a mystical island where a man who's been "not dead" for 2,000 years was reanimated. Phrases like "release the body" and "say goodbye" lead to an explosion from Elena. She clings to her desperate belief: if the Gilbert ring fails, Bonnie can magically fix it. Everything *will* be okay again.

It's only after Bonnie explains her solution — explains the cost of the magic fix to this unthinkable scenario — that Elena realizes that to pretend any longer would be denial, not hope. In a perfectly executed moment (from Nina's performance to the sound design to the framing), the heated debate between Caroline, Matt, and Bonnie about dropping the veil between this side and the other becomes muted as Elena blocks out everything, barely holding it together, only to be interrupted by April's call. Elena cannot lie to this girl on the phone, she cannot put the whole universe at risk to bring back her brother, and then she finally says it. Once she does, it's all she can say as everything she was keeping at bay slams into her. When she looks at him lying in his bed, she sees a corpse, fully understanding that he is truly gone. The cold facts of death — his decomposition already something a vampire can smell — are no longer possible to ignore. In a contrast to the scene with Dr. Fell, Elena knows now that magic has failed her — the hoped-for solution is too horrible to contemplate — and all that's left is the science. It's shocking and raw and tragic. Like Caroline's effort to scrub out the burn mark on the floor where Kol died, some things can't be erased or made right.

And so Elena accepts reality: her little brother is dead. And there are practicalities to attend to. What Elena wants to do in her state of heightened grief turns out to be the same thing she wants after Damon commands her to flip the switch: to burn down the Gilbert home. The house, still in shambles after the siblings' fight with Kol, is destroyed by fire. Everything is burned: the memories, mementos, the stuff that makes up a life and a family's history — Jer's art, that birthday card he drew for Elena, all their family photographs, Elena's teddy bear, her favorite sneakers, the diary in

© Annette Brown/The CW/Landov

which she made sense of her world, those doors everyone was always popping up behind, Ric's bourbon, all the comforts of the home she grew up in — gone.

And Elena walks away from it with nothing but the clothes on her back and the two Salvatores at her side. Stefan takes a last look, but not Elena. With her humanity off, there's no reason to. Was Damon right to make Elena flip her switch? As she begins to break down, she asks in a sob, "*How can you help me?*" and that line makes explicit the useless feeling her friends have had all day as they stand by and watch her go through something utterly devastating. There are two things you wish you could do for someone experiencing that kind of loss: bring their beloved back, and take away their pain. In "Stand By Me," Bonnie is resolved to undo the permanence of death, and bring Jeremy back, while Damon is able to take Elena's pain away through the sire bond. He can literally make her stop grieving. But what's the consequence? Will Elena still be herself if she doesn't have her humanity?

In "Down the Rabbit Hole," Bonnie was side by side with Jeremy in his last moments; they helped each other reach the Cure, and they failed together. In "Stand By Me," Bonnie's emotional state moves from vehemently believing that necromancy is unnatural — telling Shane "You can't bring back the dead" — to seeing it as the perfect solution to their problem. Drop the veil, bring back Jer, bring back Grams, bring back all the Bennett witches. Silas-as-Shane is there to guide her into that belief, in her shell-shocked and vulnerable state. While Silas-Shane tells her he refuses to "let her fall apart," falling apart is a natural reaction to losing someone you love. He capitalizes on the strength of her grief (as he did to Shane himself by appearing in the form of Caitlin) and deliberately misleads her. Once she's under his spell, he matter-of-factly answers her question: the humans who were killed in the massacres will *not* be returned to life. Silas doesn't have that power, Bonnie doesn't have that power. But Bonnie's resolution to "do whatever it takes" mitigates that horror: she's determined to "fix" the situation, to save Jer, to protect herself and her best friend from further loss — and, perhaps, to prove that she is in control, something she was so confident of before they entered that crypt.

While Bonnie's resolve is strong, Matt "Poison your best friend once and suspicion follows you forever" Donovan is near broken by episode's end. He's there for Elena: the two have their isolation and grief in common, as well as their need to hold out hope. Matt says it's what keeps him going, and we see him lose it when he's alone, just him in his truck. As in real life, in "Stand By Me" friends play different roles in assisting the grieving: Caroline goes into Caroline mode — lists, casseroles, plans, and strategies — though she herself is grieving Tyler's departure, and trying to stay connected to him. Damon makes his choices based on what he believes Elena needs the most: for Stefan to be by her side; for Damon to bring Bonnie home; and, eventually when the realization that Jer is not coming back hits her, for her overwhelming pain to be dulled, so she can survive this.

Though Stefan and Damon have since the beginning of the season disagreed about how flipping her switch would ultimately affect or damage Elena, their scene on the porch highlights how, in times of loss, we're reminded to appreciate those still with us. It's barely a sentence that Stefan gets out to Damon, but his brother gets it, and the hand on the shoulder returns the sentiment. These guys love each other, and each would be devastated to lose the other.

While Julie Plec's script and Nina Dobrev's performance deserve huge admiration, the direction of "Stand By Me" works to highlight both of those strengths and helps them pack an emotional punch. As Elena refuses to acknowledge Jer's death, she is framed in very tight spaces — walls or shadows or doorframes box her in, giving us the claustrophobic feeling of someone just barely able to function. Reprieves from that framing play into the emotional arc of the story: when Matt arrives, she not only cracks a joke (about tea poisoning) but she has some breathing room in the frame as well, which continues when he takes her to the stoner pit to look at the graffiti. Those moments of friendship and of reaffirming hope are communicated to us not only through dialogue and performance, but through the visual cues. And in the scene with the broken picture frame that bookends the episode, Elena is tiny in the large space — her family gone, her big house empty, her emotions off.

"Stand By Me" is a difficult episode to watch, but one that can be incredibly cathartic because of its nuanced and poignant portrait of loss and of how loved ones support those in grief. A series highlight.

COMPELLING MOMENT Nina Dobrev's performance from beginning to end. From the subtle moments to the big breakdown that was painfully believable, once again the impact of this episode hinged on her ability to make us empathize with Elena, and once again she portrayed the emotional arc with nuance and heart. Stunning.

CIRCLE OF KNOWLEDGE
- No Tyler.
- The title of the 1960 song "Stand By Me" (written by Ben E. King, Jerry Leiber, and Mike Stoller) was borrowed by the 1986 Rob Reiner film — which in turn inspires this episode. The film, based on a Stephen King novella, tells the story of a group of boys in the fictional town of

Castle Rock, Oregon, in 1959. The four boys decide to go on an adventure to find the body of a kid who's gone missing; it's the summer before junior high when their childhoods will come to an end, and the confidence that "we knew exactly who we were and exactly where we were going" falters. In addition to the real-life bloodsuckers in the unforgettable "Leeches!" scene, *Stand By Me* also connects with this episode in a number of important ways — the confrontation with the harsh reality of death, the loss of family, the importance of friendship, and the end of an era of innocence. Gordie (Wil Wheaton) is quietly mourning his older brother (John Cusack), who died four months earlier in an accident; his parents are absent in their grief, and he feels like an invisible boy. In a pivotal scene, Gordie breaks down, needing to see the body of the kid in order to confront his own brother's death. As Gordie wishes it had been him instead of his brother who died ("I'm no good") and questions why his brother had to die, hard-scrabble Chris (River Phoenix) steps up to take care of his friend in his grief. When the bad-boy gang led by Ace (Kiefer Sutherland) tries to take the body — to get the credit for discovering it, which was the younger boys' plan as well — Gordie pulls a gun, unwilling to let the dead be dishonored. In a way, that decision runs parallel to Elena's vehement vote against dropping the veil to resurrect Jeremy. The moral choice is more difficult and less rewarding, but necessary. The boys return to Castle Rock changed, having learned (as the grocer tells Gordie), "In the midst of life, we are in death." The title of Stephen King's novella is *The Body*, also the title of the season five episode of *Buffy the Vampire Slayer* that sees Buffy dealing with great loss in an achingly realistic manner, in much the same spirit that Julie Plec and company achieve here with "Stand By Me."

- Points for accuracy! Rebekah says they are 1,200 miles from home and Stefan says the flight bringing Bonnie and Damon should take a couple of hours; based on the nearest major town to Mystic Falls, Virginia, and the fact that Silas island lies 200 miles from Nova Scotia, these little details are bang on.
- In "Catch Me If You Can," Klaus warns Elena and Jeremy that Kol will stop at nothing and will burn their house down to get at them. In "A View to a Kill," Klaus threatens to burn the house to the ground after they kill Kol. In the end, it's Elena who actually carries through on the threat.

THE RULES Silas-as-Shane says he's not "an actual witch"; when Silas became an immortal, his time as a witch ended. The massacres of 12 mark "the earth with power," which a witch can then draw from using Expression. The three massacres will form an "Expression triangle."

PREVIOUSLY ON *THE VAMPIRE DIARIES* Caroline and Tyler were apart during another major death: her father's. He leaves her a voicemail with his condolences and apologies in "Dangerous Liaisons" (3.14) after she leaves him multiple messages in "Bringing Out the Dead" (3.13), as she does here.

Elena says Ric died four times before he started going crazy: "A Few Good Men" (1.15), "Crying Wolf" (2.14), "Disturbing Behavior" (3.04), and "The New Deal" (3.10). His evil alter ego kills medical examiner Brian Walters in the following episode ("Our Town," 3.11). Jeremy has been resurrected by the ring three times: "The Return" (2.01), "Before Sunset" (3.21), and "We All Go a Little Mad Sometimes." When Jeremy was shot dead by Sheriff Forbes in "As I Lay Dying" (2.22), his ring was of no use, and Bonnie resurrected him using magic.

Matt's arrival in Jer's room and his embrace with Elena was reminiscent of when Vicki's body was found, and Elena arrives at the Donovan house in "Let the Right One In" (1.17).

Elena jokingly asks Matt if the tea is dosed; he knocked her out by dosing her tea in "The Departed" (3.22).

Matt takes Elena to the stoner pit, the site of the very first scene between Jeremy and Vicki ("Pilot," 1.01).

Matt says Vicki wasn't completely gone, referring to her presence on the Other Side and her ability to talk to him in "The Reckoning" (3.05) and "Smells Like Teen Spirit" (3.06).

Jer lies dead on that same couch in "We All Go a Little Mad Sometimes" after a demented Elena stabbed him in the neck, thinking he was Connor.

Elena tosses out well-worn cover stories for Jeremy's death as alternatives to burning down the house with him in it: when Damon attacked Vicki and others in season one, it was blamed on animal attacks — a local tradition that Anna explains dates back at least to the '40s ("Bloodlines," 1.11) and which we hear about in flashback to the 1860s in "Memory Lane" (2.04). The "tumble down the stairs" excuse is used for John Gilbert after Isobel tosses him down a flight during a historical society luncheon in "Know Thy Enemy" (2.17).

Ode to the Gilbert House

Julie Plec joins us in remembering favorite Gilbert house moments, from the bloody to the hilarious to the poignant, room by room.

Elena's Bedroom

Julie Elena tells Damon, "If anyone's going to save him, it's going to be you" ("Ordinary People," 3.08).

Vee & Crissy Drunk Damon snaps Jer's neck ("The Return," 2.01).

Jeremy's Bedroom

Julie Elena/Damon "He's dead" ("Stand By Me"). Damon tells Jeremy that feelings suck ("Founder's Day," 1.22). "And tomorrow, and tomorrow . . ." (Ric to Jeremy in "As I Lay Dying," 2.22). Jeremy tells Anna, "I want you to turn me" ("There Goes the Neighborhood," 1.16).

Vee & Crissy Anna sneaks in to say goodbye to a sleepy Jeremy ("Blood Brothers," 1.20).

Jenna's Bedroom

Julie Jenna cries after learning the truth about Isobel ("Know Thy Enemy," 2.17).

Vee & Crissy Ric wakes up to find a concerned, if snarky, Damon sitting by his bedside ("Break On Through," 3.17).

The Bathroom

Julie Elena follows the blood trail into the bathroom and finds the murderous message ("The Killer").

Vee & Crissy Katherine-as-Elena takes a bite out of Dr. Jonas Martin ("The House Guest," 2.16).

Upstairs Hallway

Julie Chunky Monkey, obviously.

Vee & Crissy Chunky Monkey, obviously ("The Sacrifice," 2.10).

The Stairs

Julie Bonnie is Emily ("History Repeating," 1.09).

Vee & Crissy Jenna throws an apple at Jeremy ("The Night of the Comet," 1.02).

Entryway

Julie Stefan arrives and Elena makes out with him ("Family Ties," 1.04). Elena hugs Alaric ("Break On Through," 3.17). Damon scares Elena: "Be careful who you invite in" ("Lost Girls," 1.06).

Vee & Crissy Alaric decks John Gilbert ("Know Thy Enemy," 2.17).

Living Room

Julie Elena "turns it off" and lights the match ("Stand By Me").

Vee & Crissy Damon plays a video game with Jeremy on family night and advises him, "Hot trumps weird" when it comes to the ladies ("Children of the Damned, 1.13).

Kitchen
> **Julie** "Hello John. Goodbye John."
> **Vee & Crissy** Is there any other choice? Katherine-as-Elena chops off Uncle John's fingers ("Founder's Day," 1.22).

Front Porch
> **Julie** SO MANY! Elena and Stefan's first breakup ("Lost Girls," 1.06). "Elena" and Damon kiss ("Founder's Day," 1.22). Elena and Damon actually kiss ("The New Deal," 3.10).
> **Vee & Crissy** Little Gilbert beheads a hybrid ("The New Deal," 3.10).

An honorable mention to the Gilbert front lawn, ground zero for Klaus's most epic (and fun!) temper tantrum to date. If Klaus could lift it, it was hurled with maximum prejudice through the Gilbert windows and front door ("Before Sunset," 3.21).
> R.I.P., Gilbert House.

OFF CAMERA Julie Plec recalled getting a phone call after the table read for this episode. "Apparently the performance [Nina Dobrev] brought to the read-through was so astonishingly good, everyone knew we were doing something special," she told *ET Online*. She considers Elena's meltdown in the living room her proudest season four moment: "I didn't overthink it, I just let it flow. I barely rewrote it once I put it on the page, and then Nina knocked it out of the park."

Composer Michael Suby considers Elena losing her humanity the stand-out moment of the season. "Last year, for the season finale, Chris [Mollere, music supervisor] had a song, and there might have been some issues with clearance on the song for the season three finale, and they called me and said, 'Oh my god, we need a four minute cue for Elena drowning and Stefan's underwater and all this, and we need it now.' So I wrote this big, huge cue, and they ended up clearing the song ["Dauðalogn" by Sigur Rós], so they tucked the cue away and they pulled it out at this moment [in "Stand By Me"], and it literally cut into the show and hit the moment so perfectly it was serendipitous. That was one of my favorite moments for sure."

In an interview with *Entertainment Weekly*, costume designer Leigh Leverett recounted telling Nina Dobrev that the show would be burning down Elena's old wardrobe, and asked the actor to choose favorite pieces to save. Nina picked a pair of brown, knee-high lace-up boots and a navy suede jacket, both of which she is wearing as Elena and the Salvatores exit the burning Gilbert house.

"I thought Jeremy's death was crucial to tell Elena's story," says Caroline Dries, "so I was all for it. Obviously [this] was a heartbreaking, riveting, truthful episode, and it made his death very sad, but gave it the respect it deserved."

FOGGY MOMENTS Silas-as-Shane explains to Bonnie that Qetsiyah gave Silas two choices: stay trapped in the crypt for an eternity, or take the Cure, eventually die of old age, and then pass on to the Other Side (where he'd be apart from his lady love forever). But if Silas took the Cure and was no longer an immortal, but still trapped in that crypt, he'd die of starvation long before he reached old age. (Assuming that he is in the same demographic as every other character in the history of CW shows, and is not already an octogenarian.) If Shane is dying, and soon to be abandoned by Silas (since he didn't bring him home from the island), why did Silas bother bringing him up from the cave?

QUESTIONS
- Did Elena ever return that first edition copy of *Wuthering Heights* to Stefan (which he gave her in "Night of the Comet," 1.02), or did it go up in flames in the house fire?
- Who are "Shane" and Bonnie planning on killing in massacre #3?
- Silas must have pulled both Bonnie and Shane all the way out of the well — how strong is he?
- Does the Hunter's Curse apply to Silas? Is he being haunted by Jeremy's ghost?
- What will Katherine do with the Cure? Is Stefan right: is she going to use it to leverage a pardon from Klaus? Or will she go on the offensive and try to jam the Cure down the Original hybrid's throat?
- Does Katherine also have the super valuable Qetsiyah-blood tombstone?
- Vaughn reveals that Katherine tracked him down in Colorado and had intel from Hayley. When Katherine attacked Vaughn in Silas's crypt, she must never have been planning on killing him (knowing he's a hunter and knowing about the curse), but did he know that she planned to abscond with the Cure? Or had she convinced him she was down with his plan to kill Silas?

- Where is Katherine? Where is Klaus? What will our Big Bads' next moves be?
- In "Down the Rabbit Hole," Shane was left with a broken leg and with Silas-as-Caitlin consoling him. Will the real Shane, assuming that was the real Shane whom Rebekah tripped over in the woods, survive?
- Silas-as-Shane interacts with the physical world (tending a fire, and so on), and Bonnie trips over fake-Jeremy. Does Silas have the ability to change his physical form? Would someone else see what Bonnie sees (i.e., Shane or Jeremy) or would Silas appear to a third party as his true self? If Silas can't be a witch because he's an immortal, how is he changing form — does he have extremely advanced mind-control skills?
- Will April Young clue in to the fact that Elena told her Jeremy was dead, speaking to her on the home phone, before he "officially" died in the house fire?
- How *do* you hide from the devil when you don't know what he looks like?

"When I saw the first version of the 'previously on' for episode 4.01, my head almost exploded over how complicated it was. You always want to start the season with as much of a fresh start as possible in case new viewers are dropping in, or if casual viewers are dropping back in after an absence. The recap was just too complicated. We loved the 'saga sell' version, which cleanly teed up the season's premise. But after a while, the saga sells became just as complicated as the recaps, and took twice as much work, so we reverted."

— Julie Plec

Elena: Be honest. You like me better like this.

4.16 *Bring It On*

Original air date: March 14, 2013
Written by: Elisabeth R. Finch and Michael Narducci
Directed by: Jesse Warn
Guest cast: Regan Deal (Woman), Katie Garfield (Blonde Girl), Aaron Jay Rome (Will)
Previously on *The Vampire Diaries*: Ian Somerhalder

With her humanity switch flipped off, Elena wreaks havoc at the cheerleading meet and on Caroline. Damon and Rebekah try to track down Katherine, while Klaus entertains Hayley.

Life sucks. Bring on the fun. This new version of Elena — manipulative, impulsive, brutally honest — is not afraid of embarrassing people, spilling secrets, or breaking all the rules. She's like a parent's worst nightmare. Except, of course, Elena's an orphan and it's up to Caroline, Damon, and Stefan to watch over her and deliver the unwanted and condescending lectures. In a hilarious twist, the sire bond doesn't work when there are no emotions to fuel it, and so not even Damon — who commanded her to flip the switch in the first place — has any authority over Elena. She will do whatever she wants. She feels amazing and sees no reason to exercise restraint.

The well-meaning trio tries their best to keep Elena entertained: the old lying-in-the-road trick with Damon, some cheerleading gone wrong with Caroline, and an easily outwitted Stefan who "grounds" her at the Salvatore house. Elena is now a little reminiscent of Damon when he first rolled into Mystic Falls: no concern about leaving a bloody trail, disrupting school activities by feeding on athletic types, and displaying a sexual freedom that is vexing to others. While showerheads at the Salvatore mansion may have an extra special vervain-removing filter, switched-off Elena has no filter whatsoever, and the kicker is that what she says, though way harsh, is true. Stefan's world *does* revolve around Elena; Damon *is* scared the old Elena will judge him and find him reprehensible; and Caroline *is* desperate to have Tyler back while harboring some lusty thoughts about Klaus (and she hasn't even seen his tattoos!).

Elena's also smart as heck: she knows her audience and she plays to them,

© Emiley Schweich/PRPhotos.com

and keeps her plans to herself. She could give Katherine Pierce a run for her money. But is this the better version of Elena, as she suggests? Are you your best self if you are completely ruled by your id, with no morals, compassion, or concern for others? And for those who love her most, how difficult it must be to see her truly carefree probably for the first time since her parents died — smiling, dancing, letting loose — but know they are obliged to drag her back to her "real" self, a girl whose life sucks. As Caroline asks, why would she want to turn her emotions back on?

And while Elena says she feels amazing, is that *all* she feels? She seems just a tad jealous of Caroline and Stefan's good times at the party, and she certainly punishes Caroline for her "meddling" and lectures: why do that if you *truly* do not care? There's always that little gray area of the switch-flipped vampire — the cracks where the light can get in, to paraphrase Leonard Cohen. Though Elena threatens Liz and shoves her against the wall, though she is right on the edge of killing Caroline, she doesn't do anything irreparable. She lets the Salvatores take her away. She sits on Damon's bed and waits as he roots through his trunk of old stuff. She gets in the car with him, not knowing where they're going, when she could easily just run away.

Elena suggests to Damon that he likes her better this way: there's no fear of being judged by *this* Elena. She doesn't care if he's immoral. Whether it's true that he prefers bad-girl Elena remains to be seen. He certainly gets the appeal of misbehaving, better than most. He tells Rebekah at the party that being ordinary means being nothing (and BTW thanks for that, Damon, on behalf of mortals everywhere). It's the first hint of the argument against taking the Cure that is perhaps more obvious from a human's perspective than from an immortal's: humans still have emotional problems, experience loneliness or ostracism, fight with their families, or lose them entirely. The Cure won't guarantee Rebekah — or anyone — a happy life, just one that has an end date; it won't erase past mistakes. Damon's attitude toward humanity suggests he might prefer an Elena who enjoys being a vampire, who is non-judgmental and fun-loving — if a little crazy and reckless. He's never wanted the Cure for himself or for her, but he did want her to have what *she* wanted. And up until her switch was flipped, she wanted to take the Cure. So while Damon spirits her out of town to the City that Never Sleeps and says that "emotions are overrated," he's still chasing Katherine and the Cure.

As Damon and Elena head out of town, Caroline faces the fact that

Tyler is never coming back. At least not until Klaus is dead. In one last act of protectiveness, Tyler signs over the deed of the Lockwood mansion to Matt (how will Donovan afford the upkeep on a place like that?) so Caroline will have a safe house. Though Caroline has been standing strong for her friend, trying to help Elena, she herself is experiencing loss and having a pretty sucky day: her best friend tries to kill her, attacks her mom, suggests she take Stefan for a spin in bed, and calls her out on her lusty feelings for Klaus, while insulting her for still caring about Tyler. (And no doubt the Mystic Falls cheer squad lost the competition thanks to Elena's mean-spirited sabotage.) But what finally makes Caroline break down is Tyler's goodbye letter: no matter how many voicemail messages she leaves him, and no matter how much they still love each other, he is not coming back to Mystic Falls. Just when Caroline could use a best friend in Elena, Elena could not care less.

While Klaus is bent on ensuring Tyler stays far away from Mystic Falls, he doesn't immediately seek revenge for Kol's death. While the Cure is in play, and the potential still exists for Elena to become a hybrid-making machine, the interests of our heroes and Klaus continue to align, and as long as Klaus feels in control, he's happy — as he explains to his new lupine companion Hayley. Hayley seems attracted to Klaus's darkness, and there's a similar twistedness in her approach to family. She was willing to befriend the hybrids and orchestrate their beheading in order to discover more about her heritage, valuing family but devaluing life. Klaus has a similar kink to his values. Klaus's speech about art as a metaphor for control is a little heavy-handed, but it aligns with his desire to be an architect of lives, determining who lives and who dies, who is tormented and who is wooed. With Hayley, he is coy about his interest, as is she, but, plucky kids that they are, that doesn't stop them from getting down.

While Klaus has shown a romantic fondness for Caroline, this is the first explicitly sexual moment for the character (save for that Caroline-instigated makeout with him in Tyler's body in "Growing Pains"). It's been an interesting character choice, this apparent chastity, running contrary to someone like Damon, who's always been depicted as a vampire who knows he's handsome, attracts ladies, and enjoys sex. The Originals — save for Rebekah, who similarly gets it when she wants it — have all been rather asexual; even Finn with his longtime love of Sage didn't exactly register as *passionate*. But Hayley and Klaus on the table? Passionate.

COMPELLING MOMENT "I didn't mean me!" Stefan and Caroline's friendship is just the salve both need while they go through serious Elena drama. Stefan tossing his choice of "hot girl" over his shoulder was adorable, fun, and inspired.

CIRCLE OF KNOWLEDGE

- No Bonnie, and no Tyler (though he does make a voiceover appearance as Caroline reads the letter).
- *Bring It On* is a 2000 high school cheerleading movie, starring Kirsten Dunst as T-T-T-Torrance Shipman, head of a squad that goes up against the (way better) Clovers as they battle to win the championship. The movie spawned four lesser sequels.
- By putting vervain in the water, Mayor Hopkins has done more for Mystic Falls than, like, any other mayor in the history of Mystic Falls. Well played.
- Damon mocks Rebekah's wish to "turn into a real girl." In the tale of Pinocchio, popularized in the Disney film of 1940, the titular marionette wants to become a living, breathing boy instead of a wooden puppet. In Disney's version, he can achieve that by being brave, truthful, unselfish, and by listening to his conscience (a.k.a. his best pal Jiminy Cricket). No magical cure required.
- In a well-timed music cue, Elena smirks at Stefan as the party-goers stream into his house just as the lyrics of Icona Pop's "I Love It" declare, "I don't care." Elena later repeats that declaration in the forest with Caroline — right before she tries to kill her. The song has another tie to Ms. Gilbert's saga with lyrics about a car crash on a bridge.
- The detective-story aspects of *TVD* are gently made fun of in this episode, with Rebakah calling Damon "Sherlock Holmes with brain damage" and Damon refusing to "Scooby-Doo our way through the Case of the Stolen Blood Supply."

THE RULES Without any emotion to fuel it, the sire bond is rendered inert when a vampire has turned off his or her emotions.

PREVIOUSLY ON *THE VAMPIRE DIARIES* Elena tries out the old lie-in-the-road trick that Damon's been perfecting since 1864 ("Children of the Damned," 1.13). We first see him luring victims this way in "Pilot" (1.01),

Editor Tyler Cook on the Show's Tone

The best thing about *Vampire Diaries* is that it is many things. There's action, horror, suspense, comedy, romance, and drama. Sometimes the images are very sweeping, beautiful, and elegant. Sometimes they are dark, disturbing, and gritty. The visual style changes in terms of the story that is being told in a particular episode and in a particular scene. The editing is there to help complement that style as much as possible. In our romantic moments, we want the editing to be as invisible as possible. We tend to cut less, stay in takes longer, let moments play out. We cut to emphasize specific lines and hold on a character's face to watch an expression change. In the action sequences that are dark and gritty, we tend to cut more frenetically, trying to engineer a sense that all hell has broken loose.

The editorial style of the show was created by Lance Anderson and Joshua Butler who were on the show from the beginning. They were the ones who really helped shape and create the pace, tone, and sound of the show. They've both gone on to direct some really memorable episodes and Lance is a producer on the show as well. Their importance to the show cannot be overstated.

he reprises it in "The Descent" (2.12), and he's just getting comfy on the road in "The Departed" (3.22) when he hears Elena's voice in the May 2009 flashback.

When Elena came back to school after her parents' deaths, she briefly rejoined the cheerleading squad ("Friday Night Bites," 1.03) but found her heart was not in it (and the routines were not that easy).

One of the cheerleading squads participating in the competition is from Grove Hill; the first photo Elena saw of her birth mother, Isobel Flemming, shows her in her Grove Hill cheerleading squad uniform with her blond bestie ("A Few Good Men," 1.15). Damon and Rebekah also visit the nearby town in search of Katherine's minion, Will, marking the second time Damon's chased a lead there: in "Blood Brothers" (1.20), he and Alaric go to Henry the Tomb Vampire's place (and kill him too).

Stefan reminds Elena that he had his switch flipped in this town: in "The Reckoning" (3.05), Klaus ordered Stefan to turn it off, and he was just as delightfully unruly then as Elena is proving to be now.

Hayley and Klaus's scene where she flips through his art but fails to be impressed mirrors the one between Caroline and Klaus in "Dangerous Liaisons" (3.14).

Last big blowout at the Salvatores' was Caroline's idea, not Elena's. Caroline threw her a bash in "The Birthday" (3.01) to celebrate Elena's 18th, but there was, sadly, no dancing on tables for the guest of honor.

Damon uses his firsthand knowledge of werewolf bites to figure out how to find Katherine's minion; he nearly died from the toxin in "As I Lay Dying" (2.22). Rebekah had a dosing earlier this season when Connor slipped the venom into the keg in "The Rager."

OFF CAMERA "Season four has been a difficult transition for me," Paul Wesley admitted to *Zap2It*. "Season three was my favorite season because of the things I was able to do as an actor. I had my fun, and now they're putting Stefan . . . it's almost like, you play a game of basketball, and then the coach puts you on the sidelines for a minute, and you're like, 'Put me out there, Coach!'" As for Stefan's highly unsuccessful hands-on approach to wrangling a new humanity-free Elena and the future of the two characters as a couple, Wesley explained, "The key to Stefan and Elena, as far as I'm concerned, is time and distance. The more you keep them away from one another, the less Stefan is trying to help Elena, trying to fix Elena, trying to run after her and pick up everything she drops — the more she just screws up on her own, he screws up on his own, they have all these experiences, and then something maybe happens. That's the only way that Stefan and Elena can be together."

FOGGY MOMENTS If your friend (a powerful witch) is talking about murdering a dozen people and then raising all the supernatural dead, maybe do more than just call her and be like, "You cool?" as Caroline does. Rebekah hangs back when Damon rushes over to Will, giving him time to recognize him and kill him. Why? She's faster than him and was standing right beside him.

QUESTIONS
- Is Stefan's theory right — is it Silas who is stealing all the blood from hospitals? (How much does Silas know about things that have been invented in the past 2,000 years, like blood bags?)
- Who was Damon's old pal Will and why did Damon kill him when Rebekah had some of her brother's blood, a.k.a. the cure for a werewolf bite, with her? He knows from personal experience that there is no "too far gone" when it comes to a werewolf bite.

- Now that Klaus knows some info about Hayley — thanks to her unique birthmark — will she spill what she knows about Katherine's network of allies? Can these two master manipulators trust each other at all? What does he know about a clan of werewolves that used to thrive in the Louisiana area?
- Is Hayley interested in Klaus or is she following the winning strategy she's observed in Katherine Pierce — building a network of allies willing to do anything for her?
- Could hybrids flip their emotion switch and be free of the sire bond?
- What will happen to the sire bond if Elena decides to turn her emotions back on?

Klaus: Don't underestimate the allure of darkness.

4.17 *Because the Night*

Original air date: March 21, 2013
Written by: Brian Young and Charlie Charbonneau
Directed by: Garreth Stover
Guest cast: Cynthia Addai-Robinson (Aja), Judson Blane (70s Guy), Holly Lynch (70s Girl), Taylor McPherson (Punk), Aaron Jay Rome (Will)
Previously on *The Vampire Diaries*: Ian Somerhalder

Damon takes Elena to New York City, where she quickly guesses his ulterior motive for relating his past exploits.

Ridiculously attractive cast members aside, *The Vampire Diaries* is a consistently good-looking show with the ability to jump through time and place and give us a believable and rich flashback experience. In "Because the Night," the music cues are also incredibly slick: the opening teaser's wonderfully timed "Psycho Killer," as punk-rock Damon saunters down a Manhattan street, transitions into a cover of the song to signal the move back to present day. The same trick is used in the reverse order later in the episode: Dead Sara plays the cover of Patti Smith's "Ask the Angels" at the club, while the vamps get vampy, and we transition back to the same era-appropriate song at Billy's in the '70s. Just as a vampire who has her wits about her can seamlessly transition between decades to avoid arousing suspicion (see: Lexi's perfect style makeovers from era to era), so can *The Vampire Diaries* shift through time to deliver important backstory that resonates.

Despite things taking a turn for the worse for the brothers Salvatore (double fail, boys), "Because the Night" was wildly entertaining. It was an episode full of manipulators — and manipulators being manipulated. As Damon tried to play Elena and she returned the favor, while Rebekah jockeyed for position, the trip down memory lane let us know how little things have changed in the past 36 years between switched-off vampires and their would-be saviors. Back in Mystic Falls, Silas convinces Bonnie to massacre 12 of her witch sisters to complete that triangle, while Caroline and Klaus, as two mystical parts of Stefan's detective triangle, come to a standoff in their relationship. In each case, the manipulator knows his or her audience well enough to play to a vanity or weakness — or in Elena's case, to her appetite for blood and fun — and give the patsy the illusion of control.

Besides showcasing Lexi's perfect hair, this flashback to 1977 was important as it finally explained why she arrived in Mystic Falls in "162 Candles" hating Damon. The previous flashbacks had only given us a partial picture of the Damon-Lexi dynamic. Though they have never been chums (far from it), their regard for Stefan made them allies of a kind. He asked her to take care of Stefan in 1864. Though Damon tempted Stefan into drinking human blood in "1912," by 1942 he put Stefan's interests ahead of his own and stayed behind as Stefan shipped off to war. What Lexi asked for Stefan's sake, Damon did. But this 1977 trickery is the crucial missing piece, the reason why she was pissed and why Damon didn't hesitate to kill her in season one. Fooling her into thinking that not only had she been successful in bringing him back to an emotions-on state, but he'd fallen in love with her in the process, cuts to the heart of who she is — her Florence Nightingale/Mother Teresa complex. Damon mocks that cruelly . . . and later comes to regret it. Of course, the joke was also on Damon back in 1977. He felt so clever for tricking Lexi, but he was unwittingly helping Katherine elude capture, as he nicked ID after ID for a 5-foot-7 brunette. Duped by the doppelgänger, then and now!

Elena is the most entertaining of all the manipulators in this episode, precisely because, despite warnings, Damon simply underestimates her. She uses the same tricks on Damon that he uses on other people, but there are certain boundaries he won't cross now (thanks to having his emotions activated) that

© Emiley Schweich/PRPhotos.com

Elena simply does not care about. She can be ruthless, and as she says to Rebekah, she's just manipulating Damon the same way he's trying to trick her. While she plays the fun and flirty card with Damon to appeal to his ego (and his undying love for her), with Rebekah she feels free to keep up her truth bombs from "Bring It On," calling the Original sister a pile of neuroses and insecurities. What a Katherine thing to say. Certainly the old version of Elena would argue that Rebekah's desire to be human again is her saving grace, not what makes her useless as an ally. Elena and her friends are usually the "big emotional variables"; now the tables have turned and Elena is the stone-cold planner of a rational, if obvious, strategy of seducing Damon. If she gleaned anything from Damon's history lesson, it wasn't that she'll later regret her dastardly deeds, but that there's value in not being *totally* reckless. You'll only get more annoying lectures from well-meaning bores.

And in an acknowledgment that even when the switch is off, it can't be *entirely* off, Elena points out that Damon's actions with Lexi were fueled by emotions, just hate-based ones. And even now Elena can't be 100% emotionless — it just doesn't work on a story level. She wouldn't care enough about Damon to let him live if he threatened to jam the Cure down her throat or got in the way of doing what she wanted. But she doesn't kill him — she just steals his lead on Katherine and steals his kickass car. In season three, as Stefan slowly came back to himself after "Homecoming," the term "dimmer switch" was used regarding his emotional state, and that is a more fitting image. There's never a completely emotion-free state (just a really, really dim setting) and you *can* have a few feelings sneak back in without flipping the switch entirely and being smacked with it all at once. With those brothers determined to get her humanity back in both senses (her emotions and her mortality), what Elena will do remains to be seen, but thanks to her new BFF, Rebekah, they'll have a little grand theft auto fun while they can.

That aborted friendship between the two (cut short by Elena daggering Rebekah and Rebekah killing Elena and all that) is finally gelling again, and it's as entertaining as Rebekah smacking down that punk who dared touch her. New-glam-hair Elena doesn't mind Rebekah's sharp tongue, she smirks in response to her (hilarious) insults rather than getting all riled up and shirty the way old Elena would. Long may this unholy alliance last.

As fun as it is to watch everyone play each other, there's a bigger issue underlying Damon's nostalgia and reminiscences that resonates nicely with what's happening in Mystic Falls between Caroline and Klaus. Damon wants to save Elena from the regret that will, inevitably, hit her, and hit hard. It's the kind of regret that Klaus seems to have (maybe?), and that Caroline has had since she killed the guy at the carnival back on day one of being a vampire. And now she's killed an entire coven of witches, which will make her partly responsible for a crazy apocalyptic supernatural bloodbath if things continue to go south. When she's angry with Klaus and "spiraling," Caroline tells him, "People who do terrible things are just terrible people." But she can't really mean it — it's an indictment of everyone she knows and loves, and of herself. Can any of them be "fixed" once they've done something they cannot undo?

Back in the '70s, Damon was so cocksure that his way was the right way, telling Lexi that he wasn't a victim like Stefan, he was *choosing* this. But eventually, the thing that Damon fears will happen to Elena happened to him (since it's happened to every vampire in the history of vampirism): he *felt* and that made him think differently about his choices in his hedonistic days. Eventually they all feel the intense regret only a vampire (with heightened emotions and innate tendencies to do super terrible things) can experience.

"Don't underestimate the allure of darkness," says the darkest of all vamps. "Even the purest hearts are drawn to it." And though he's speaking of Elena, and in earshot of an attentive Caroline, the third of the trio of girlfriends could have benefited from that warning. With a great display of power and some help from "Shane," Bonnie Bennett, the good witch, tricks her own father into calling in a full coven of witches to help her — and instead turns those witches into lambs for the slaughter. Silas manipulates Bonnie and turns her dark wish, to have her loved ones back no matter the cost, into an irreversible action. What a heartbreaking moment when Stefan realizes that she doesn't know Jeremy's dead, that she still possesses the hopefulness she went into that crypt with, and he has to crush her with the truth.

With the Expression triangle complete, Silas turns his attention to the missing piece, the Cure, and he wants Klaus to get it for him. Nothing like a little show of strength to motivate the Original hybrid — and that's the thing: Klaus is not invulnerable. He can die, and Silas has just demonstrated how easy it would be to kill him. Klaus's reign as the most fearsome of all immortals may have come to an end. Will Klaus do as he's told and help Silas get the Cure? As Damon warns Elena, there will come a day when that one thing happens that you just can't take back — has it happened already for Bonnie and Caroline? Will Klaus add one more terrible, horrible, no good thing to his list?

COMPELLING MOMENT Caroline saving Bonnie and realizing she's responsible for massacring 12 witches and completing Silas's Expression triangle.

CIRCLE OF KNOWLEDGE
• No Tyler or Matt in this episode.

- "Because the Night" is a song originally written by Bruce Springsteen and later reworked (with new lyrics) by Patti Smith for the Patti Smith Group album *Easter*. Though Springsteen didn't release a studio version of the song until 2010, he and Smith have shared cowriting credits since the Patti Smith Group released "Because the Night" as a single in 1978. It is one of her most commercially successful songs and it has been widely covered. The night may belong to lovers, lust, and "us," but New York City — not love — is the banquet on which Elena and Damon (and Rebekah, the Original third wheel) feed, while Damon seduces Lexi with a sentiment similar to the song's.

- In the teaser, Damon's soon-to-be victim says, "You're that serial killer, aren't you? Son of Sam?" David Berkowitz, the self-proclaimed Son of Sam, killed six and wounded seven people during a murder spree that lasted from the summer of 1976 until his capture in August 1977. Claiming demonic possession, Berkowitz targeted and shot young women with long dark hair, couples, and pairs of people in cars. When he was arrested, his first words were reportedly, "You got me. What took you so long?"

- Klaus ascribes the descriptor "the young Brutus" to Tyler, Brutus being Roman dictator Julius Caesar's friend and infamous assassin. (You see where Klaus is going with this analogy.) William Shakespeare famously dramatized the circumstances surrounding Caesar's assassination in his play *Julius Caesar*, in which Caesar's last words are "Et tu, Brute?" The phrase has become synonymous with ultimate betrayal. Klaus is nothing if not dramatic. His later "How Shakespearean" comment about Silas and his lost love is most likely a vague handwave in the direction of the star-crossed lovers Romeo and Juliet.

- Damon says Mystic Falls isn't "Vamp Xanadu." Xanadu (née Shangdu) was the summer palace of Mongolian emperor Kublai Khan, made famous by explorer Marco Polo's description of its decadent wonders after a 13th century visit and by Samuel Taylor Coleridge's 1797 Romantic poem *Kubla Khan* (published in 1816). Coleridge claimed his poem was inspired by an opium dream and the work is credited with bringing Xanadu into the popular lexicon as a synonym for a man-made paradise of pleasures.

- Since Katherine's birthday is June 5, 1473, she was 17 when she had her baby girl.

Michael Suby on Composing for Silas

For Silas, I tried to do something new, something fresh. I used some chants with more tribal percussion because of his age, so I mixed those two things. I started Silas's theme with Shane and, of course, it turns out that Silas overtook Shane, which I didn't know, but it turned out to be a good thing. As Shane started to describe Silas, I started to write him these themes and it morphed from Shane's theme into Silas's theme. Most of his stuff is really atonal, there's not a lot of "music"; you know, tapping-your-foot music. It's really very dissonant and choral and I tried to keep it outside of the normal harmonic palette of the show. It just feels really disconnected and hopefully the chanting and the tribal hand percussion, stuff like that, makes it feel a little bit older, more mystical; there's a lot of witchcraft involved. The human voice is really powerful, you only use it when it's really called for or needed or the screen can handle it.

- Damon calls the band performing at Billy's "The Runaways 2.0"; The Runaways (1.0) was the Los Angeles all-female rock band best known for their 1976 single "Cherry Bomb" from their debut self-titled album.
- Believe it or not, thanks to the wacky *TVD* timeline, the addresses that Damon finds for Katherine, which date back two months, cover the timespan from "The Birthday" (3.01) to "Because the Night." (Rest assured, this compressed timeline is contradicted later in the season.)
- Klaus's friend, renowned Portuguese explorer Ferdinand Magellan, served King Charles I of Spain. His early 14th century expedition was the first to travel from the Atlantic to the Pacific Ocean via what is now known as the Strait of Magellan, south of the South American continent. It was also the first to cross the Pacific, thus circumnavigating the globe, though Magellan himself died in battle in the Philippines before that accomplishment was achieved. He probably could've handled a map app.

HISTORY LESSON In 1977 New York City was at a cultural turning point, which this episode revels in, heaping references into the flashback scenes. The birth of America's punk rock movement — at its height in New York City between 1974 and 1976 — is largely featured, with Damon wearing a rather hilarious anarchy symbol T-shirt (punk rock shorthand for noobs?). Later, when setting the 1977 Billy's scene for Elena, he name-drops Manhattan clubs like CBGB. CBGB is widely considered the birthplace of punk rock, serving as a launch pad for notable bands and musicians such as Patti Smith, The Ramones, The New York Dolls, Blondie, and Talking Heads (whose "Psycho Killer" is featured in the opening scene). Damon also refers to The Factory, Andy Warhol's art studio and a nerve center of the American art and music scenes, particularly in the late '60s.

THE RULES Because Silas specifically says to Bonnie, "You invited me into your home," it seems he is subject to the invitation rule, like a regular vampire. Aja tells us that a full coven of witches is 12. While a witch can use Expression to draw power from any sacrifice (as Val did when she tricked Damon into killing a dozen people for her), an Expression triangle requires two of the three mass sacrifices to be of supernatural creatures, which "compounds the mystical energy." Silas tells Klaus that Rebekah's mind was easier to read than his; it seems Silas has the mind-reading power that Sage had ("Break On Through," 3.17), in addition to his ability to change form (or appear to change form) as he wishes and to cause hallucinations (as he did to Shane, Bonnie, and the miners in the cave). Stefan believes that Bonnie's memory loss is a result of the witches' attempt to rid her of Expression, not damage from Silas.

PREVIOUSLY ON *THE VAMPIRE DIARIES* The opening kill scene is a callback to the couple Damon killed in "Pilot" (1.01), who were also on their way home after a lovely evening out when they came across a dead-looking dude lying in the road.

Lexi reminds Damon of the first time they met, which is shown in flashback in "The Dinner Party" (2.15).

In "162 Candles" (1.08), Lexi wakes up from a nap to find Damon lying next to her: the first time they've seen each other since he locked her on the sunshiny roof. Lexi mockingly says to him that she's "finally realized after a century that death means nothing without you. Do me," before declaring that he's "not a nice person" and he only exhibits the "bad parts" of a vampire. To which Damon replies, "Teach me to be good." In the wake of this flashback revelation, it's an extra cruel and biting exchange.

OFF CAMERA As for the episode's surprising reveal that Damon and Lexi had once been lovers, Ian Somerhalder was pragmatic about Damon's womanizing ways. "[There's] a possibility of any woman Damon is around, he's going to try and seduce," he told *TV Guide*. But, he told *ET Online*, Lexi and Damon have something important in common: Stefan. "There are just so many different agendas at play, but at the end of the day, both Lexi and Damon love Stefan, so to see them interacting throughout an episode where they're not trying to kill each other or making derogatory jokes to one another the entire time is amazing. There was a real relationship there, so it was fun to explore."

The band playing Billy's is Dead Sara, and they specially recorded for this episode the Patti Smith cover "Ask the Angels," a 1977 single from *Radio Ethiopia*. Emily Armstrong of Dead Sara appreciates the coverage *TVD* gives musicians: "They're huge supporters of indie music . . . We were stoked to be considered among these other really cool artists."

FOGGY MOMENTS Ah, Manhattan: a place where you can drink from someone's neck in the middle of a crowd and *no one notices*. The book that Caroline finds on symbols in the dark arts is in Latin — except for the caption to the illustration that Stefan reads aloud. How did Caroline know that the symbols surrounding the triangle represented humans, demons, and witches? How does Aja know that Stefan is a vampire? Usually a witch has to touch a person to detect vampirism. Is it because Stefan is inside the circle or because Aja is linked to her full coven, or is it just a useful plot device?

QUESTIONS
- Was Damon's switch flipped in 1977 because of general Katherine malaise, or did something else precipitate it?
- When did Lexi meet her epic love, Lee ("Bloodlines," 1.11)?
- Let's say the veil comes down and all the supernaturals are back in the mortal realm. Will they be resurrected where they died, where they are buried, or will they appear wherever they happen to be when that veil drops (in their world relative to this one)?
- How will Klaus get that stake out of his back?

> *Katherine: Did it ever occur to you that you have no idea who I really am?*
> *Damon: Did it ever occur to you that you're not that deep?*

4.18 American Gothic

Original air date: March 28, 2013
Written by: Evan Bleiweiss and Jose Molina
Directed by: Kellie Cyrus
Guest cast: Mackenzie Britt (Elena Double), Reegus Flenory (Mailman), Samantha Kacho (Waitress), Emily Morris (Lanie)
Previously on *The Vampire Diaries*: Candice Accola

Elena and Rebekah track down Katherine and find she's made a "friend" of Elijah. Klaus seeks out Caroline's help.

Willoughby, Pennsylvania: creamed corn capital, beautiful place to die, and the site of the return of two of the most beloved characters on *TVD*. With doppelgänger hijinks, hilarity, twists, tricks, and ultimatums, "American Gothic" holds us captive . . . like Katherine with a fork through her hand.

When Elena turned vampire at the beginning of this season, it was inevitable that one day Nina Dobrev would have to portray vamp Elena opposite vamp Katherine. But of course, the *TVD* writers make it a little trickier than that: it's vampire Elena, emotion switch in off position, doing an impression of her doppelgänger while said doppelgänger snarks back at her. Amazing. The characters are still distinct though now both badass vampires, and we see the subtle differences everywhere, even when Elena's imitating Katherine. It continues to boggle the mind what Ms. Dobrev can do with these gradations of character, and it's ridiculously fun to watch. Just as entertaining (in a bit of a cruel way) is seeing how far reality has deviated from Stefan's oh-so-vanilla hopes and dreams for Elena's vampire future from the beginning of this season; he wanted to keep her from even a drop of human blood, so she'd enjoy a guilt-free immortality, and instead she's as devious as her doppelgänger, and as prone to stone-cold neck-breaking.

As refreshing as it is to have Katherine back in the game, it is just as wonderful to see the Salvatore boys, Rebekah, and Elena reacting to her, incredibly wary of every move and word. And while the doppelgängers still don't get along, they are singing the same refrain in "American Gothic": I'm not the girl you think I am. Katherine is well aware of what others think of her — and fair enough, given her track record — but she's insistent that she only has one thing up her sleeve: a simple plan to get her freedom from Klaus. We've seen many versions of the legendary Katerina Petrova over the past four seasons, and while Damon quips that she's not that deep, she at least has layers and layers of identity, enough to confuse Elijah and herself. Somewhere in there hides the person Elijah calls "my Katerina," but that doesn't make the vixen Katherine any less authentic. As Katherine says to him at the end of the episode, after 500 years of running, she doesn't remember who she used to be, that human girl who thought a life without love was not worth living. Though Katherine can't alter her physical form like Silas can (save for a little hair straightening), she does share that gift of shapeshifting, changing herself to suit her surroundings and to manipulate those around her. And since her goal has always been simply to survive, to outrun Klaus, she finds herself living the same life again and again. Something Stefan sees himself and Damon doing.

Now that the boys have known Katherine for a few lifetimes, they can anticipate her tricks — though Stefan seems a little more talented in this department than his big brother — but in the end that's not enough to best her. Even Elijah *knows* better, but he wants to believe in her. He calls it his "disease," his need to hope that she can be trusted, that she does love him. But he can be about as sure of her honesty as Klaus can be that whoever's standing in front of him isn't Silas, which is to say: not so much. There's no way to truly know someone, especially not in this mystical world.

Caroline schools Klaus in the rules of friendship: step one is "show me that I can trust you." Just as Elijah is wary of giving Katherine the benefit of the doubt, so is Caroline. In the Klaus-Caroline shouting match, Caroline finds herself on very similar ground to Elijah: she knows better than to give Klaus any leeway, or sympathy, or help, and yet she does. She hasn't turned her back on him. There's something in Klaus (that elusive, rarely glimpsed heart that she's digging for in his back with pliers) that draws her in, just as Elijah keeps hoping that Katherine will prove to have the capacity for decency and affection.

And Katherine gives Elijah hope at the end of the episode by taking that first step: she hands over the Cure. In doing so, she puts her fate in his hands. More than when she tried to gather all the pieces for the doppelgänger sacrifice back in the moonstone days, Katherine has a winning card in her hand with that Cure, but she can't play it herself. She needs Elijah — whether

> "My favorite scene was in 'American Gothic' where Elena wants to dress up as Katherine, and Elena strips her of her accessories and shoes and mocks her voice with Rebekah. It was clever and fun, and it switched the Katherine/Elena power dynamic."
>
> — Caroline Dries

or not she has any true feelings for him. (And c'mon, how could she not?) Does Katherine give Elijah the Cure just to keep her plan in progress? Can Katherine be trusted? Is what she's doing any different than back in "Klaus" when Elena realized that if she wanted Elijah to help her, she needed to make a show of faith?

In "American Gothic," the doppelgängers do what they do best as characters: act as foils for each other. How different from Katherine is emotionless-vampire Elena? Do Katherine's selfish ways lie in Elena's future? Certainly we get a glimpse of Katherine's shock-and-awe ruthlessness in Elena's final ultimatum to the unsuspecting Salvatore brothers. Elena asks to be left alone, for the brothers to stop trying to "fix" her and let her be herself. Because, whether they like it or not (and whether we at home like it or not), this Elena is just as authentically Elena as the "special snowflake of human frailty" they fell in love with. And even if Elena chooses to turn her emotions back on, even if she's made mortal again by taking the Cure, that "special snowflake" is dead and gone.

In a nice bit of parallelism, Rebekah's wistfulness for a "simple" human life is just as naïve as Elijah's and the Salvatores' hope that the girl(s) they fell for will come back. As Katherine tells Rebekah, there's no do-over. The bad — all the violence and betrayals, the death and loss — won't go away. But Rebekah and the love-struck men see the folly in their hopefulness and still hold on to it. Rebekah knows that a human life might not be the idyllic wonder she wishes for, just as Elijah, Damon, and Stefan can see how far gone the doppelgängers are. So are they fools to love a "ghost"? Or is it noble to hold out hope and to fight to bring back the compassionate, loving women they once knew? Stefan argues that he is doing for Elena what she did for him: refusing to give up on him. But Stefan had already been to the dark side and back, and he was crystal clear on which Stefan he wanted to be — the same Stefan his loved ones wanted him to be. Elena's just on the beginning of her journey. Isn't it rather presumptuous to think you can determine for someone else who they should be and how they should live their life?

It's that last point that Rebekah highlights to her big brother. Just like Elena and Katherine, who want their freedom, Rebekah wants to choose the way she'll live and die, free from the controlling interests of her brothers. Elena wants to be accepted as she is, and not harassed for failing to be a girl who is dead. Katherine wants to end five centuries of running and hiding. Even Stefan wants to break the cycle, to stop reliving the same dynamic with his brother and the doppelgänger and "get a life." Will any of them ride off into the sunset alone? And where would that leave Damon? At the end of "American Gothic," he's at risk of losing his brother and the girl he loves.

With everyone coming home to Mystic Falls, the Cure in the suit pocket of the impeccably dressed Elijah, an enemy lurking with powers of manipulation so great he makes Katherine Pierce look like an amateur, and a prom around the corner, all the complications are aligned for a great build to the season finale.

COMPELLING MOMENT Elena imitating Katherine while Rebekah gleefully provides pointers was a classic scene, but the fan service in having Elena and Elijah smooch was epic. Thank you, writers.

CIRCLE OF KNOWLEDGE
- No Bonnie, Matt, or Tyler in this episode.
- Although the term American Gothic is used to describe the gothic romantic writers from the States, it's much better known as the name of a famous painting. Grant Wood's *American Gothic* (1930) depicts a stony-faced Puritan farmer and his unmarried daughter, pitchfork in hand, farmhouse in the background. The title was also used by a short-lived but beloved horror TV show (1995–1996) set in a fictional South Carolina town called Trinity. (A small Southern town with murders, ghosts, and other supernatural shenanigans? You don't say!) The show starred Gary Cole as the Big Bad, Sheriff Lucas Buck, who manipulated Trinity's townsfolk into making truly terrible — sometimes fatal — choices. Say what you will about Mystic Falls PD, at least their sheriff isn't the Devil.
- *TVD* tourists and creamed corn enthusiasts please note: Willoughby, Pennsylvania, is, sadly, a fictional town (though there is a tributary called the Willoughby Run in the state).

- Klaus points out to Caroline the fact that he's not exactly chasing down Tyler to kill him, but that's kind of Klaus's M.O. as he explained to Hayley in "Bring It On." The punishment is not in the swift kill, but in the centuries of living in fear, never able to settle down. See: Katherine Pierce.
- Since Klaus's pain was all in his mind, Silas doesn't necessarily have the white oak stake and we can rest assured it hasn't been snapped in half.

THE RULES Silas has enough mind-control power to convince *Klaus* that he is dying. His capacity for psychological torture is unprecedented! It's not clear when he vanishes from a room whether he's just moving at vamp speed, or if he is magically disappearing.

PREVIOUSLY ON *THE VAMPIRE DIARIES* Rebekah reminds Katherine of the time she drove a wedge between Klaus and Elijah, depicted in "Katerina" (2.09) and "Klaus" (2.19). (But let's all remember that Klaus was intending to sacrifice Katerina for his own personal gain, so who's really to blame in that situation?)

"There goes the neighborhood," says Katherine when the Salvatore brothers enter, name-checking a season one episode (1.16).

Finally, Elena-as-Katherine gets to smooch one of Katherine's beaus! Katherine famously liplocked with Damon in "Founder's Day" (1.22) and got a little snuggle in with Stefan in "The Return" (2.01) and "Memory Lane" (2.04).

In "Klaus," Elijah tells Elena that caring for the doppelgänger is "a common mistake, I'm told. And it's one I won't make again." Guess he couldn't resist the Petrova fire.

Always check a doppelgänger's daylight jewellery: Elijah realizes he's with Elena, not Katherine, here, just as Stefan figured out it was Katherine at Elena's house in "The Return."

Katherine hides the fake cure in a vervain-water fish tank, a riff on Mason Lockwood's hiding spot for the moonstone, which he stuck down an old well full of the sizzle-the-skin vampire allergen.

Elijah can empathize with Elena losing her brother; he's lost three — Henrik ("Ordinary People," 3.08), Finn ("The Murder of One," 3.18), and Kol ("A View to a Kill").

© Tina Gill/PRPhotos.com

Elijah gave Elena the handwritten letter in "All My Children" (3.15) as an apology for kidnapping her.

Stefan confronted Damon about his humanity in "Friday Night Bites" (1.03) and he responded with a surprise-kill of Coach Tanner, just as Elena surprise-kills the waitress. Anyone, anytime, any place.

OFF CAMERA This is Kellie Cyrus's first directing gig; she is the longtime script supervisor for *TVD*.

An Elena with her humanity switched off seemed like the perfect opportunity to update Elena's look and shed the character's penchant for jeans, sneakers, and long-sleeved shirts and sweaters in favor of a more adult, accessories-friendly look. "She is going for more dresses and skirts," costume designer Leigh Leverett told *Entertainment Weekly*. "It's a little more boutique-y look, as opposed to college look." Another challenge was making sure Elena's new wardrobe and hair remained distinct from Katherine's. "I try to keep Elena a little more organically based, whereas Katherine kind of wears shiny leathers and blacks and has a little bit more of a, I don't want to say an edge, but she doesn't wear flowy stuff," Leverett explained. "She's always really tight and sexy . . . [Elena's look is] a totally different color palette than Katherine."

Scenes with the doppelgängers together present their own special logistical challenges. "The scenes where we have Nina playing both Katherine and Elena are usually shot with Nina playing one role against a photo double [a stand-in] and then we shoot the scene again with her in the opposite role," explains Dave Perkal, director of photography. "Sometimes the double is replaced digitally so that you are looking at both Ninas or sometimes you're actually looking at the back of the photo double's head but onto Nina."

"Like most creative types, I'm greedy and want to do it all," says writer Jose Molina when asked about the drastically different tones of "Memorial" and "American Gothic." "'American Gothic' was initially quite different — much wilder and funnier, and probably a little off-tone for the show. I really like breaking up drama with humor (and vice-versa), so in a perfect world I'd smash the two episodes together."

QUESTIONS
- Does Elijah know Kol is dead and who killed him?
- What will Elijah, man of honor, do with the Cure?
- What will the boys do in the wake of Elena's ultimatum?

Rebekah: Name me a more human experience than the prom.
Elena: Death.

4.19 *Pictures of You*

Original air date: April 18, 2013
Written by: Neil Reynolds and Caroline Dries
Directed by: J. Miller Tobin
Guest cast: Scott Parks (Silas)
Previously on *The Vampire Diaries*: Paul Wesley

Worst. Prom. Ever.

On the eve of the backdoor pilot for "The Originals," the Mystic Falls teens (and creepily too-old-for-high-school Damon) head to prom to pay homage to a time of their lives that is drawing to a close. But as they find themselves already grieving both the actually dead and the dead-to-you friend in Elena, the high school rite of passage that is senior prom plays out worse than the Best Night Ever that Caroline hoped and dreamed for her pals. But hey, isn't that what prom is all about?

A night about memories and friends fittingly sees the return of two dearly departed cast members, with both Michael Trevino and Steven R. McQueen making appearances, as the rest of the gang — led by the Salvatore brothers — try to get that heartless Elena to feel *something*. The nostalgia of seeing old pictures flash by her doesn't work. The heartfelt pleas from Matt and Bonnie don't work. A little reminder of lusty times gone by from Stefan fails too. The only thing that Elena is capable of feeling? Fear. The fear of death is so primal it can't be shut off, not even in a delightfully cruel Ms. Gilbert. She's behaving terribly — stealing prom dresses and eating the prom queen — but Evil Elena is highly entertaining. She's always been able to understand people: to get to the heart of them. In the past, that power stemmed from empathy — she knew just how to talk someone out of a crisis and help them. But now she uses that power to cut the heart out of someone and leave them gasping. She mocks Caroline's love for all things prom, she calls Bonnie a brainwashed crazy person, she makes Rebekah feel like she'd make a *terrible* human being. And with the boys who love her, she's just plain dismissive, knowing that her apathy hurts them the most. Her "What heart?" line says it best: their attempts to stir up some positive feeling in her are in vain. The only thing that works is Bonnie's huge smackdown of witch power on Elena, bringing her so close to death that she pleads for her life. So now, after she's tried to kill both of her best friends, her two (ex?)boyfriends realize what they have to do next: trap her in the Salvatore holding cell and try to scare some feeling into her. It's a nice bit of history repeating, the brothers now watching over their prisoner and figuring out how to bring her back to herself, like she has done for both of them in the past.

As Elena eschews any glimmer of humanity like she's allergic to it, her temporary roommate Rebekah tries to be good. Elijah's "be human for a day" test leads Rebekah to that paragon of human decency, Matt Donovan. The loyal, honest busboy with a heart of gold, Matt helps Rebekah appreciate the spirit of being decent, though she technically flunks her test. It's interesting that both Klaus and Elena have rather cynical views of what it means to be human: Elena suggests death is a more human experience than hitting senior prom, while Klaus rhymes off all the clichés we trot out time and again after a tragedy or death. And they're both right: being human isn't necessarily about saving lives or being good or having special prom memories. It's all the terrible stuff too. But the appeal — what Rebekah wants so desperately — is in grasping for greatness with no extra help, only our mortal abilities to get us there.

That difference lies at the heart of the discord between Elijah and Klaus. Elijah hopes that his only living brother will spare Katerina for him, for the sake of his own chance for happiness, while Klaus thinks of him as a lovesick fool who has betrayed him. And when Klaus threatens to run down Katerina, Elijah feels only pity for his brother and his "hollow" life. Of course what we see is that Klaus is as wrapped around Caroline's finger as Stefan accuses him of being: Klaus lets Tyler escape so Caroline's perfect evening can be realized, in all her Princess of Monaco hotness. Despite all his bluster, Klaus wants the same thing as Elijah does, as Damon and Stefan do: to love and be loved in return.

Those human feelings — the desires and insecurities — are just the things that our astral-projecting Phantom of the Opera preys on: Silas uses these vulnerabilities to manipulate minds and to get his way. But what drives him is at its heart no different: he wants to be reunited with *his* true love. He's just willing to destroy the world to get to her. And that's the question at the heart of all these love stories: is it worth it? It's what Klaus asks of Tyler, and it's what Elijah decides for Klaus: his personal discomfort is not sufficient reason to put the entire world in jeopardy. Just as fear is still a very real emotion for Elena, Klaus has experienced the power of Silas and he fears an eternity of being subjected to that kind of psychological torment. No doubt his half-century suffering from the Hunter's Curse fuels his determination to give Silas what he wants; he's been subjected to seemingly endless torment before, and is willing to betray Elijah and Rebekah, and risk hell on earth, to avoid experiencing it again.

Bonnie too must ask herself the question of whether the risk justifies the reward as she contemplates bringing Jeremy back from the dead by taking down the veil to the Other Side. What price is she willing to pay to have him alive again? Silas pushes Bonnie too far in "Pictures of You" and she pushes back. The nightmares and waking dreams of Jeremy make Bonnie feel she's losing herself to Silas's mind games, and with a display of power (that has the strange side effect of making all the car alarms in the parking lot go off) Bonnie tries to break herself free from Silas's hold. What will happen next with the whole Bonnie-Silas superpower duo? He can't get what he wants without her help, and she's insistent she doesn't need his. Why does she seek him out in his creepy cave? With her insane Expression ability, could she single-handedly destroy him? Does she want to?

COMPELLING MOMENT "Yeah, well, hindsight is almost a bigger bitch than you." Damon's more vicious snarks are very rarely aimed at Elena, so this particular comeback crackled with the ferocity of what kids these days call *an epic burn*.

CIRCLE OF KNOWLEDGE
- "Pictures of You," the episode's title and prom theme, is a 1989 single from The Cure's album *Disintegration*. A cover of the song, performed by Class Actress, is featured when Elena, Damon, and Stefan arrive at the prom.
- Caroline wants to look as hot as Princess Grace of Monaco at prom, after Evil Elena steals her dress. American actress Grace Kelly (1929–1982) became princess of Monaco after marrying in 1956 and has long been a style icon known for elegance and, well, grace.

THE RULES Bonnie shows off her new powers in this episode: she heals from Elena's bite, she can overpower vampires easily, and she is able to do a locator spell without a talisman of the person she's looking for.

Michael Suby on the Music of *The Vampire Diaries*

On the show's musical palette: The music's definitely changed a lot. It started much more sparse in season one and it's been ramping up ever since. I think it was at its largest, sort of, orchestration-wise in season three with the Originals 'til the end; I think I kind of went bananas on Elijah and Klaus, which was a lot of fun. I really enjoyed that. And then we kind of pared it back again here in season four, as far as the palette for the show goes. It's constantly changing; I'm always trying to introduce new elements and themes and sounds for the season four cues. Once you play the cues you should be able to know what season it's from. But at the same time the themes can work universally — in a perfect world.

On cues and themes: There are some obvious cues related to character development and relationships. Stefan and Elena started out with three or four major love and development themes in season one, and as Damon leaked in, essentially what I would do is try to help the writers create confusion. What they're writing on the page, I'm trying to also do that with emotional response to music. So you take the Stefan and Elena theme and put it over Damon and Elena. Even though it's not going anywhere, people might think it might be going somewhere. Maybe change the key, maybe change the instrumentation. I may use a fragment of that theme, but what it does do is, as soon as you hear this certain motif, it makes you think of Stefan and Elena and it's over Damon and Elena, and you're causing that confusion. So that's one way to use it.

Of course another way is the characters have come and gone in the relationships, and Stefan and Elena have been separated for a while and so it's really easy to go back to one of their big season one themes and make people think love is kind of growing again. The themes get a lot of mileage.

Caroline and Tyler have themes — they have a big one, one of my favorites — and it just really helps to fragment it, to take pieces of those themes to catch people's attention. They don't know it, but once they hear a couple of bars of a theme, it just takes you to that place. It ties the show together in a way that is hopefully not as obvious as cuts and lines of dialogue.

I'll watch the footage and sometimes it will be obvious [that characters are on the road to romance]. But sometimes I'll be in a meeting and I'll be like, "Is this going somewhere?" In this show there isn't a lot of that — unlike *Pretty Little Liars* where there are a lot of misdirects on relationships and there are little flirts here and there. That's not really happening on this show, so most of the time I know we're going to develop themes on a broad level.

On scoring action sequences: The action stuff — I mean, once you set the palette of what the action is on the show, that hasn't changed a whole lot. The more interesting stuff is the levels of darkness in guys like Silas or when the Originals arrived. Trying to make things sound like they're 1,500 years old, 2,000 years old. The action is just kind of what it is: someone's running, someone's fighting, someone's dying — you give the screen what it's asking for and that's what action is, for me at least. But the kind of weird, creepy sounds and palettes used for the different characters and different time frames, that's a lot more time-consuming and interesting.

On deciding between licensed music and score: That's mostly decided with Chris [Mollere, music supervisor] and Julie [Plec] and some of the other producers. But if we're in a meeting and I really feel like a song isn't doing it justice, or vice versa, if the score isn't doing it justice, Chris and I absolutely put our heads together and come up with solutions all the time.

On his favorite character: Well, I'm a sucker for Elijah. He's my favorite guy, he's such a badass. I remember watching him come in in "Rose" [2.08], through the doors of that house, and he's just such a fucking badass. And I just loved writing that theme for him. There are times when I absolutely, *absolutely* love this job and that was one of them. Writing Elijah's theme was just absolutely great — I love that guy.

On a long-awaited score soundtrack release: We've talked about that so many times. That is something that Chris and Warner Bros. do, and they did have a deal to do one, and then some sort of business thing happened, the publishing, something happened where they changed labels or I don't know what it was, but for the last three seasons we've been talking about releasing a score. We get a lot of requests for it. I'd like it; it would be fun.

PREVIOUSLY ON *THE VAMPIRE DIARIES* The dream Bonnie has in the teaser is not her first creepy cemetery dream: Emily Bennett and the old cemetery featured in Bonnie's dreams in "162 Candles" (1.08) and "History Repeating" (1.09), and Bonnie dreamed of Klaus in a coffin in the cemetery in "The New Deal" (3.10).

The brothers Salvatore toss the football around the great room of the boarding house: is there any greater signifier of them bonding? They first played football together in 1864, seen in "Lost Girls" (1.06), and hit the MFHS field in "History Repeating."

Rebekah has made the same crack about compelling herself a date that Elena does here. It happened in "Heart of Darkness" (3.19) when she was organizing the 1920s Decade Dance.

Elena arrives at the prom with a Salvatore on each arm, recalling Isobel's line from "Isobel" (1.21) and her arrival at the Mikaelson ball in "Dangerous

Liaisons" (3.14). At that ball, Caroline showed up in a dress given to her by Klaus.

Stefan vervains Elena and tosses her in the Salvatore holding cell, just like he did to Damon after "Family Ties" (1.04) and just like Elena and Damon did to him in "Miss Mystic Falls" (1.19). Damon threatened to do just this (though his exact scenario involved chains) to Elena in "Because the Night."

OFF CAMERA "[The girls] tried on a bunch of gowns, probably six to 10 each," costume designer Leigh Leverett told *Entertainment Weekly*. Elena's red gown, a.k.a. "the watercolor dress," was sold out in Nina Dobrev's size, so Leverett tailored the Theia dress from one originally four sizes too big. Bonnie's navy blue gown was also Theia, while Rebekah's was Jolene. "It felt like the big, yellow, quintessential prom dress," said Leverett — appropriate for Rebekah's first honest-to-goodness school dance! The extenuating circumstances surrounding Caroline's vintage-inspired Sherri Hill gown allowed Leverett to "go a little more feminine." The Salvatore brothers both wore Armani, Matt a Brooks Brothers tuxedo. Leverett shares the fan appreciation for Elijah's dapper style, even if he didn't attend the prom: "That man can wear a suit." Amen.

The moment where Klaus threatens Elijah and the older brother pats Klaus's face was unscripted. "We shot that [scene] from several angles," Daniel Gillies explained to *Entertainment Weekly*. "And for some reason, he was just so close to me in that take, and I felt so sad for him threatening me, and he seemed particularly lost and lonely in that one — I was just overwhelmed, and I touched his face. I remember even Joe commented right after the take. He said, 'I loved how you did that.' I was so delighted to see that in the final cut."

FOGGY MOMENTS Klaus has amazing vintage gowns in Caroline's size hanging around his mansion? A good friend to have. Bonnie had her memory wiped, but she does know what Silas's powers are and how he's manipulated her in the past; yet she doesn't immediately clue in to the fact that she's dancing cheek to cheek with Silas, not Jeremy? Similarly, despite Klaus's very clear warning that Silas can appear as anyone and has sufficient powers to fool him, Elijah hands over the Cure to "Rebekah" no questions asked? Elijah was right last week: Rebekah doesn't have a smart brother!

QUESTIONS

- In Bonnie's dream, is it the real spirit of Jeremy warning her to wake up, or Silas-as-Jeremy, or just Bonnie's subconscious? Did Silas set Bonnie on fire while she slept or did she do that to herself?
- Can Silas appear to more than one person at a time, or is he stuck with one-on-one trickery? How deeply into a mind does he go? Does he know *everything*? Did he need the tip-off from Klaus about Elijah giving Rebekah the Cure if she passed the test? Couldn't he just have read any one of the three Originals' minds? (Or Elena's for that matter.)
- Why isn't there vervain in the water in Mystic Falls anymore? Has Bonnie's dad given up or dried out his secret supplier? (eBay?)

Klaus: This town was my home once, and in my absence, Marcel has gotten everything that I ever wanted. Power. Loyalty. Family. I made him in my image and he has bettered me. I want what he has. I want to be king.

4.20 *The Originals*

Original air date: April 25, 2013
Written by: Julie Plec
Directed by: Chris Grismer
Guest cast: Charles Michael Davis (Marcel), Daniella Pineda (Sophie Devereaux), Leah Pipes (Camille), Callard Harris (Thierry), Eka Darville (Diego), Malaya Rivera Drew (Jane-Anne Devereaux), Karen Kaia Livers (Fortune Teller), Jonathan Weiss (NOLA Tour Guide), Chris Osborn (Vampire #1), Derek Roberts (Vampire #2)
Previously on *The Vampire Diaries*: Joseph Morgan

Klaus follows Katherine's tip to New Orleans and faces off with his former protégé Marcel. Elijah urges his brother to allow their family to start over, together.

Remember the old days when the Originals were introduced and they were so incredibly compelling that a chorus of "spin-off" arose from the fandom? TV dreams do come true, but rarely do they look so good (and sound so good) as "The Originals." Serving as the backdoor pilot for the series, which will debut alongside season five of *The Vampire Diaries*, the episode is framed with Mystic Falls action, but its heart is in New Orleans.

Klaus's return to a city he loves, a city he was once happy in with his family, is complicated by two progeny: Marcel, a vampire he turned and mentored, and a little hybrid-werewolf fetus, growing inside Hayley. All that Klaus has ever wanted, Marcel has; he has "bettered" him. But with Mikael no longer the driving force behind Klaus's choices, the source of his fear and sense of powerlessness now gone, Klaus *can* have a home, a family, an empire, and true power that stems from love and loyalty — or so Elijah argues. Elijah is crucial in directing Klaus's ultimate choice to stay and build a home with his family: his pep talk encourages his brother to make a choice that seems to scare him more than a little bit. This is what Klaus earnestly wants, and together they might just be able to pull off the coup.

What is certain is that Joseph Morgan can pull off the task of leading a series. He's long shown us that Klaus is more than just a villain, he's a compelling leading man in his own right. In *The Originals* he'll be able to deeply explore his character, and the pilot episode alone already takes us deeper into the nuances of Klaus. Besides Klaus's deep affection for Caroline, what reason does he have to stay in Mystic Falls? Stefan will not be his best mate; Silas has the Cure, thanks to Klaus; and Tyler and Katherine will keep on running no matter where he settles down. With Elena a vampire, and there being next to no chance of her becoming human again, Klaus has no doppelgänger blood source with which to rebuild his hybrid gang — and they were a flop anyway. Long established as an appreciator of beauty and art, Klaus is drawn to the city's culture and vibrancy, and to the potential it holds for giving him all he's dreamed of.

But there's the pesky problem of Marcel. Here's hoping that Klaus and the witches never, ever, ever succeed in getting rid of Marcel, because the charisma of this badass vampire king seems limitless. Has there ever been or will there ever be again a karaoke debut scene that's so killer? Marcel has a devil-may-care attitude, but his every choice and his every word is precise and deliberate. He gives Klaus a warm welcome to town, but he is careful to demonstrate how in control of the vampires, witches, local humans, and out-of-towners he is — and that he learned his rules for ruling from Klaus himself. While Marcel pops vervain (again, very deliberately in front of Klaus to let him know he can't be compelled), Klaus makes it clear that he has one thing Marcel will never have: true immortality. There is only one weapon in the world that can kill Klaus, and he is in possession of it. In addition to that power, he now has some valuable allies: the witches of the French Quarter, once a force to be reckoned with.

This episode is heavily witchy, establishing an entrenched tension between the witches and vampires, which has never been front and center on *The Vampire Diaries* in such a vital way. Instead of focusing on an individual witch and her struggle (as we do with Bonnie), there is a community of oppressed witches ready to rise up, and a powerful clan of vampires determined to keep them down. With Marcel's mysterious ability to clip the witches' wings, so to speak, we're entering a world on *The Originals* that stays true to the *TVD* mythology but avoids its occasional overreliance on magic as the way out of tight plot corners. If you do magic in New Orleans, you risk a swift, public execution. And what Sophie figures out — that Hayley is Klaus's baby momma — helps her rope in the Original brothers to their side. While the pregnancy twist received a mixed reaction from viewers, to put it mildly, what it has done, by episode's end, is give hope to Elijah and Klaus, a renewed sense of family to the Mikaelsons (even if Rebekah is a holdout for now), an uneasy alliance between the witches and the Original brothers, and a reason for the one and only Phoebe Tonkin to stick around. The established rule that vampires can't procreate is just barely skirted thanks to Klaus's unique hybrid blood making this situation unprecedented, and Hayley seems to have her own mysterious lineage yet to be revealed.

Family has always been at the core of *The Vampire Diaries*, whether it's the Salvatores or the Gilberts or the Mikaelsons. In the witches' bargain, Elijah sees a chance to help his siblings get what they have always wanted: an end to the isolation that drives Klaus, and a family that Rebekah so earnestly wishes for. Elijah himself is willing to say goodbye to Katerina in order to be a brother to Klaus and build a home in New Orleans.

While the New Orleans sections of "The Originals" shine — with a distinct look, feel, and sound that is nonetheless related to *The Vampire Diaries* — the Mystic Falls portion of the episode suffers from the clunkiness of bookending the backdoor pilot. Katherine in particular feels off: instead of being snarky and cruel, she's open about her insecurities . . . to *Rebekah!* Compare their scene here to the diner scene in "American Gothic." There are certain character notes that need to be delivered, to set up the rationale for Klaus leaving Mystic Falls behind to strive for a kingdom in New Orleans, but the overly emo Katherine comes off a little false.

But given the difficulty of hitting pause on a series that races from episode one to its finale in order to introduce this spin-off, viewers can forgive "The Originals" its minor misstep, which is more than overshadowed by compelling new characters, Hayley's predicament, and the potential for Original family fireworks and camaraderie in the future. The *TVD* team should take pride in creating this supernatural offspring, and take to the streets with a celebratory brass band parade. Let the good times roll.

COMPELLING MOMENT Marcel declaring himself king. Thank the powers-that-be that we have more Marcel to look forward to in *The Originals*.

CIRCLE OF KNOWLEDGE
- No Tyler, Caroline, Bonnie, or Matt.
- Jane-Anne calls the werewolves of the Bayou "*rougarou*," a Cajun word that stems from the French term *loup garou*. Some legends of the *rougarou* align with *TVD*'s werewolf mythology, whereas others tell of a creature with a human body and wolf head, or even a swamp monster.
- A human fetus has developed a heart that pumps blood (and thus a heartbeat) by week 6 or 7 of pregnancy. Hayley and Klaus had sex about two weeks prior to their crypt reunion here, so that hybrid fetus is developing at a nonhuman rate.
- Rather hilarious now that they're on a *very* rocky road to co-parenting: Klaus said to Hayley in "Bring It On" that "Matters of family are sacred."

HISTORY LESSON Named after the French city of Orléans, Louisiana's largest city straddles the Mississippi River and is a major American port with a slew of nicknames: the Big Easy, NOLA, the Crescent City, N'awlins, and the City That Care Forgot — though it seems the Original siblings never have.

According to Klaus, the family helped found the city (alongside the French) in the early 1700s, building it up from "a backwater penal colony," and they remained there for two centuries before Mikael drove his children out in the early 20th century. In the 19th century, New Orleans had the largest slave market in the U.S. and it's likely Marcel, or his ancestors, came to Louisiana through that market (as suggested by Klaus's comment to him about the "lashes of the whips of those who would keep you down"). During the Civil War, the city fell early under Union control, so was spared the devastation other cities in the South (such as Atlanta) suffered. Because of the city's prime location on the river, and its long-time status as a major international trade port, its population is rich in European, African, and Caribbean heritage, and its architecture is renowned worldwide for reflecting this multicultural heritage.

New Orleans' diverse ethnic and cultural makeup, alongside strong Catholic influences and the proliferation of Louisiana Voodoo, is often cited as the reason the city has such a long and vivid association with the supernatural. But author Anne Rice's The Vampire Chronicles — starring the charismatic (and wildly popular) vampire Lestat de Lioncourt — is largely credited with entwining New Orleans and vampires within the pop culture lexicon. In *Interview with the Vampire*, the first book in the Chronicles series, Louis de Point du Lac is an 18th century New Orleans plantation owner who becomes increasingly suicidal after the death of his brother, engaging in duels and brawls in the hopes that someone will kill him. This is how he crosses paths with Lestat, who falls in love with him and turns him into a vampire, beginning their centuries-long love-hate relationship. Though Charlaine Harris set Sookie Stackhouse's fictional town of Bon Temps in Louisiana, it is undoubtedly Rice who capitalized on the decayed and haunted qualities of her once-hometown to make New Orleans specifically a decadent haven for the undead.

THE RULES Jane-Anne snatches some of Hayley's hair to use in her pregnancy-test spell. When a hybrid and a werewolf ~~love each other~~ get very drunk . . . Though vampires cannot procreate, Klaus is a werewolf-vampire hybrid and he managed it with Hayley, which Sophie describes as one of "Nature's loopholes."

PREVIOUSLY ON *THE VAMPIRE DIARIES* Damon recalls when he was trapped and starving in "You're Undead to Me" (1.05), saying he would've leapt for an orange peel.

Kol says the Original family lived in New Orleans at the turn of the century in "Catch Me If You Can."

Damon told Elena in "Bloodlines" (1.11) that vampires can't procreate — "but we love to try."

© Janet Mayer/PRPhotos.com

OFF CAMERA The shape of the season wasn't compromised by the backdoor pilot for *The Originals*, explains Caroline Dries. "We knew from early on that episode 4.20 was going to be 'The Originals,' so we had time to build to it and not make it feel like this weird episode that comes out of nowhere. We end season four in a place that we've been leading to since episodes 4.01 and 4.02, and it would have felt this way with or without the spin-off. However, the spin-off did help shape some character dynamics — like Klaus and Caroline, Elijah and Katherine — but nothing that couldn't have happened if the spin-off didn't exist. I think Julie did a really elegant job of making the spin-off its own dramatic world, but also keeping it familiar with all the characters we love."

"[The pilot] is stunning," says Pascal Verschooris. "I think, artistically, we've broken new ground, and we did it in the middle of a series, which I feel gives us even more to be proud of."

Joseph Morgan's favorite scene was opposite Leah Pipes (who plays Cami) where Cami and Klaus observe the street painter in the French Quarter. He told Alloy Entertainment, "I think it's some of the best acting I've done," and added, "For me, [Leah] was really solid. She made some interesting choices as an actress and came across so strong in the pilot."

Candice Accola was a fan of the episode's huge twist, telling *Entertainment Weekly*, "I thought that Klaus finding out that he was going to be a father was really smart. That's the most human thing that can ever be done. It feeds into the storyline of the Originals. They have had such a strong want and need for family."

FOGGY MOMENTS Why didn't Klaus know Marcel had been running things in New Orleans? He seems like a guy who keeps tabs. How did the witch know that Klaus was "the hybrid"? Why didn't Jane-Anne and Sophie let nature take its course and figure out if Hayley was pregnant that way — in other words, what's so urgent about their situation that it's worth Jane-Anne losing her life? How did Sophie, who apparently has the gift of telling when women are pregnant, know that Hayley was not just pregnant, but pregnant with Klaus's child? Witch powers?

Filming "The Originals"

"The moment we launched the origin story of the Original family, I hoped we would one day be able to tell their story," says Julie Plec. "While Klaus led us into the spin-off from *The Vampire Diaries*, the series is much more of a family piece, so we'll be able to keep Klaus deliciously naughty while Elijah represents more of the moral center." The plan is to imbue *The Originals* with its own distinct look and tone but "with the Originals being much more gothic and mannered characters, the challenge will be to keep them still grounded in simple human points of view and universal emotionality," explains Plec. "We're always trying to avoid getting too Shakespearean with the dialogue."

The Originals was initially going to be set in Chicago to capitalize on the Original family's history there, established in "The End of the Affair" (3.03). But the rich history and decadent atmosphere of New Orleans seemed a more appropriate playground for 1,000-year-old vampires. "When I talked about it to the network and the studio, I said, 'In its own way, the French Quarter, with its less than 3,000 inhabitants, is the ultimate small town,'" Julie told *Entertainment Weekly*. "So it's still a small-town story, it's just a town that we all know pretty well. We all have our own party fantasy that we've either lived or wanted to live in New Orleans."

"'The Originals' was a big logistical success, but to put it together was ubercomplicated," explains Pascal Verschooris. "Filming in NOLA, building new sets in record time, traveling our entire crew to Louisiana. This was an adventure." Filming on location meant the opportunity to shoot in and around such diverse and haunting locations as the Hotel Royal, St. Louis Cathedral (the oldest cathedral in the United States), and Lafayette Cemetery. The pilot also features establishing shots of the city that show the Superdome, home of the Saints football team, and reference is made to the Ninth Ward, which was particularly devastated during Hurricane Katrina. In the French Quarter, we return to Bourbon Street, and watch a witch's execution at Royal and St. Anne. Pirate's Alley, where Elijah and Klaus have their post baby-news altercation, was where Julie Plec fleshed out the character of Marcel.

"One of the things that our director Chris Grismer said is the best [thing] about New Orleans is the history is all right there," she said. "If there's a coat of paint on the walls, it's covering 10 other coats of paint. If there's a building, it's built on the remains of the building before it. Even in the cemeteries, all of the bodies are buried with each other, so an entire bloodline of ancestors are all commingling in the dust below these gravestones." Joseph Morgan told Alloy Entertainment that Grismer "wanted to exploit the vivaciousness of [New Orleans] so, in tone, it's a much more colorful show [than *The Vampire Diaries*]."

© David Giesbrecht/The CW/Landov

Transitioning from mostly closed sets on *The Vampire Diaries* to on-location for *Originals* pilot filming guaranteed cast and crew were given the full New Orleans experience: amazing food and live music performances . . . and loud, drunken, or just plain irritated pedestrians dismissive of rolling cameras. "There are these huge streets like Bourbon Street and Frenchman Street, which are incredible to film on, but impossible to control sound," Joseph Morgan explained to *Entertainment Weekly*. "In New Orleans, you just have to embrace it." While shooting the vampire party at Hotel Royal on St. Patrick's Day weekend, one particularly angry guest did not appreciate Daniel Gillies filming a press kit interview next to his room. (Julie Plec said that Gillies "almost took a punch" during that altercation.) However, the actor admitted he was having so much fun that "even *that* — this awful moment — seemed to have its own magic, its own kind of strange charm to it." For the show to embrace the city's vigor, the crew chose to showcase not only notable streets and landmarks but several locals. Jonathan Weiss, who plays the French Quarter tour guide, was Julie Plec and Michael Narducci's guide on their first research trip to New Orleans in December 2012. "We loved him so much that we cast him," she told *BuzzFeed*. "He's wearing his own real clothes, hair, and makeup." And the drummer in the scene between Klaus and Cami is Julian Addison, a local musician that Julie, Paul Wesley, and Torrey DeVitto saw on a previous visit. "We were so impressed with him that I wrote a scene with street musicians into the episode," Plec said. "Turns out he was already a big fan of *The Vampire Diaries*." The painter in that same scene owns a gallery on Royal Street, where he sells paintings of a comparable size for upwards of $80,000. Karen Kaia Livers, who plays the fortune teller/witch whom Klaus encounters in Jackson Square, is a local actor, and former specialty casting director/musician coordinator for HBO's *Treme*, and former manager of the New Orleans Historic Voodoo Museum. "Working with Joseph Morgan was the biggest delight," she told the New Orleans *Times-Picayune*. "Joseph is very nice and friendly but with a blink of an eye becomes Klaus and is very scary!"

It wasn't long after the backdoor pilot aired that *The Originals* was picked up by The CW for their fall 2013 season; the show will be produced by Julie Plec's newly formed My So-Called Company. (Best name ever? Yes.) Of the career milestone, Julie says, "I'll have a nifty title card at the end [of an episode]. It's a big deal for a writer to get that card. Kevin's had his, Outerbanks Entertainment, for years, but this is my first." Fans can expect a few familiar names from *The Vampire Diaries* to pop up in the *Originals* credits. "Someone told me that Carol Mendelsohn (of CSI fame) always had this mantra: 'You never leave the mothership,'" says Plec. "I think she's right. It would be too easy to pillage all the 'favorites' from *TVD*, but then the flagship show would suffer. That's not just bad business, it's bad karma. After four years, everyone on *TVD* is like family. That being said, I totally pillaged Nardooch [Michael Narducci], who was always one of the best writers of Klaus's voice (which we realized in 'The Reckoning'). He was born to work on *The Originals* and I knew I couldn't do it without him. I was also able to bring over Chuckles McCharbonchuck [Charlie Charbonneau] who I've been training since he was Kevin's assistant to be a badass genius producer along with his writing duties.

"I had a rule that the only crew I would take would be the ones who were truly ready to move from *TVD* to other pastures, or crew who could pull double-duty like the brilliant Lance Anderson who will be directing episodes of *TVD* while producing *The Originals*."

The Originals is shooting in Atlanta, recreating French Quarter haunts on soundstages and on location nearby, but Plec says there may be occasional New Orleans shoots. "Our job will be difficult — no one can replicate the gorgeously authentic wonder of the French Quarter. However we have a small town that will double nicely with some money and some creative effort." Cast and crew seem determined to keep New Orleans' unique spirit alive. "[That city] vibrates with history," Daniel Gillies told *Hollywood Life*. "It has a beautiful, haunted wealth of spirit. It's one of the most mystical places on earth." He added, "If I lived in New Orleans, it's so decadent, I would die . . . It's just too damn fun. It's always this jubilant party."

Tyler Cook on *The Originals* Pilot

I'm super partial to this episode because I was lucky enough to be able to get in on something at the ground floor. I said earlier that Joshua Butler and Lance Anderson were instrumental to the style of *TVD* and that is because they were there in the beginning to help shape the world and the editorial language. In very much the same way, Lance and I (we coedited the episode) were able to put our footprint on *The Originals*.

We had a lot of conversations about how editorially, musically, stylistically the show would be different than *Vampire Diaries* but still feel of the same world. The world of *The Originals* that Julie created is a little darker, more sinister, and at the same time more mature, and we wanted to accentuate that as much as possible with the pace and editing. And it's not very often that you get to introduce a character as electric and exciting as Marcel. On a completely different level it was just exciting to be able to go through the pilot process. It's a daunting, grueling schedule but it's also really invigorating because you can really see the effect that editing has on a show's success in a short period of time. In a lot of ways it was like filmmaking boot camp. But from the first frame I cut until we delivered the final air version, it just felt like we were creating something special. I really hope fans latch on to the show next season because it's going to be a fun, wild ride.

QUESTIONS

- How did Marcel's inner circle all get daylight rings? How does he know when witches use magic in his territory? Does Marcel have an informant in his back pocket?
- How wide a reach does Marcel have in terms of controlling witches? Could a witch go on vacation to, say, Mystic Falls and do magic that Marcel wouldn't know about? Is his power linked to the individual witches living in NOLA or to the geographic territory?
- Is it a coincidence that Cami the Brave Bartender is "new blood," i.e., arriving in town around the same time as Klaus?
- How far along into her supernatural pregnancy is Hayley? And do werewolf-hybrid offspring come to term in nine months like a human?
- Can *any* hybrid procreate or is Klaus's Original status in some way responsible? Given her special birthmark, is there something unusual about Hayley's werewolf line?

- How much does Katherine know about what's going on — does she know Hayley is pregnant, or that witches are looking to revolt against Marcel?
- Why doesn't Sophie want Elijah to kill Marcel right away?
- Elijah says he considers the family's time in New Orleans to be one of their only happy periods, and Klaus's and Marcel's references place that period as being between 1700 and 1913. But in "Klaus" (2.19), the implication is that Elijah and Klaus's falling-out over Katerina in 1492 was the last time they were together until they meet at the end of season two. If the Katerina situation wasn't the event that precipitated Elijah's distance from Klaus, then what led him to want revenge on Klaus in season two, and to think Klaus had hunted down their siblings over the centuries? As Elijah believes of Klaus in "The Sun Also Rises" (2.21): "he took them from me [one by one]. He scattered them across the seas where their bodies could not be found." Is this a timeline goof or is there backstory yet to be revealed?
- Who's gonna break first: Elena or the Salvatore brothers?

Damon (to Elena): Is the old you ready to come out and play?

4.21 She's Come Undone

Original air date: May 2, 2013
Written by: Michael Narducci and Rebecca Sonnenshine
Directed by: Darnell Martin
Guest cast: Scott Parks (Silas)
Previously on *The Vampire Diaries*: Candice Accola

The Salvatores try to torture the humanity back into Elena. Bonnie cuts a deal with Katherine.

For an episode that was pretty crammed with torture and torment, "She's Come Undone" is a surprising amount of fun. It would've been impossible to predict back in season one that Elena Gilbert would one day be firing from the same arsenal as the series' main villain. Mean Elena and Silas are both adept at psychological torment. They play on others' worst fears and deepest insecurities, with doses of real and imagined violence to drive home their points. And when it comes to cruel and biting takedowns, Elena wins, and she doesn't even have super-psychic mind-reading abilities. She just knows her targets all too well. And while the horror-movie vibe of Silas (freaking Caroline out, leaving her unable to trust *anyone*, with his disfigured face and otherworldly beastial growl) ups the scare factor, at the end of the day, Silas is not a truly inhuman monster; he's just willing to do anything to get what he wants. Which is to kill himself. He wants to die and be with his beloved, collateral damage be damned. It's an unusual endgame for a villain, but it carries with it a relatable selfishness, and makes the characters discover where their boundary is when it comes to "any means necessary."

The Salvatore brothers have a clear mission for their little "intervention": get Elena to open the floodgate of emotions and be her old self again, and they do it by making her present situation worse than the alternative. They are committed to doing whatever it takes to get there. It's actually pretty impressive (or creepy) that, save for one smashed glass and some hurt feelings, Damon and Stefan keep it together and don't crumble under Elena's seeming imperviousness to their assault. Elena is smart: she knows that when the boys say they'll "do anything" to bring her back, they don't really mean *anything*, because they want her alive. She lights herself on fire, knowing that they'll save her — she's not at risk of losing her life in this intervention, so who cares what they do to her? She'll survive.

Why Elena is such a holdout is a subject of much theorizing by Stefan, and there's a laundry list of reasons: her brother is dead, she killed an innocent woman, she tried to kill two of her best friends, she has no home, the only life to return to is the end of senior year and no dreamed-of future. But what she does have are her pals: those who "fawn" over her and never give up on her, even when she tries to kill them. Ultimately, that staunch loyalty brings her back to herself: Matt is brave enough to test out that Gilbert ring's efficacy, and Damon risks driving Elena further away from him by snapping Donovan's neck.

Elena jokingly refers to her little prison — a safe, quite a symbolic choice — as "solitary," and it's an apt description of the social state of a flipped-switch vampire. She's isolating herself, in what she later realizes is a cheat. Katherine is right: the easy way out is avoidance; the hard thing is to face what you've done and what you've lost, whether you're a vampire or a mere

© Janet Mayer/PRPhotos.com

mortal. After an episode of Elena provoking emotional responses in those trying to do exactly that to her, she is finally broken by the sight of Matt dying. So why does she crack here? Maybe it's the cumulative effect of the intervention, maybe there's something about the innate decency of Matt Donovan, the guy everyone loves, that brings out the best even in those who seem past redemption. She's known him since he was the little kid with a goofy smile, as Damon describes, they've been there for each other through all the crazy that is Mystic Falls, and she willingly died so that Matt could live. Showing the "intuitive" instincts that Professor Shane praised him for back in "O Come, All Ye Faithful," Damon figures out how to shock Elena back to her humanity.

Elena emerges from her no-emotion state in horror, and it's useful to compare her breakdown here to that in "Stand By Me." As her crimes sink in and the loss of Jeremy hits her again, it is Stefan who shows her a path forward, advising her to focus on that which makes her want to live. It works: she's shaky, and she says she's not okay, but she will get better. She doesn't seem to hold a grudge against the boys for torturing her (and yeah, Stefan, inflicting physical pain until someone breaks? that's torture). She knows that, just like using an Italian app on your smartphone instead of learning the language, choosing a life without emotions is a cheat. Of course, since this is *TVD*, there's an awesome twist lying in wait: the brothers learn that Elena has gathered herself together not by focusing on love, or friendship, or even her proven capacity to carry on in the face of great tragedy, but on hate. Much like Stefan last season when he was determined to get his revenge on Klaus after having his switch forcibly flipped, Elena comes back *angry*. And she's right: Katherine has brought a world of misery to Mystic Falls. This turn in Elena isn't unprecedented. When she was struggling in her early days of vampirism, Stefan saw her channel her emotions into rage: "It makes her feel like she has a purpose." It's time for revenge!

While "She's Come Undone" makes it clear how much Elena has lost, she's not alone in that bleak state: Rebekah is without her brothers, without a hope of becoming human again, without direction. Katherine's been dumped by Elijah. Matt has no money, no family, failing grades, friends with supernatural-sized problems, and he's had enough grief to last a lifetime. Stefan is feeling lost, still talking about ditching Mystic Falls for good and breaking this history-repeating Salvatore cycle. Caroline's been left behind by her "two boyfriends" and, while we don't know what she has planned past graduation day, Silas's peek into her subconscious tells us, even if she'd say no, she'd at least like Klaus to ask her to join him in New Orleans.

And what of Bonnie Bennett? She says she hasn't switched sides, and yet she promises Silas she'll help him perform the spell. She also makes a deal with Katherine, promising to help her reach true immortal status, which would amount to an eternal break from five centuries of running from Klaus for Ms. Pierce. Putting aside for a second the great collision course that promise creates — Elena vowing to kill Katherine while her BFF vows to make her un-killable — it's also an indication of how far Bonnie will go. She's no stranger to extreme measures: she fake-deactivated the Gilbert device; she temporarily killed herself and Jeremy, and then herself again; she body-swapped Klaus and Tyler; under Silas's influence, she coordinated a witch massacre; she used so much Expression that she's become the most powerful witch on the planet. And while she is fiercely loyal to her friends, she doesn't feel the need to share her plans with them. She's isolated herself from the group, not telling them about her arrangement with Silas or her deal with Katherine. How desperate is she to get Jeremy back? To get Grams back? Is Bonnie planning on cheating death?

Some would call it a cheat that death doesn't always take on *TVD*. In this episode alone, we get two death fake-outs: Liz seems pretty dead, but she ain't (Caroline begging her to come back to life is heartbreaking and so very Caroline), and Matt turns out to be wearing the Gilbert ring of resurrection. And of course, there's the Other Side where dead supernatural creatures hang out in a state of limbo, ready to sneak back through any chance they get. The impermanence of death will surely get a big display as we near the much-ballyhooed veil-dropping. If Bonnie does destroy the Other Side like Silas wants her to, it would not only bring back every deceased supernatural creature, it would mean that, from that moment on, anyone who dies — whether witch or hybrid, werewolf or vampire — would be gone for good. Is that a world the writers are willing to enter?

COMPELLING MOMENT Elena setting herself on fire, and then laughing about it.

CIRCLE OF KNOWLEDGE
- No Tyler in this episode.

Caroline Dries on Making Product Placement Work

Every year we have to include a few product integrations into our show. Most shows go through it, and it helps to see it as a fun challenge instead of a task (did I just write that? I'm lying. It's a task). We usually try really hard to make them elegant and then they tend to come out clunky. This season though, Mike [Narducci] and Rebecca [Sonnenshine] did one in "She's Come Undone" where Caroline is backing up her Ford and Silas appears in the rearview camera. We knew we had to feature the camera at some point this season and we came up with that and I think it worked great. My friend was watching the show with me and she jumped in that moment. That is a *much* better reaction than a groan.

- *She's Come Undone* is the title of Wally Lamb's 1992 novel (itself titled after a line in the Guess Who song "Undun"); the novel follows Dolores, who struggles with depression and other mental health issues after a series of disturbing and traumatic experiences trigger her self-destructive behavior. She eventually finds some peace, and a relationship that isn't a total train wreck. The book was selected to be part of Oprah's Book Club in 1996 and exploded in popularity thereafter. Alternatively, the episode title could be a reference to the 1993 Duran Duran song, "Come Undone," whose lyrics include the fitting "Might take a little crime / To come undone" (torture and neck-snapping fit that "crime" bill) and images of falling apart at the seams and a heart breaking into pieces.
- Damon tells Elena she took a giant leap over the cuckoo's nest, a nod to Ken Kesey's 1962 novel *One Flew Over the Cuckoo's Nest* — a book made into an Academy Award–winning film in 1975 starring Jack Nicholson as a patient committed under false pretenses to a psychiatric institution who engages in a battle of wills with the sadistic head nurse of the ward. The nurse wins the battle.
- In "Stand By Me," Elena removed Jeremy's Gilbert ring and tossed it to Damon while she was having her breakdown; that's how he had it handy to give to Matt Donovan.

THE RULES Katherine reminds us that big spells require a power source — a full moon, a comet, a mystical object (like the moonstone), or a connection to uber-powerful dead witches like "Qetsuya or whatever." (Never change, Katherine.) Bonnie says she's the only one who can see Silas's true face, implying that she always sees his true face and will never be fooled; Silas also shows Caroline his Monster Man face twice in this episode. While Silas had previously only appeared in the form of dead people (e.g., vampires or the human deceased), he appears as Liz Forbes and Matt (who, fair enough, died briefly that one time), so Silas is not limited in terms of his appearance.

PREVIOUSLY ON *THE VAMPIRE DIARIES* Damon manipulates Elena's dream, like he did to Stefan in "Family Ties" (1.04) and to Rose in "The Descent" (2.12).

Caroline tried to have a "friend-tervention" with Elena in "My Brother's Keeper" by telling her her feelings for Damon were bad news, but she opposes the boys' "interventioning" . . . until Elena tries to kill her again.

Rebekah was fluent in Italian in the 12th century: in "The Five," we see her and her brothers living *la dolce vita* in *Italia* in 1114.

Damon tells Matt to "let the adults handle this," which he also said to Stefan back in "The Turning Point" (1.10) after Sheriff Forbes came to Damon about the town's latest vampire problem.

This marks the second time Damon has snapped the neck of a person close to Elena, the first being Jeremy in "The Return" (2.01). Both Matt and Jeremy came back to life thanks to that Gilbert ring.

Chairs in the Salvatore mansion see a lot of action. Stefan and Damon tying Elena to a chair in their living room recalls Stefan tying Katherine to a chair in the Salvatore basement in "Memory Lane" (2.04), and Mason Lockwood's final moments before being killed by Damon in "Plan B" (2.06). Damon's had two turns: in "Crying Wolf" (2.14), after Jules, Stevie, and company storm the house, shoot him full of vervain, and put a collar of wooden nails around his neck, and in "Ghost World" (3.07), when Mason Lockwood returns as a ghost to give Damon a taste of his own torture medicine.

Damon used Matt as bait in "Growing Pains," bringing him to the Young farm and biting him so that the pastor and his pals would come out to save him. When he tried to kill him in that episode, Elena came to the rescue.

Bonnie's big on secret side plans. In "Isobel" (1.21), she fake-deactivated the Gilbert device; in "The Last Dance" (2.18), she and Damon orchestrated a fake death to trick AlariKlaus; in "The Departed" (3.22), she worked with Klaus to body-jump him into Tyler; and here she teams up with Katherine to get the tombstone.

OFF CAMERA If you're wondering why Elena is suddenly wearing a hoodie when she's in the woods outside the Salvatore house, Julie Plec explained on Twitter that it was thanks to "very cold weather when shooting," and that the hoodie is one of Stefan's.

Candice Accola believes Caroline and Elena's friendship will remain intact, despite Elena's cruelty. "What I love about Caroline is that her perspective has grown tenfold as the series has gone on," she told *TV Guide*. "So, I don't think she's going to hold Elena fully accountable for all those moments when she hasn't been the kindest."

FOGGY MOMENTS When Caroline calls her mother in a panic, it seems like Liz, town sheriff, doesn't already know about Silas and his special psychic powers. PSA for Mystic Falls residents: anytime a crazy mind-controlling super-immortal comes to town, alert your friends and loved ones immediately.

QUESTIONS
- How did Silas get into the Forbes house? Does his First Immortal status grant him immunity from the invitation rule or was Liz fooled into inviting him in? Was Caroline hanging out with Silas-as-Liz the whole time? (The call-the-cell-phone evidence isn't reliable at all: if Silas can make you believe you've been staked, he can make you hear a phone ring.)
- Will the Salvatore brothers help Elena or try to stop her?
- Will Matt pass history, Italian, and math?

Bonnie: Oh my god. I'm dead.

4.22 *The Walking Dead*

Original air date: May 9, 2013
Written by: Brian Young and Caroline Dries
Directed by: Rob Hardy
Guest cast: Scott Parks (Silas), Mackenzie Britt (Elena Double)
Previously on *The Vampire Diaries*: Kat Graham

Inside the Expression triangle, the veil between the living world and the Other Side is dropped, bringing back the supernatural dead to Mystic Falls.

Like "Ghost World" last season, "The Walking Dead" brought back many a familiar face as Bonnie's attempt to get a little advice from Qetsiyah has far-reaching consequences. And just as Bonnie is unwavering in her ultimately self-destructive plan, Elena is also full-on obsessed with getting her revenge on Katherine — who's a smart, crafty vampire 500 years Elena's senior, as the Salvatore brothers point out. A woman with a mission, Elena very deliberately chooses what she will and won't let herself feel: she tells Caroline at the Grill that she can't apologize to her for all the awful things she said, she can't even allow herself to feel bad. Feeling bad means feeling all the bad things — primary among them her grief over losing her little brother. It's an interesting mix of denial and self-awareness that Elena displays in "The Walking Dead." Consider her conversation with Damon in the school hallway (just before she stakes him for disagreeing with her). How much of what she says in that scene does she believe? That killing Katherine might free her from all the grief and guilt and release her to feel good, positive things? Or is she just saying that to appeal to Damon? Probably a little of both. She says herself that she's not thinking clearly, which suggests she doesn't *really* know what will help her. When a manic Elena is ultimately stopped from killing Katherine, it's enough to break her spirit.

When Stefan tells her that Bonnie would die along with Katherine, she refuses to believe him, calling him a liar and accusing him of still having feelings for Katherine. But by the time she is alone and kneeling at her brother's grave — visiting for the first time, as her reaction to the tombstone's engraving tells us — Elena has realized that Stefan is right. That her mission to kill Katherine was a distraction, just like smashing cinderblocks or playing

© David Gabber/PRPhotos.com

darts or getting angry enough with Stefan to clock him in the face. (Isn't it nice of Elena to be equal opportunity about doling out violence to her loved ones? No one has escaped unscathed.) In that heartbreaking scene at Jer's grave, Elena gives up. She can't move on and doesn't want to, because to do that means accepting that Jeremy is gone. Once Kol arrives, his own revenge scheme against Elena in play, she tells him he would be doing her a favor to kill her . . . and she means it. In "The Killer," she wrote in her journal that her one purpose in life, her reason for living her horrifying vampire existence, was Jeremy. She had to be strong for him, to persevere so that he would not be left alone. Without him, what's left? It seems Damon was right when he said to Stefan on the porch in "Stand By Me" that he wouldn't be enough to keep Elena going in the wake of Jeremy's death. None of them are.

But with the veil down inside the Expression triangle, it's not just worst enemies who return but the beloved dead, and Jeremy is there to save his sister both from the physical threat Kol poses her and from the grief in which she's lost herself. Elena gets the chance to see Jer again, to hug him, to have a proper goodbye — that moment wished for by so many who have lost loved ones. Stefan tells Elena there are no shortcuts, that loss is part of the deal when you're a vampire, and she finally faces her grief in a way that none of us gets to: while holding the dearly departed and getting that last moment. And while the Gilbert siblings' time together is fleeting, it's hugely restorative for Elena. She sees Jeremy and becomes her old self again.

Elena needs that moment with Jeremy in order to start making amends, and for other characters, seeing lost loved ones is just as powerfully restorative. Alaric returns to roam the halls and slug back bourbon with Damon once again. The catharsis of that moment is beautiful for the characters, and for the viewers at home who missed seeing the drinking buddies together. And just when Stefan's resigned to the fact that he won't see Lexi, there she is, with nothing but praise for Lexi 2.0, Caroline. It's in these moments that the allure of dropping the veil is crystal clear: imagine having your buddy back, your brother, your guardian. Bonnie is once again helped and comforted by her Grams (leading up to what turns out to be her own final moments), and with her help Bonnie realizes that she holds the power to take down Silas. She doesn't need advice from her distant ancestor; she needs the confidence her Grams inspires in her. But as Grams knows so well, Nature demands a balance: it's not all rainbows and unicorns with the return of the dead; the danger is made manifest by an avenging Original and a town square full of hunters. (Seems those pesky tomb vampires had something better to do than go after the founding families *again*.)

The parallel but separate journeys that Elena and Bonnie have been on this season finally come together in their scene at the cemetery. Each acknowledges how lost they've been, and how far they've drifted from who they used to be. It's a brief glimpse of the old Elena-Bonnie dynamic, and one that may be forever lost seeing that Bonnie's now made the ultimate sacrifice to keep Jer in the living world.

All these emotionally resonant moments happen in the midst of a crazy supernatural storm (to quote Matt Donovan, "This wind is weird"). "The Walking Dead" has an apocalyptic feeling that we've not seen before in Mystic Falls, but it ends the way all previous second-to-last *TVD* episodes have: with total insanity ready to break loose. There are resurrected hunters: Alexander, Vaughn, Connor, and Jeremy. There is a calcified Silas statue in the trunk of Damon's car. There is one dose of the Cure that was fished out of a "dead man's pocket" and it's now in Damon's possession. And at long last, Elena is herself again, and she's ready to apologize for how she treated her loved ones while she was in mean-vamp mode. Will either of Caroline's "boyfriends" return to see her graduate? Will Katherine stick around for the big finale? Who will stay dead and who will rise again? The caps and gowns have been ordered, the big day approaches, and who knows what the future holds for our young graduates and their undead friends and enemies.

COMPELLING MOMENT The final throes of compassion-free Elena are amazing: after punching Stefan in the face, she delivers this killer line: "Just like the cinderblock. Nothing." Sad to see you go, Queen of Insults!

CIRCLE OF KNOWLEDGE
- No Klaus or Tyler in this episode.
- While there have been a few films called *The Walking Dead,* the title likely refers to the American cable television horror-drama based on Robert Kirkman's comic book series of the same name. The TV series, which premiered on AMC in 2010, centers on a group of humans struggling to survive in a postapocalyptic world overrun with "walkers," or flesh-eating zombies. Joseph Morgan is a huge fan of the show, which — like *The Vampire Diaries* — films in Atlanta.
- Elena rejects Rebekah's attempt to resurrect their Thelma and Louise–esque friendship. In the 1991 Ridley Scott film *Thelma & Louise,* housewife Thelma Dickinson (Geena Davis) and waitress Louise Sawyer (Susan Sarandon) head out on a road trip but run into serious trouble along the way, leading to a slew of crimes that give the two women full-on fugitive status.

Caroline Dries on Creating Silas

We debated Silas a lot. We knew all along the endgame with Silas, but episodes 17–22 required a lot of Silas discussion — not because of [anticipating] fan reaction, but because we wanted him to feel like a villain who was fresh and threatening, but also [we needed to] find ways of presenting him that would disguise his true identity.

The character of Silas was a new type of supernatural creature for us. He's the first immortal, and possesses traits different than our Originals and our regular vampires, so we had to, as a group, understand why. Everything we do is grounded in some sort of reality, and then we stick to rules. We can't just create a villain and then change their capabilities each episode. It'd get confusing for the audience and it'd be hard to lock into. So a lot of discussion went into the rules. It started when we knew we needed someone who was badass and scary. Then we came up with the idea of this "cave of sorrows" where there was lore that if you gave a drop of your blood to a well, you could see your dead loved one. Once we decided we liked that idea, it became how? why? And we talked a lot about that before season four began.

Then once we introduced Silas, we knew we couldn't reveal [his face] so we tapped into his psychic ability to create visions. And watching it now it seems so obvious what the right choice was, but we debated various things like should he be a monster, should he wear a mask, should he appear as visions? Visions felt like it tied into his psychic powers the best and therefore his abilities were grounded in who he was as a character. Once we decided we wanted to go with visions, we discovered the challenge was that Silas could be anyone at any time. So you had moments like when Tyler surprised Caroline with a prom dance, that some audience members feared it was Silas playing a trick on her. Fear and romance are opposite emotions! I didn't want to taint that moment but there was no way around it. So Silas/not Silas became this tricky thing of having to explain. Also, there became very few ways to prove someone wasn't Silas — hence the Locker 42 gag in 4.22. Brian [Young] and I were banging our heads against the wall trying to find a solution to that. We just played into Alaric's character and thank god Brian came up with something.

- The wind storm knocks over some *Mystic Falls Tribune* newspaper boxes, the third of three newspapers seen on the show — there's the *Daily*, the *Courier*, and now the *Tribune*. It may be a small town but they need three papers for all those obituaries.
- Stefan and Silas-as-Caroline realize that the mystical hotspot is beneath the high school; in *Buffy the Vampire Slayer*, the Hellmouth is beneath

the high school, and Buffy and company spend more time in its basement than they'd care to admit too, Damon.

- Bonnie turns Silas to stone, so naturally Damon nicknames her Medusa, the Greek mythological monster (or Gorgon) who had the face of a woman and living snakes in place of hair; looking at her would turn a person to stone.

THE RULES Silas demonstrates new heights of power: he has been fooling Bonnie (and Caroline) with his Monster Man appearance, he can throw off the Hunter's Curse in minutes, and even when Bonnie knows he's fooling her, he nearly suffocates her. Only the ghosts who want to come back to the living realm do; they have corporeal form (within the confines of the Expression triangle), as they did in "Ghost World" (3.07). Bonnie says she has access to spirit magic, Expression, and dark magic — a toxic combination when she attempts to bring Jeremy back from the Other Side permanently. Grams warns her it would go against the will of Nature.

PREVIOUSLY ON *THE VAMPIRE DIARIES* After drinking people blood, Stefan tries to deal with his ripper tendencies by working out in his bedroom, doing pull-ups from the ceiling beams in "Under Control" (1.18) as he makes Elena do here.

Matt says he isn't holding his breath for a graduation check from his mother; Kelly Donovan was last seen in "Under Control" when Matt told her "I'm better off without you" and kicked her out of the Donovan house.

Caroline and Elena sit at a table outside the Grill doing their graduation cards, in a moment that recalls the scene in "The Night of the Comet" (1.02) with the two of them and Bonnie putting together programs.

Elena mentions their family friends in Denver (we can see Mr. and Mrs. S. Anderson on the envelope) whom Jeremy went to stay with in "Our Town" (3.11).

Bonnie links herself to Katherine; in "Masquerade" (2.07), Katherine used a similar trick when she had the witch Lucy link the doppelgängers so any injury inflicted on Katherine by the Salvatore brothers would also injure their precious Elena. While in that episode the whole gang conspired to kill Katherine, here it's just Elena who wants blood.

Lots of past episode titles get name-checked here: Elena says she doesn't want a trip down "Memory Lane" (2.04) and Alaric refers to the Other Side as "Ghost World" (3.07). Kol makes a pseudo reference to "Fool Me Once" (1.14) with his "Kill me once, shame on you. Kill me twice . . ."

Rebekah says, "Looks like something wicked finally came." In "The Rager," she said to April and Elena that it feels like "something wicked this way comes" at her party.

"Tick tock, Bonnie." Ah, a classic Katherine-ism, last heard after she snapped Aimee Bradley's spine in "Masquerade" (2.07): "The moonstone, Stefan. Tick tock."

Kol makes light of Rebekah's interest in Matt ("finally got the quarterback to pay attention") and taunts Matt about his arm; Kol crushed his hand at the Mikaelson ball in "Dangerous Liaisons" (3.14) after Rebekah called off a plan to kill him.

Matt previously got attacked with a broken bottle at the Grill in "The House Guest" (2.16).

Silas mind-whammies Caroline into cutting herself, just as Klaus compelled Katherine to stab herself in the leg all the livelong day in "The Last Dance" (2.18).

Stefan suggests they drop Silas's body into the ocean like they planned on doing to Klaus when he was immobilized in "Before Sunset" (3.21) and "The Departed" (3.22).

Damon says he thought Alaric was cutting back on the booze, a reference to their last conversation before Alaric died in "Do Not Go Gentle" (3.20). Alaric reminds Damon he was supposed to be "taking care of the kids," which Damon said in "Memorial" while sitting at Ric's grave.

Like Bonnie dying here to resurrect Jeremy, Caitlin Shane died trying to resurrect her dead son using Expression ("Into the Wild"). In "Growing Pains," Grams warned Bonnie about messing with resurrection: "It is not Nature's plan; touch it again and the Spirits will unleash their anger in ways that will make you suffer."

OFF CAMERA Of the unlikely pairing of Bonnie and Katherine, Plec told *TV Fanatic*, "The beauty of Bonnie is that in spite of being led down some very dark paths over the course of the year her moral compass is stronger than ever and she's definitely up to something. And if you're up to something and you're up to no good, you may as well partner with the one girl in town who's better at being up to no good than you are." But Katherine herself may

Making Threats

This season was a goldmine of brilliant, gross, and downright hilarious threats, usually not followed through on, but still fun. Here's a handful of favorites.

- Klaus-as-Tyler threatens to rip out Bonnie's tongue and to tear out Tyler's heart with Tyler's own hand ("Growing Pains").
- Damon has a simple plan: he's going to rip Connor's heart out and then feed it to him ("The Killer").
- Stefan's fine, really: "I just want to rip into someone's artery and feed until I can't breathe anymore" ("My Brother's Keeper").
- Rebekah wants to "ram [the Cure] down Niklaus's throat and look into his eyes as he realizes he's mortal again" ("After School Special").
- Damon helpfully informs Kol that he's going to rip out his spleen ("Catch Me If You Can").
- With a very creative work-around to the Hunter's Curse, Kol sets to chopping off Jeremy's arms ("A View to a Kill").
- Klaus suggests he'll look different to Tyler after Bonnie's spell wears off, or "I won't look like anything because I'll have gouged your eyeballs from their sockets" ("Into the Wild").
- Since Rebekah and Damon can't kill Vaughn, she suggests they will tear him apart "piece by piece, nerve by nerve, until the pain is so severe that your brain shuts it off to give you one tiny moment of blessed relief, and then we'll heal you and do it again and again and again" ("Stand By Me").
- Caroline's not overly fond of humanity-free Elena: "I'm going to wring her skinny little neck" ("Bring It On").
- Katherine threatens to rip Elena's throat out so she won't have to listen to her whine, then threatens to feed Elena her own eyeballs ("She's Come Undone").
- Elena gets in on the action with the plan to kill Katherine: "Maybe I just want to feel the warmth of her chest cavity as I rip out her heart and watch her face as she realizes that I took it from her" ("The Walking Dead").
- Bonnie brushes off Katherine's threat with "I can crush your skull without even flinching" ("Graduation").

finally be cracking after five centuries' worth of survival and backstabbing: "The thing that's interesting about Katherine this year is she's always been . . . a survivor, a fighter, very selfish, looking out for number one, and I think that's taken its toll on her and made her a little bat-shit crazy in certain ways."

FOGGY MOMENTS When a dead supernatural pops over from the Other Side, can they not choose where to arrive? Like, why do Lexi, Alaric, Grams, etc. arrive right by their intended targets, but Kol arrives at the Grill, wondering where Elena is? He had clearly been following her around, as his later admission ("I've been breathing on you and whispering threats") would indicate. Rebekah's super vamp hearing somehow misses the sound of Caroline cutting herself and making little pain noises; she only hears her when she's in human-range earshot.

QUESTIONS

- What would happen if they had taken Kol's body and flung it outside the boundaries of the Expression triangle? Would it disappear back to Ghost World? Stefan says he's going to put it somewhere safe until the veil goes back up: where did he stash him?
- Silas says he will always be one step ahead of Bonnie. And then she fairly easily turns him to stone, despite the fact that he's been fueling up on blood and is an uberstrong being. So is Bonnie's magic that powerful or is Silas being a lying trickster again?
- What will Damon do with the Cure? Will he give it to Elena or will the hunters take it from him and kill Silas?
- Did Bonnie's spell succeed?
- How dead is Bonnie? Is she corporeal within the Expression triangle?

> *Stefan: I'm not happy about Elena, but I'm not not-happy*
> *for you either. I just want you to know that.*
> *Damon: Thanks, brother.*

4.23 *Graduation*

Original air date: May 16, 2013
Written by: Julie Plec and Caroline Dries
Directed by: Chris Grismer
Guest cast: Cynthia Addai-Robinson (Aja), Vincent Farrell (Stefan Double), Micah Joe Parker (Adrian)
Previously on *The Vampire Diaries*: Paul Wesley

After high-school graduation, real life begins — or at least it can feel that way, and the last rite of passage of the teenage years promises that what happens next is a choice. For most of the seniors assembled in Mystic Falls (congrats for living to see this day!), the question of what comes next is a huge one. That spirit of limitless potential comes into neat contrast with the guys willing to blow up Grandma and Grandpa at the Grill just to see their own destiny fulfilled. The hunters return to this realm more determined and goal-oriented than Caroline Forbes on a prom-steering committee. There's no two ways about it: Silas must be destroyed with the Cure. Their presence drives the action of "Graduation," as do the resurrected victims of the massacres interested in keeping that veil down so they can live again. But that single-mindedness of purpose is far from the average graduate's state of mind, and it acts as a supernatural foil to the big decisions the seniors have to make now that high school is over and they're moving on to the next phase of their lives — whether in this realm or on the Other Side.

In the season premiere, Stefan told Matt that he doesn't *"have* to live" with the guilt of surviving Elena in the car crash, he *gets* to: "You better earn it." And after nearly getting blown to bits by a vampire hunter, after graduating with his friends, Matt decides to relish the fact that he's alive (and that there's a hot vampire offering to show him the world). Rebekah teaches him that the first rule of truly living is to do the thing you're afraid of — for her, that's kissing Matt — and for him, it's leaving the only place he's ever known to explore the world. In the context of a theme of the episode, "you reap what you sow," both Matt and Rebekah get what they deserve. Rebekah has been

© Curtis Baker/The CW/Landov

striving to be a better person and longing for love (and for Matt), while Matt has been consistently a stand-up good friend. But he's lonely without family, often a pawn for supernaturals, and he slogs away at his crappy job because there's no one for him to lean on. Now he can enjoy a reward for once, and he embraces the offer that Rebekah makes him after she selflessly saves him from peril. (And keep in mind: though she can't be killed by the blast, she does suffer the pain of it.)

There's a parallel between former sweethearts Donovan and Forbes: Caroline also has an Original courting her, and that infatuation comes in handy as Klaus arrives in the nick of time to save Damon. But tellingly he didn't come back to town for Damon's sake, he came to see Caroline graduate. (Of course Caroline sent him a graduation notice. Oh, Caroline, never change.) And, to boot, he saves her from Aja's witch attack with what is, perhaps, the most creative beheading of all time. Caroline hasn't accepted Klaus's past offers to travel the world with him, as Matt does here with Rebekah, and instead of asking again, Klaus wisely gives her what she truly wants: a pardon for Tyler. This magnanimous gesture speaks volumes about how far Klaus has come through knowing and loving Caroline, and it's the one thing he could do to prove how earnestly he wants to be in her good graces. His line about wanting to be her last love is just about the most swoonworthy of all lines ever on *TVD*, and to think it's spoken, convincingly, by the man who for two seasons was the gang's worst nightmare. As Klaus begins his New Orleans adventure, he is, like all the graduates, on the precipice of big change, big choices, and new experiences. Like the actors, writers, and crew "graduating" from *TVD* to *The Originals*, whose absence will be felt and presence missed when season five rolls on, Klaus has been a huge part of the past few seasons, and here's hoping he finds his way back to Mystic Falls on occasion.

Elena's journey this season has in part been an exploration of a question you'd never want to personally find out the answer to: is it worse to lose someone you love or to lose yourself? Elena Gilbert, overachiever, goes for door number three: lose both simultaneously. And after a season of torment, Elena is finally (finally!) able to enjoy herself, as she sits in the cemetery, eating burgers and drinking bourbon with Alaric and Jeremy, able to laugh at what's she done (like burning down their house) before feeling the weight of it. She's able to allow her feelings in without losing herself to grief or rage.

Emerging on the other side of her battle to acclimatize to vampirism, having experienced an emotionless version of herself, having become fueled by rage, and finally having the catharsis of reunion with her dead brother, Elena also finds that she's no longer subject to the sire bond. Whatever she feels, *she* feels. The question of whether Elena earnestly felt love for Damon has plagued the brothers Salvatore since the bond was discovered. Elena felt sure and at ease with her feelings for him, and here she's able to finally express herself to Damon without restraint or coercion. Of course, because it's Damon and Elena, the conversation is passionate and argumentative, but it manages to address a lot of the problems that Stefan and Caroline saw in their pairing. Elena knows that Damon is "wrong" for her, but that is in part what fuels her love for him. They challenge each other, and change each other, and never is that more apparent than in their pyrotechnic-filled, feisty disagreement that surges into proclamations of love and epic kissing. Neither will apologize for who they are, or how wrong they are for each other — and that's what makes them so right.

Though Damon gives Elena the Cure as a kind of graduation gift, Elena believes that Stefan deserves to have it. She knows that he would have taken the Cure himself if he could, to free himself from the guilt and pain of being a vampire. In an episode of gift-giving (and re-gifting, in this case), Elena's gesture marks an important turn in her relationship with Stefan, despite the fact that he doesn't keep it in the end. She wants to take care of him in the way that he's always done for her. Now that she has come to peace with who she is as a vampire — able to feed on blood bags, free of the sire bond, and her emotions in control — she understands that his struggle is greater than her own. What she says as she gives it to him is that he deserves "whatever you want out of life." It's a testament to the love that's still shared between them, despite her not being *in* love with him, that she would make this gesture. But Stefan, being Stefan, can't keep it: he wants her to have what was taken from her in "The Departed." She chose to die, but she didn't choose to be a vampire. If she has the Cure, she gets to make that choice — to take it or not.

But not for long. In the wake of getting dumped by Elijah, Katherine wants to get even with her doppelgänger. She believes (rather hilariously) that Elena has a better life than she does. The happiness in Elena's life is not "deserved" because Elena's a "good girl" — it's just luck, if you ask Katherine Pierce. But she messes with the wrong shadow self on the wrong day. In the doppelgänger showdown of the century, Katherine's bad day only gets worse, and she certainly doesn't get what she wants. Besides it being so freaking cool to see Elena and Katherine have a realistic-looking and kickass fight, it's an important moment for Elena. She would rather use the only Cure in the world on Katherine than be killed, because she's no longer willing to die, as she was under Kol's attack in "The Walking Dead." So restorative was it for her to see Jeremy again, to have that family moment with him and Alaric, to be able to have a peaceful reconciliation, that Elena fights for her vampire life. Instead of Katherine getting the super immortality she wanted, she has the Cure crammed down her throat. What will Katherine Pierce be like as a human? Will she try to turn again?

While Katherine's revenge-seeking attack on Elena comes off as sour grapes (followed by just desserts), Damon proves that he may not actually know what the word "selfish" means. After being infected with the werewolf toxin, Damon goes into hero mode. When Elena realizes what's happening and that Damon will die soon, she urges him to take the Cure, but he refuses. Instead he decides to be the brother who concerns himself with the supernatural apocalypse, and he distracts Vaughn with a wild goose chase for Silas in order to protect his loved ones, and graduation day, from the obsessed hunters. Even after Vaughn's been dispatched — how amazing was it to see Ric grinning at Damon after saving his ass, kicking Vaughn's, and holding on to the Cure? — Damon refuses to take the Cure. He wants Elena to have it, and he would rather die than be mortal again. (A choice which earns him a serious slap from Elena.) While he's still his Damon-y self, the bad brother has been pretty good this season and he is gifted with one of the happiest fates of the finale (if you put aside nearly dying): he gets the girl.

Not all of Mystic Falls' "hero protectors" have their dreams come true like Damon does though. What Stefan jokes he should be doing during the supernatural apocalypse instead of enjoying his brief moment with Lexi, Bonnie actually does: she puts her friends and the town above her own interest, safety, and happiness — even though she's dead. She promises Caroline a "friend day" and she delivers, but for Bonnie it is bittersweet. She knows that when she hugs her friends before graduation it'll be for the last time and that when she thanks her father, for everything, it's her last moment with him. When Kol tries to make Bonnie permanently take down the veil, she explains how desperately she'd love to do just that — to stay in the world of the living, rather than haunt it from the Other Side. But she knows she can't do unspeakable and irreparable damage to the world for her own personal happiness. Unlike Kol who flipflops on his opinion regarding Silas and the Other Side after spending, like, five minutes dead, Bonnie has the strength of her convictions. She'll risk her own life to bring back Jeremy, but she won't risk the lives of anyone else for selfish gains.

And Bonnie's sacrifice goes further: for the first time her friends are okay, and she doesn't want them to suffer, knowing she's died. So she doesn't say goodbye while she can. Bonnie is successful in putting the veil back up, and in returning Jeremy to life, but now that she's on the Other Side, in season five, in addition to losing a best friend, the gang won't have a witch to call on for magical fixes to Big Bad problems.

And Jeremy will have to live knowing that his life came at the cost of Bonnie's. (He should talk to Matt about survivor guilt.) While there are many questions regarding Jer's future — like, um, everyone thinks he's dead so how will that be explained? — what's certain is that he and Bonnie's romance has rekindled this season and is cemented in this episode with what might be their last kiss. Jer's had some experience loving a ghost before (his relationship with Anna ended his romance with Bon), and he'll be able to still see Bonnie and talk to her, if not touch her. His resurrection, done in great part for Elena, will have a huge impact on his sister; her identity is so wrapped up in being Jeremy's only family, just as the Salvatore brothers are linked to each other.

With Lexi back, for once Stefan chooses to enjoy himself, getting drunk and rocking out to Bon Jovi's greatest hits with her. He jokes about his "hero hair," but Stefan usually does choose the selfless option: putting the needs of others over his own well-being and happiness. The events of season four began in the wake of Stefan respecting Elena's choice over his own first preference, and that act led to her becoming a vampire. Here in the season finale, he comes full circle: he returns the Cure to Elena so that she will again have the choice — to live as a human or to live as a vampire. Her call, her choice.

Stefan, Damon, and Elena are so inextricably linked that anything that affects one affects the other two. It's to that point that Stefan (who, granted, has been day-drinking) believes that, now that the sire bond is broken, the question of who Elena loves is more important than *saving the world*. As much as it is utterly heartbreaking to see his face as he hears every word Elena says to Damon (and their mouth noises), Stefan has developed a single-minded focus on Elena, something she no longer reciprocates. Lexi's advice to him — to move on, to let go — is just what he needs to hear, and follow.

Stefan's journey this season has been to get Elena back to herself and to find out the truth of how she feels. With her reconciliation with Damon, the Cure in her pocket, and her self-assurance and free will present and accounted for, Stefan's quest comes to an end. What kind of life is left for him in Mystic Falls? It's a sad denouement for him, and one that's made ever more tragic by his fate at the falls. While he is not happy about it, Stefan accepts the fact that Elena has chosen Damon over him. As he loads stony Silas from Damon's trunk into his own, he offers an olive branch and sets his brother at ease by saying he's "not not-happy for" Damon. Compare that sentiment to his bitterness in "My Brother's Keeper": "Let's not pretend like this isn't the best day of your life." Or his judgment in "We'll Always Have Bourbon Street": "It's impossible for her to be so blind that she doesn't see how wrong you are for her." Here, Stefan and Damon finally come to a kind of peace and resolution, after spending much of the season at odds over Elena, over who she loved and who they thought she should be. It's a huge moment that acts as a kind of blessing for the relationship.

Before the final twist, it seems Stefan's fate at the end of the season is to have his best friend disappear back to the Other Side, to graduate high school for the 17th time, to mark the end of this era of his life, and to see his brother win the heart of his epic love. Before Lexi disappears back to the Other Side, she tells him that she believes an unfettered Stefan will one day find another epic love — if he can let go of Elena. But that's a problem for another day.

Instead of going to Portland or discovering that there's no need to live in a yurt in Australia (they have perfectly nice modern dwellings), Stefan is dealt a life-changing mythology smackdown — he is a doppelgänger, and of *Silas*, the original immortal and formerly a super-powered witch — and then he's immediately imprisoned in a safe and tossed over the falls, a spot he chose for its remoteness. In a horrifying final scene, the water seeps into the safe and Stefan gasps for air — he will drown and heal and drown again until he desiccates and he'll stay that way until someone finds him. Is this what Stefan deserves? Decidedly not. As with Bonnie Bennett, Stefan gets a raw deal in the season finale, but it's a setup for a fascinating story-turn in season five in terms of character and mythology.

And we're left duped by the doppelgänger one more time. The Katherine-Elena fight seemed like it would end in Katherine's favor, that Katherine would be the one assuming her doppelgänger's life. But the rug was pulled out from under us: yes, one evil doppelgänger would be destroying a shadow self, but it was Silas, not Katherine. How the *TVD* writers manage to one-up themselves in jaw-dropping finales season after season is a mystery best left unsolved (Expression triangle?), but what they've accomplished with "Graduation" is an emotional end to an important chapter in the series. No more high school. No more Originals. Tyler is coming back, Bonnie's on the Other Side, and Elena and Katherine aren't the only doppelgängers. It's time to let go and move on from many of the familiar places and faces: the joys of the college years are just around the corner.

COMPELLING MOMENT For an episode jam-packed with memorable moments, it's hard to pick a solitary standout, but for all her stoic sacrifice, raise your cap to Bonnie Bennett.

CIRCLE OF KNOWLEDGE

- "I can't believe it. We're actually all here. We are all here together!" Well, Caroline, actually, Tyler is not in this episode.

- None of the graduation signage has a "Class of . . ."; instead, the set designers opted for "Congratulations, Seniors!" banners. A subtle way to avoid exposing the wonky timeline! Since Elena's parents died in 2009, she started her senior year in September 2010, making them the class of 2011.

- Damon snarks that Stefan and Lexi are living *Dance Party U.S.A.,* a dance television show that aired on the USA Network in the late '80s and early '90s. The show is notable for being the first TV dance show for teens to allow interracial couples on its broadcast.

- Vaughn says he starved to death, but he likely died of thirst. Depending on overall health, weight, and genetics, a human can live for up to two months without food, whereas three days without any hydration is a serious threat to survival. Either/or, an awful way to go.

- Compelling your way into college, says Caroline, is one of "the perks of being a vampire," a reference to the 1999 novel *The Perks of Being a Wallflower* by Stephen Chbosky, which was adapted into a 2012 film costarring Nina Dobrev.

- Distracting Matt from their explosive situation, Rebekah rhymes off a few of the world's wonders that she would like to show him. She begins with San Vittore in Brienno, the church Rebekah and Alexander were to be married in and where she buried him with his sword. Next, the northern lights, or the *Aurora Borealis* — named after Aurora, the Roman goddess of dawn — are a natural phenomenon of colored light caused by charged energy particles colliding with the earth's atmosphere. Rebekah's fellow Vikings believed they were the ghosts of virgins reflected in the sky. The northern lights are at their height in the early autumn and early spring and can be seen in the sky at higher altitudes, in places such as Iceland, Siberia, Alaska, the Northwest Territories of Canada, and Arctic Scandinavia. Seventy-five miles outside Beijing City in China is the Simatai Great Wall, built in the latter half of the 14th century and stretching over three miles of challenging terrain, making it a marvel of medieval technology. Simatai is on Yan Mountain and is considered one the "Wild Great Walls," renowned for its natural beauty and being the only Great Wall that retains its original Ming Dynasty style. As for Rebekah's promise to show Matt every inch of the Louvre, that's an impressive feat even for an Original: located on the bank of the Seine River in Paris, France, and founded during the French Revolution, the Louvre is one of the world's largest museums (located in a palace!), covering over 650,000 square feet and featuring over 35,000 works of art.

- Rebekah and Matt debate whether the Gilbert ring would work if she's the one that explodes the bomb that kills him: since she's supernatural, if she causes the explosion, does that count as a supernatural death? Alaric's ring worked when he was hit by a car driven by a hybrid in "The New Deal" (3.10), so there's a chance the exploded bits of Matt would re-form . . . Best not to take chances on that one.

- Before *Buffy the Vampire Slayer* got its own spin-off (*Angel*), its season three finale was a two-parter called "Graduation Day" that showed the gang graduating high school in a near apocalypse, before heading off to a nearby college the following season. Angel was plunked in the ocean in a metal coffin by his son, Connor, in the *Angel* season three finale, "Tomorrow." Angel and Stefan aren't the only vampires to suffer that fate; in the comic book *American Vampire*, Skinner Sweet is trapped 66 feet underwater in a coffin. (Don't worry: he escapes to exact revenge.)

- Lexi and Alaric commiserate about life on the Other Side. "Not exactly a party, is it?" Lexi says, insisting that "something else" has to be out there and that perhaps those trapped on the Other Side are serving time for the bad things they have done before they can let go and move on. Alaric implies that their purgatorial state has more to do with attachment to loved ones who are still alive and less to do with their own deeds, which only partially explains how Anna and Pearl were able to find peace after being reunited in "Ghost World" (3.07), or why Jenna is thought to have sidestepped supernatural purgatory altogether after dying as a vampire in "The Sun Also Rises" (2.21). (There's no canonical evidence that Jenna has found "peace," but Julie Plec has said as much in interviews.)

- Both Katherine and Silas refer to their respective doppelgängers as their "shadow self," a Jungian term for the weaker or darker aspects of one's psyche. In Stefan's case, he is a version of Silas that can be killed, thus he is indeed "weaker." When Katherine calls Elena her shadow self, the implication is that Elena is an all-round lesser version of Katherine. For more on doubles in *TVD*, check out the chapter "Doppelgänger Hijinks Ensued" in *Love You to Death — Season 2*.

THE RULES After flipping her emotions back on, Elena is no longer subject to the sire bond. The amount of werewolf venom determines how quickly a vampire will expire from it. Silas reminds us of two key elements of magic in the TVDverse: Nature demands a balance, and every spell has a loophole. Silas is released from Bonnie's spell when the veil goes back up, and she no longer has access to her power because she is dead-dead. When Silas made himself immortal, Nature created a version of him that could be killed — the shadow self, or doppelgänger. So Stefan is a Silas knock-off, 2,000 years after the fact.

PREVIOUSLY ON *THE VAMPIRE DIARIES* Carol Lockwood was worried about Tyler missing graduation if he did a body-jump spell with Klaus and was encased in concrete in "O Come, All Ye Faithful"; turns out both Lockwoods miss graduation.

In "Under Control" (1.18), Damon sees Stefan being the life of the party and quips to Elena, "Have I entered an alternate universe where Stefan is fun?" The alternate universe is back, as Lexi and Stefan have good end-of-days times.

"Buzzkill" is a nickname usually reserved for Stefan and often paired with "Bob" ("A Few Good Men," 1.15).

Jeremy experienced the terror of standing on one of Connor's exploding platforms in "The Killer," just as Matt gets to here.

Stefan offers to beg Klaus for some of his blood, but that strategy for saving Damon from a werewolf bite didn't go so well for Stefan in "As I Lay Dying" (2.22).

Katherine stabbing Elena with a broken broom handle brings to mind Elena's badass moment in "Unpleasantville" (1.12) when she snapped a broom handle over her knee to defend herself against Noah.

There are a few echoes of Damon and Elena's conversation in "My Brother's Keeper" in their epic fireside chat here: Damon said to her, "I'd say I'm sorry, but I'm not," about her break-up with Stefan, and also told her, "I don't think I've ever seen you more alive."

Matt also told Caroline, "This'll never work" in "Unpleasantville" before continuing to smooch her big time; Rebekah, officially get your hopes up for some romance on the road.

Lexi refers to Elena as Stefan's "epic love," which is how Rebekah referred to the Stefan-Elena romance in "After School Special" and Caroline did in "My Brother's Keeper."

It's not easy to dump the Big Bad into watery depths: the boys were on

Tyler Cook on "Graduation"

The season finale was so wonderful in the way it serviced all of the characters and relationships as these high school kids were ending one chapter in their lives and starting another. One thing this show is great at is balancing the big, huge action genre moments with the honest, more poignant ones and this episode was no different. My two favorite scenes to cut were the Damon/Elena kiss and the Elena/Katherine fight sequence.

Editorially the Damon/Elena kiss was exciting because you start to work on it knowing it's such a huge moment and the fans are going to love it, but it's also a lot of pressure because you want to do it justice. It was amazingly written on the page and it was amazingly directed and performed and so you are sitting here with a couple hours of footage thinking to yourself, "Don't screw it up." Ha ha. But it came together very organically and naturally, and I just looked at that scene as popping the cork on a bottle of champagne. All the fun and the excitement exists in the anticipation, so I really just wanted to make sure the scene was as slow as it needed to be at the top so that way when we started picking up steam it really felt like a shift and an acceleration into the kiss. Of course, one of my greatest tools in that scene was the song "Belong" by Cary Brothers. The build of that song is in perfect lockstep with the emotional build of the scene and when I married them together for the first time, all these emotions started to fly around in my stomach and I knew I had found the perfect song. What made it even more perfect was the way it breaks down and shifts on the cut to Stefan eavesdropping and the lyrics of "I don't belong" ring out over his realization that he wasn't chosen. Soul-crushing.

And the Elena/Katherine scene was just a whole lot of fun to cut. Not very many opportunities arise in your career to cut a fight scene where both of the participants are played by the same person. So it was an exciting editorial challenge to sell this fight as real and believable. And on top of that you still need to make it exciting and high-stakes! So you have to pull out your bag of tricks and sell an audience on a giant conceit. But that's the magic of filmmaking in its purest sense: making an audience believe something that is not real. As you get farther and farther away from reality, the more rewarding it is when you make it feel like it is real.

And finally, "Graduation" is a special episode for me because it's most likely going to be the last episode I edit of *The Vampire Diaries* (although never say never). Next year I will be editing *The Originals*. It's a bittersweet thing because I'll be moving on to a new show and there will be new challenges and I'm going to love exploring that new world but I've spent the last three to four years with *TVD* and it will be sad not to be part of it anymore. I grew up as an editor on *The Vampire Diaries* and was promoted from an assistant to an actual editor, so *TVD* holds such a special place in my heart and it's going to be strange not to be an active part of its creation.

their way to do it to Klaus in "The Departed" (3.22) but had to turn back, and Silas pulls a fast one on Stefan here.

OFF CAMERA Several members of the graduating class of seniors announced during the ceremony are named after members of *TVD*'s crew: John Albrecht is the payroll accountant for *TVD* and assistant production accountant for Bonanza Productions; William Duncan works in the art department; Matt Freeman is a production assistant; and in a weird, random bit of trivia, when the name Katherine Wilson is said, the closed captioning reads "Trish Stanard," and Trish is the unit production manager on *TVD*.

When asked about her favorite season four moments, episode cowriter Caroline Dries says, "I love the whole finale. Julie and I wrote it together and frankly the hardest part about it (once we figured out the story) was keeping it around 44 pages. We had so much we wanted to do and no space for it all."

Julie Plec called the finale "bananas" on Twitter, and joked with *ET Online* about Mystic Falls' ever-dwindling student population. "We had so many conversations about how big the graduating class of Mystic Falls should be! I mean, it's a small town, there were probably only 40 seniors and we've killed 20 of them!" The moment in season four Julie Plec most wishes she'd written herself appears in this episode: the Damon-Elena "I'm not sorry" speech. Says the showrunner, "I read it for the first time and wept at its Dries-y perfection." But Caroline Dries' favorite characters to write for are the baddies: "I like the villain voices — Damon, Katherine, Rebekah, and Elena without humanity; Elijah is pretty fun too. And Klaus of course — I LOVE THEM ALL."

For Pascal Verschooris, the finale was "fun, but nerve-wracking!" and he considers it "a showcase of our entire season": "Fire, explosions, waterfalls, tons of guest cast who all have a different schedule, weather . . . Over the course of the season, we came up with explosive devices, we went back to Middle Ages Italy, we met a lot of new characters. The finale brought everyone back together, including Jeremy. It also made use of all the tricks we learned over the past year. It was epic." The waterfall, in particular, was a long time coming. "We had the means to do it, but never had the right place," Verschooris explains. "Or so we thought. Julie has been asking about the waterfall since day one but we were never able to do it. This season we had the means, so I wanted to give it to her and the show. We had to bring special pumps to bring the water to the top of the cliff, which then dropped back in just like a . . . fall. It was truly beautiful."

Name Calling

Whether it's a friendly nickname or a clever insult, no one is spared from name calling on *TVD*.

- **Elena** Judgey (Damon), Special Snowflake of Human Frailty (Katherine), The Dress Thief (Caroline), Cupcake (Katherine), Little Girl (Katherine)
- **Stefan** Ripper You (Caroline), Shady Stefan (Damon), Baby Bro (Damon), Ripper Stefan (Caroline), O Selfless One (Damon), Ripper of Monterey (Lexi), Handsome (Katherine)
- **Damon** Lurker, Man Slut (Caroline); Pretty One (Val); Sherlock Holmes with Brain Damage (Rebekah); My Sire (Elena); Brother, Mom (Stefan); Buzzkill (Lexi)
- **Jeremy** Little Gilbert (Damon, Katherine); Van Helsing, Connor 2.0, Karate Kid, The Little Hunter That Could, Big Jer (Damon); The Gilbert Boy (Klaus)
- **Bonnie** Wicked Witch of the West (Damon), Bonnie the Teenage Witch (Damon), Bon (Matt, Caroline), Bonnie Bloody Bennett (Rebekah), Medusa (Damon), Bon-Bon (Katherine), Little Witch (Kol)
- **Caroline** Blondie (Damon), The Queen (Elena), Care (Matt, Tyler)
- **Tyler** Lockwolf, Ty (Hayley); Little Orphan Lockwood, Young Brutus (Klaus)
- **Matt** Quarterback, Least Most Valuable Player, Prom King, Donovan (Damon)
- **Klaus** Sunshine (Tyler), Niklaus (Elijah), Nik (Rebekah)
- **Rebekah** Scaredy Cat (Damon), Terrible Twosome (with Elena, Damon), Cinderella (Elijah)
- **Katherine** Katerina (Klaus, Elijah); Psychotic Doppelgänger, Evil One, Smiley, Auntie Katherine (Damon); Very Old Lady with Dreadful Taste (Rebekah)
- **Connor** Mr. Busybody Guy (Damon), My Jarhead Friend (Vaughn)
- **Shane** Witchipedia (Damon), Professor Creepy (Damon), Creepy Professor Guy (Caroline), Professor Shadypants (Damon), Dr. Evil (Damon), Atty (Caitlin), The Nutty Professor (Damon)
- **Hayley** Wolf Girl (Klaus, Kim), Little Wolf (Klaus), Killer (Shane), Little Backstabber (Damon)
- **Klaus's Hybrids** The Lollipop Guild (Damon)
- **Kol** Little Brother (Klaus)
- **Vaughn** Shrek, Laddie (Damon)
- **Silas** The Big, Bad Silas, Psychic Freak (Damon)
- **Silas's island** Numbskull Island (Damon)

FOGGY MOMENTS Looking back to the beginning of the season, what exactly was Pastor Young going on about in the letter he left for April? He wrote, "There's always been an evil that spread through Mystic Falls, but now a greater one is coming. My death is but the first in the war ahead." But we're later told that Shane convinced the pastor that if he sacrificed himself and 11 others, his wife would be resurrected, along with the others killed in the massacre. (Which was a big old lie on Silas's part; he can't raise mortals, only convince a very powerful witch to eradicate the Other Side.) Why did Pastor Young consider himself part of a war against a greater evil? He was on a personal quest, just like Shane.

Vaughn tells Damon he starved to death in Silas's well, right before he informs Damon that Qetsiyah found him on the Other Side to remind him of his destiny, confirming that Qetsiyah is still an active force. But with the veil down, why couldn't Qetsiyah herself pass through to take out Silas? Even dead witches have an incredible amount of power inside the Expression triangle, as Bonnie and Aja both demonstrated. Is there a reason — other than it not being convenient, story-wise — why Qetsiyah is staying behind-the-scenes?

Damon refuses to take the Cure, even though he's seconds away from death, because he doesn't want to become human. Could he not just take the Cure, be human for the drive home, and then turn again?

When Bonnie did the spell on Silas, she turned him *into* stone (as opposed to encasing him in stone); when the spell breaks, he turns back into his non-calcified self — so where do the stone casing bits that Stefan finds come from? Did Silas stick them in there for dramatic effect, or was his Monster Man form a little larger than his natural Stefan form and those were the extra bits of shed stony coating?

QUESTIONS
- When will Rebekah find her way to New Orleans for *The Originals*?
- Is Stefan the first Silas doppelgänger?
- Stefan is trapped in a safe at the bottom of a quarry. How long 'til someone realizes that Silas-Stefan isn't the Stefan they know and love?
- Katherine is human. She's going to have to start paying for those $500 boots she's so fond of. What ever will she do?
- What will Jeremy's "Oops, I'm not dead" explanation be? Where will he live since his sister burnt down their house?

- Tyler has been granted a pardon. Will he return to Mystic Falls? Can he compel himself a diploma or will he just chill chez Lockwood with Matt?
- Matt has the awesomest summer plans. But will it be back to the Grill when his jaunt with Rebekah is over? What will Donovan do?
- How will Damon and Elena fare, as she heads off to college?
- Have we seen the last of the hunters? Of April Young?
- Did Bonnie ever intend to give Katherine Silas-level immortality? Or was Bon-Bon just playing Katherine to get the tombstone?
- When Silas explains that the spell that turned him to stone broke because Bonnie died, Stefan says, "But Bonnie's not dead." And Silas replies, "It doesn't matter, does it?" Is Silas just giving Stefan the brush-off because he's about to dump him over the falls, or is there a supernatural significance to Silas's comment?
- Since Silas and Stefan are doppelgängers, was Silas 17 years old, like Stefan is, when he became an immortal, Qetsiyah imprisoned him, and she created the Other Side? Or is he more, like, 30, but could pass for 17 on a TV show?
- Silas has demonstrated a voracious appetite for blood. Is Stefan's status as Silas's doppelgänger somehow connected to his tendency to go into full-on ripper mode?
- The Other Side is a place of isolation for the supernatural dead, but witches seem to have a position of power there (Qetsiyah reaffirms Vaughn's mission, for example). Since Bonnie can see Grams as she leaves the cave with her, does that mean that Bonnie will be connected to other witches too?
- If Qetsiyah invented the Cure to the immortality spell and she's on the Other Side with Bonnie, could Bonnie get the recipe?
- Silas will think that Elena is in possession of the Cure, since that's what he will have psychically gleaned from Stefan before tossing him over the falls. How long will it take before Silas discovers that the Cure has been taken? What will he do when he realizes his one goal in life — to die — is unachievable? Go to college? Raise some hell?

Looking Back and Looking Ahead

Caroline Dries on the Big Moments of Season Four: In season four, we knew Jeremy's death would be a big moment. We call it a tent pole episode — it's holding up the spine of the season. Major story leads up to it, and the event pivots the story into a new direction. We built to it by giving Jeremy his first real mythology storyline: we made him a hunter. Even though he was triggered to want to kill Elena, it ultimately brought him closer to her, and when he died, we knew it was going to throw a massive twist into Elena's emotional journey. She turns off her humanity and we have the second half of our season.

[In terms of the sire bond] the only thing we discussed in great depth was: once Damon knew Elena was sired, could they have sex? And we decided no, that would be weird. We debated that a lot.

At first, fans didn't seem to like the concept of the Cure. To me, I expected its reveal to be super cool, but I guess people groveled at the mention of it. They were probably feeling the convenience of it emerging the season Elena became a vampire. We didn't let it affect us and stayed the course with our plans for it.

Julie Plec on Reactions to Season Four that Surprised Her: I was quite chagrined over the online reaction to the Cure. Bloggers and experts alike seemed very cynical about it and weren't very kind. The Delena fandom was furious about the sire bond, and to this day I'm still not hearing the end of it. That all being said, when we turned off the social media chatter and asked our friends, random fans, and regular viewers of the show, they all loved those developments and thoroughly enjoyed the mystery, tension, and romantic drama that we got out of both elements.

Julie Plec on the Choice to Burn Down the Gilbert House: It just felt right. Awful right. Tragic right. But right. Elena's losses had been so horrific, and we knew that she would have her humanity off until the end of the season, at which point she would be leaving home to go to college. So if there was a time to make a big bold move, that was it.

Joshua Butler on the Challenges of *TVD: The College Years*: The trick is to make the college environment work on two levels: (1) as a place that feels like a real college and (2) as a potentially neverending supply of blood for our vampires. The whole series works so well because we see high school and now college through the eyes of immortals who have the same hopes, dreams, yearnings that human beings possess. We, the human viewers, can identify with these complex characters and imagine ourselves having the additional burden of immortality and of needing blood in order to survive forever.

Jose Molina on the Opportunities that Lie Ahead: The show's gonna have to reinvent itself in several ways at the beginning of season five. High school is over, the Originals are gone ... it's time for a re-boot, which I think can only benefit the show. Every show could use a good kick in the ass once in a while, and *TVD* is no different. I wish my old colleagues luck! [Molina has moved on from *TVD* to write for Fox's 2013 series *Sleepy Hollow*.]

Caroline Dries on What Evil Might Lurk in Season Five: Our challenge every season is trying to top ourselves without going over the top and becoming broad with black-and-white bad guys. It's less about out-villain-ing (new word!) the previous season and more about creating a new level of intrigue. To me, our best villains are the ones who are directly connected to us — e.g., Elena without her emotions, season one Damon, Katherine always, Stefan without his humanity. I love those characters because you want them to be redeemed, but you're also along for the ride while they're evil. Someone like Connor is a great external villain, but it wasn't until Jeremy became a hunter who then wanted to kill his vampire sister that I think the hunter mythology really clicked in for us.

Caroline Dries on Keeping Things Fresh: Strangely, the big stuff of season four felt pretty easy to break, because Elena being a vampire and being sired to Damon generated so much story for us. The love triangle felt fresh. The journey of a new vampire felt fresh. So the big stuff wasn't too difficult. It's not like we run out of ideas. We run out of ways of telling the story — do we do another kidnapping/torture episode? What other story paradigms are there? Reaching to do things that we haven't done before, or that TV hasn't done before, gets a little more difficult, especially as we're diving into season five.

Music in Season 4
Songs by Scene

4.01 "Growing Pains"

1. "Twice," Little Dragon: *Elena remembers Damon's "selfish" confession of love.*
2. "Whirring," The Joy Formidable: *Caroline and Klaus-as-Tyler make out in the woods.*
3. "Wait for the Morning," Amy Stroup: *Elena and Stefan, on the rooftop, watch the sunrise.*

4.02 "Memorial"

1. "Hurt," The Gods of Macho: *Elena and Stefan make out in the woods.*
2. "Woe Is Me . . . I Am Ruined," The Lonely Forest: *Sheriff Forbes and Damon chat at the Grill about the Young farm explosion.*
3. "Change," Kopecky Family Band: *Stefan and Elena celebrate Elena's first feed with champagne.*
4. "Fear and Loathing," Marina & the Diamonds: *Elena finds Damon at the Grill, where he feeds her his blood.*
5. "How Can I Keep From Singing," St. Philips Boy's Choir: *Matt lets Elena feed from him during the memorial service.*
6. "Youth Knows No Pain," Lykke Li: *Connor chats with Matt and Jeremy at the Grill.*
7. "Ungodly Hour," The Fray: *The gang lights lanterns for their lost loved ones.*

4.03 "The Rager"

1. "Ho Hey," The Lumineers: *Hayley arrives at the Lockwood mansion.*
2. "Disparate Youth," Santigold: *Stefan and Elena arrive at Rebekah's party.*
3. "Keep You," Wild Belle: *Elena and April talk in Rebekah's kitchen.*
4. "Girl Like Me," Ladyhawke: *Elena does a keg stand.*
5. "Don't Say Oh Well," Grouplove: *Stefan takes Elena for a motorcycle ride.*
6. "Too Close," Alex Clare: *Elena hallucinates Damon while making out with Stefan.*

4.04 "The Five"

1. "Kill Your Heroes," AWOLNATION: *Klaus and Rebekah chat at the Grill; Damon, Elena, and Bonnie arrive at Whitmore College.*
2. "Sweat," Hard-Fi: *Stefan finds Rebekah with April at the Grill.*
3. "Glamour," Anders Manga: *Elena, Damon, and Bonnie arrive at the frat party.*
4. "Feel So Close (Benny Benassi Remix)," Calvin Harris: *Elena and Damon, high on blood, dance at the frat party.*
5. "Happening," Olivia Broadfield: *Elena and Damon talk on the Gilbert porch, Stefan interrupts.*

4.05 "The Killer"

1. "Smother," Daughter: *Elena and Stefan write in their journals.*
2. "Tick," Yeah Yeah Yeahs: *Klaus's hybrid Dean triggers Connor's booby trap in the Grill.*
3. "Keep On Runnin'," Cat Power: *Elena digs Connor's grave.*
4. "The Light," The Album Leaf: *Damon and Stefan discuss the Cure in Stefan's room.*

4.06 "We All Go a Little Mad Sometimes"

1. "Same Ol'," The Heavy: *Tyler wakes up to Hayley and Chris still partying in honor of Dean, their fallen hybrid friend.*
2. "Bedroom Eyes," Dum Dum Girls: *Caroline keeps Klaus occupied at the Grill.*
3. "Away Frm U," Oberhofer: *Caroline admits to Klaus that she's been distracting him and that Stefan has let Elena loose.*
4. "The Thread of the Thing," Fay Wolf: *Damon tells Elena there is a cure for vampirism.*

5. "It's Alive," A Fine Frenzy: *Matt and Damon have a chat in the Grill about Shane.*
6. "Walking Blind," Aidan Hawken and Carina Round: *Elena and Stefan break up on the Gilbert porch.*

4.07 "My Brother's Keeper"

1. "Let's Go," Matt & Kim: *As they set up for the pageant, Elena talks to Caroline about her break-up.*
2. "Ain't Fair," Deap Vally: *In an abandoned barn, Hayley talks hybrid Kim through breaking the sire bond.*
3. "Ordinary World," Vitamin String Quartet (Duran Duran cover): *Caroline and Klaus talk at the pageant; Hayley and Tyler arrive.*
4. "Little Deschutes," Laura Veirs: *During the Miss Mystic Falls dance, Damon and Elena make eyes at each other; Caroline stages a "friend-tervention."*
5. "Falling Slowly," Vitamin String Quartet (The Swell Season cover): *Caroline and Klaus discuss whether they'd take the Cure.*
6. "Kiss Me," Ed Sheeran: *Elena and Damon give in to their feelings; Caroline realizes Elena is sired to Damon.*

4.08 "We'll Always Have Bourbon Street"

1. "Eyes on Fire," Blue Foundation: *Elena and Damon wake up together; Caroline and Stefan talk about the possibility of the sire bond.*
2. "It Don't Mean a Thing (If It Ain't Got That Swing)," TVD NOLA Band (Duke Ellington cover): *Charlotte kills a man for spilling Damon's drink.*
3. "Take It Back," Junior Prom: *At the Salvatore house, Elena tells Caroline and Bonnie that she no longer has to snatch, eat, erase.*
4. "Stop Breaking Down," TVD NOLA Band (Robert Johnson cover): *Stefan and Damon decide to see if Charlotte is still at the corner of Bourbon and Dumaine.*
5. "The Mall," Fort Lean: *At the Grill, Hayley convinces Tyler to assert his alpha authority over Kim.*
6. "Let It Go," Dragonette: *Bonnie, Elena, and Caroline dance in the Salvatore living room.*
7. "So What Do You Say," PJ Parker: *Damon tells Charlotte to forget about him and move on with her life.*
8. "Hooray for You," Felicia Carter: *Lexi urges Damon not to go off to war with Stefan.*

9. "Speechless (Acoustic Version)," Morning Parade: *Elena and Damon talk about the sire bond at the Salvatore house.*

4.09 "O Come, All Ye Faithful"

1. "Covering Your Tracks," Amy Stroup: *Elena and Damon wake up together, clothed.*
2. "Christmas Treat," Julian Casablancas: *In the town square, Tyler reveals to Caroline his and Hayley's plan for taking out Klaus.*
3. "Take You to the Mistletoe," The Kicks: *Caroline and Stefan plot to get the hunter's sword from Klaus.*
4. "Christmas Wrapping," The Waitresses: *At the Grill, Caroline tells Klaus that there's something lonely about his postmodern snowflake painting.*
5. "The Christmas Song," The Raveonettes: *Tyler and his mother have a heart to heart at the Winter Wonderland festivities.*
6. "Jingle Bells," Sugar + the Hi-lows: *Klaus opens up to Stefan about his issues with trust and loneliness (before committing multiple murders).*
7. "O Holy Night," Cary Brothers: *Klaus slaughters his hybrids.*
8. "Oblivion," Bastille: *Stefan learns that Damon and Elena have slept together.*
9. "Have Yourself a Merry Little Christmas," Digital Daggers: *Klaus kills Carol Lockwood.*

4.10 "After School Special"

1. "Shooting the Moon," Mona: *Caroline calls Stefan and tells him to get it together.*
2. "Go Right Ahead," The Hives: *Jeremy and Matt train at the Gilbert lakehouse.*
3. "Female Robbery," The Neighbourhood: *Bonnie and her father talk in the Grill about rules and protecting the town.*
4. "New York," Snow Patrol: *Over the phone, Elena tells Damon she loves him.*
5. "Nothing Will Ever Change (This Love of Mine)," Jimmy Jules: *In a bar full of newly transitioned vampires, Klaus and Damon encourage Jeremy to go on a killing spree.*

4.11 "Catch Me If You Can"

1. "They Told Me," Sallie Ford & The Sound Outside: *At the bar, Klaus sics the vampires on Matt to motivate Jeremy.*
2. "Sleep Alone," Two Door Cinema Club: *Stefan discovers Rebekah in his room, reading his journal.*

3. "Baby I Call Hell," Deap Vally: *Damon and Jeremy return to the bar and find a pile of dead vampires . . . and Kol.*

4. "Missing," The xx: *In Shane's office, Rebekah and Stefan talk about crazy sex.*

5. "16 Years," Phantogram: *Damon and Elena arrive at the Grill looking for Jeremy.*

6. "Skin," Zola Jesus: *Stefan locks Damon in the Salvatore cellar.*

4.12 "A View to a Kill"

1. "Another Girl," Wild Belle: *Stefan wakes up in bed with Rebekah.*

2. "99 Red Balloons," 7 Seconds (Nena cover): *Bonnie and Elena chat on the phone as Bonnie inflates balloons in the school gym.*

3. "12 Gauge," Bundle of Hiss: *Kol is listening to this song when Elena calls to lure him to the Gilbert house.*

4. "Maneater," The Bird And The Bee (Hall & Oates cover): *Stefan returns to Rebekah's house where she's choosing an outfit for the dance.*

5. "Half Asleep," Trever Keith: *Stefan turns on the lights in the high school gym.*

6. "Lovesong," The Cure: *Stefan cues this up after Rebekah requests "nothing cheesy."*

7. "Wanted Dead or Alive," Bon Jovi: *Rebekah twirls through balloons in the gym.*

8. "If You Were Here," Cary Brothers: *Stefan teaches Rebekah "The Breakfast Club slide" in the school hallway.*

4.13 "Into the Wild"

No songs in this episode.

4.14 "Down the Rabbit Hole"

1. "Been a Long Day," Rosi Golan: *Caroline and Tyler say goodbye.*

4.15 "Stand By Me"

1. "Family," Noah Gundersen: *Elena burns down the Gilbert house.*

4.16 "Bring It On"

1. "White on White," FIDLAR: *Elena tosses her victim onto the road and walks away; Hayley gets jumped at a truck stop.*

2. "5 to 9," FIDLAR: *Elena finds the memorial flier for Jeremy on the school bulletin board.*

3. "Temporary," White Rabbits: *Elena arrives at the cheerleading meet.*
4. "Lions of Least," Pontiak: *Caroline confronts Elena about feeding on the competition.*
5. "I Love It," Icona Pop: *Stefan and Elena go downstairs to find people flooding into the Salvatore mansion.*
6. "Miracle Mile," Cold War Kids: *Caroline arrives at the party.*
7. "Control," Garbage: *Klaus and Hayley have sex.*
8. "Professional Griefers," deadmau5 feat. Gerard Way: *Sheriff Forbes arrives to break up the party.*
9. "Dance With Me," Ra Ra Riot: *Damon and Rebekah arrive at the Salvatore mansion.*
10. "Anymore of This," Matthew Perryman Jones and Mindy Smith: *In the Salvatore living room, Caroline leaves a voicemail for Tyler, then talks to Stefan; Elena tells Damon that she feels amazing.*
11. "White on White," FIDLAR: *Damon and Elena head to New York City.*

4.17 "Because the Night"

1. "Psycho Killer," Talking Heads: *Damon attacks a couple on the street in 1977.*
2. "Psycho Killer," Harper Blynn (Talking Heads cover): *Damon and Elena walk down the street in New York City in the present.*
3. "Bite Your Lip," New Cassettes: *Damon takes Elena to Billy's.*
4. "Loudmouth," The Handys (Ramones cover): *Damon and Billy talk about a mysterious client.*
5. "Shut Up and Dance," Rookie: *Rebekah finds Damon and Elena at Billy's.*
6. "Evil Soul," The Young Werewolves: *Elena tells Rebekah that she plans to find the Cure before Stefan and Damon do.*
7. "Ask the Angels," Dead Sara (Patti Smith cover): *Elena, Damon, and Rebekah feed on a woman at the club.*
8. "Lemon Scent," Dead Sara: *Rebekah approaches Elena about forming an alliance to find the Cure.*
9. "In the Search of an Audience," The Godz: *Lexi asks Damon about Katherine.*
10. "Let's Dance," The Ramones: *Damon reveals that he and Lexi slept together.*
11. "Arms and Enemies," The Quiet Kind: *Stefan realizes Bonnie has lost her memory; Klaus and Caroline bury the dead witches.*
12. "Heartbeat," Kopecky Family Band: *Elena and Rebekah steal Damon's car and leave the city.*

4.18 "American Gothic"

1. "Forget Me Not," The Civil Wars: *Elena and Rebekah shake down Katherine in the diner.*
2. "Days Long Gone," Don Gallardo: *Elena demands Katherine's jewelry, jacket, and shoes.*
3. "Why Try," Young Summer: *Damon admits to Stefan that he didn't try to stop Rebekah from taking the Cure.*

4.19 "Pictures of You"

1. "Whispers," Dave Baxter: *In a dream, Bonnie visits Jeremy's grave.*
2. "Keep Together," Hunter Hunted: *Elena and Rebekah shop for prom.*
3. "Bottled Up Tight," Luke Sital-Singh: *The Salvatores pick up Elena for prom.*
4. "Pictures of You," Class Actress (The Cure cover): *Damon, Stefan, and Elena arrive at prom.*
5. "Desert Song," Hot As Sun: *Bonnie and Matt arrive; Damon swipes Elena's flask.*
6. "Stay," Rihanna feat. Mikky Ekko: *Jeremy appears to Bonnie; Rebekah chats up Matt; Stefan and Elena slow dance.*
7. "Remember," Kari Kimmel: *Caroline arrives.*
8. "Paper and Gun," The Cold And Lovely: *Rebekah tries to sweet-talk April to win prom queen.*
9. "Lights," Josh Ritter: *Matt and Rebekah dance.*
10. "Song for Zula," Phosphorescent: *Tyler surprises Caroline; Damon and Silas-as-Stefan talk Elena and history.*
11. "Stay Away," Charli XCX: *Rebekah warns Matt that Elena intends to kill Bonnie.*
12. "You Send Me," Caught a Ghost (Sam Cooke cover): *Caroline and Tyler dance and say goodbye.*

4.20 "The Originals"

1. "Revolution," Dr. John: *In New Orleans, Hayley gets her gumbo on.*
2. "Ball & Chain," Martin Harley: *Klaus arrives in the French Quarter; Elijah tells Rebekah he's following Klaus to New Orleans.*
3. "How You Like Me Now?" The Heavy: *Marcel does karaoke.*
4. "Walking Backwards," Leagues: *Klaus and Marcel catch up.*
5. "No Sugar in My Coffee," Caught a Ghost: *The vampires of the French Quarter gather for the "trial" of Jane-Anne Devereaux.*

6. "Testified BK," Steve Nathanson: *Klaus pays Sophie Devereaux a visit.*
7. "Mojo Fix," Martin Harley: *Klaus buys Marcel's lackeys the bar's oldest Scotch.*
8. "How," The Neighbourhood: *Klaus tracks down Marcel at his hotel party.*
9. "New Cannonball Blues," TV on the Radio: *Marcel makes it clear he's in charge.*
10. "Terrible Love," The National: *Klaus reminds Marcel he is truly immortal, then crosses paths with Cami in the Quarter.*
11. "Do Whatcha Wanna," Rebirth Brass Band: *Klaus calls Caroline.*

4.21 "She's Come Undone"

1. "Tightrope," Walk the Moon: *Elena arrives at Mystic Falls High and realizes she's dreaming.*
2. "Bitter," Benny Marchant: *Matt finds Rebekah "celebrating" at the Grill.*
3. "Blue," Israel Cannan: *At a diner, Bonnie tries to convince Katherine to give up Silas's tombstone.*
4. "Found," Christel Alsos: *Elena finally lets her emotions come flooding back.*
5. "Open Mind," Wilco: *Katherine and Bonnie meet again to talk about dropping the veil.*

4.22 "The Walking Dead"

1. "Sail," AWOLNATION: *As Elena works out, Stefan tries to convince her not to kill Katherine.*
2. "Lean On Me," Telekinesis: *At the Grill bar, Matt explains graduation notices to Rebekah.*
3. "Things We Lost in the Fire," Bastille: *While playing darts, Elena makes it clear to Rebekah that they are not friends.*
4. "Fragile Love," Adam Agin: *Kol surprises Matt and Rebekah at the Grill.*
5. "Dream," The Boxer Rebellion: *Elena hugs Jeremy; Stefan finds Lexi at the Grill; and Alaric gives Damon the Cure.*

4.23 "Graduation"

1. "You Give Love a Bad Name," Bon Jovi: *Lexi dances in the Salvatore living room.*
2. "Dance in the Graveyards," Delta Rae: *Alaric, Jeremy, and Elena eat hamburgers in the cemetery.*
3. "Gone," Olivia Broadfield: *The gang gathers at graduation.*

4. "Belong," Cary Brothers: *Elena tells Damon she loves him.*
5. "When I Was Younger," Liz Lawrence: *Alaric and Lexi disappear back to the Other Side.*
6. "In the Stream," S. Carey: *Bonnie asks Jeremy to keep her secret; Matt agrees to travel with Rebekah.*

The Vampire Diaries Timeline

Despite the fact that *The Vampire Diaries* makes no pretense of establishing and then adhering to a timeline, here is an attempt to organize the information provided in the first four seasons: a history of the last 2,000-odd years in the *TVD* universe. A question mark indicates that a date is only an estimate; a ● marks a full moon.

The Origin of the Species

c. 10 C.E. — Silas becomes immortal, Qetsiyah kills Silas's true love, creates the Other Side and the Cure, and entombs Silas. The witch Qetsiyah was alive 2,000 years ago according to Shane ("After School Special"); Silas has been entombed for 2,000 years ("Down the Rabbit Hole").

c. 975?–1000 — Esther and Mikael lose their first child to a plague, travel to the New World, and live in peace as they raise their six children ("Ordinary People").

c. 1000 ● — Henrik is killed by a werewolf ("Ordinary People").

c. 1000 — Esther turns her remaining children and Mikael into vampires and places the hybrid-binding curse on Klaus ("Klaus," "Ordinary People"). The white oak tree is burned. Klaus kills Esther; Ayana preserves Esther's body with magic. Klaus and Elijah begin faking documents that tell about the curse of the Sun and Moon ("Klaus"). At some point in this era, the "witches," perhaps Ayana, forge the daggers that can put an Original into a death-like state when coated in the oak's ash ("Klaus").

Between c. 1000–1114 — At some point while still in what would become Mystic Falls, Finn and Sage fall in love and he turns her ("The Murder of One"); the Original siblings go to the Old World ("Ordinary People," "All My Children").

1110 — A "dying witch" creates the Brotherhood of the Five; the hunters spend four years translating their tattoo and killing vampires ("The Five").

1114 — Klaus slaughters the Five after they dagger all of the Original siblings; Rebekah buries Alexander along with his sword ("The Five").

Shortly thereafter — Klaus daggers Finn ("Bringing Out the Dead"), who spends 900 years in a coffin. Interestingly, Klaus daggers his first sibling while suffering from the torment of five simultaneous Hunters' Curses.

1166–7 — Klaus's Hunter's Curse breaks, after 52 years, 4 months, and 9 days, suggesting there were no active hunters from 1114 until this point ("We All Go a Little Mad Sometimes").

Dark Ages — Vampires punish those who threaten to expose their kind with 50 years in solitary confinement, according to Stefan ("You're Undead to Me").

1300s — Kol "runs with witches" in Africa ("A View to a Kill").

The 1400s–1700s

c. 1400 — The calendar markings on the cave wall indicate a white oak tree grew in Mystic Falls and was a spot for worship for the native people ("All My Children").

1400s — According to Vanessa, the Sun and Moon Curse dates back 600 years to when the Aztecs were being plagued by vampires and werewolves ("Bad Moon Rising"); later Elijah reveals to Elena that the historical documents were fakes ("Klaus").

1450 — Rose is born ("The Descent").

1464? — Pearl becomes a vampire; she has "400 years on" Damon who is not turned until 1864 ("There Goes the Neighborhood"). Presumably, Anna also becomes a vampire around this time.

June 5, 1473 — Katerina Petrova's birthdate ("Because the Night").

1490 — Katerina Petrova gives birth to a baby girl who is taken from her ("Katerina").

1492 — Katerina meets Klaus at his birthday celebration; she and Elijah spend time together ("Klaus").

Night before the sacrifice, 1492 — Katerina escapes and becomes a vampire; Trevor and Rose begin running from the Originals ("Katerina," "Rose").

Shortly thereafter, 1492 — Katerina discovers that her entire family has been killed by Klaus ("Katerina").

1600s — Kol "runs with witches" in Haiti ("A View to a Kill").

1659? — Lexi is born; she lives to be 350 years old ("162 Candles").

1692 — The Bennett family moves from Salem to Mystic Falls ("Haunted"). They are among a larger group of settlers who moved to the area to flee persecution ("The Dinner Party").

1700s? — A few hundred years prior to present-day events, Kol runs into a group of Silas worshippers and kills them ("Catch Me If You Can").

1700s — Klaus helps build up New Orleans from a "backwater penal colony" ("The Originals").

1755 — The Saltzman family comes to America from Germany ("History Repeating").

1790? — A hundred witches are rounded up and burned at the stake in Mystic Falls ("The Dinner Party").

1792 — Mystic Falls cemetery is established ("Pilot").

The Rise of the Salvatores: The 1800s

October 9, 1810 — Giuseppe Salvatore is born ("Children of the Damned").

Early November 1847 — Stefan Salvatore is born ("Lost Girls," "162 Candles").

1860 — The town of Mystic Falls is founded ("Under Control"); the town jail is built, with a special cell for vampires ("Disturbing Behavior").

1861–1865 — The American Civil War. At some point in this era, Giuseppe Salvatore impregnates a maid, who bears him a child; the child carries on the Salvatore name after Stefan's and Damon's human deaths, despite being illegitimate ("1912").

January 23, 1864 — According to his tombstone, Giuseppe Salvatore dies ("Children of the Damned"). This date conflicts with many other details in the timeline and is likely a production error.

April 1864 — According to Vanessa (and to Isobel's research), Katherine arrives in Mystic Falls ("Bad Moon Rising").

June 1864 — Johnathan Gilbert begins writing the journal that Jeremy finds ("History Repeating").

September 1, 1864 — The beginning of the Atlanta Campaign fires, which Katherine uses as a cover story ("Children of the Damned"). Presumably, Katherine arrives at the Salvatore estate shortly thereafter. This date conflicts with Isobel's research ("Bad Moon Rising").

September 24, 1864 — The first Founders' Ball is held ("Family Ties"). Katherine confronts George Lockwood at the ball ("Memory Lane"). Damon is rebuffed when he visits Katherine in her bedroom after the ball; Stefan has just professed his love for Katherine ("Memory Lane"). Some time soon after the ball, Katherine reveals to Stefan that she is a vampire ("Lost Girls").

1864 — A comet passes over Mystic Falls ("The Night of the Comet").

The Battle of Willow Creek / The Vampire Purge — Mr. Tanner says that the Battle of Willow Creek took place in 1865 ("Pilot"), but the flashbacks suggest it was actually in late 1864. On the day of the battle, Katherine meets with George Lockwood to go over their plan to fake her death ("Memory Lane"). Damon is also with Katherine at some point on that day and sees her in possession of Emily's crystal ("History Repeating"). Stefan speaks to his father about the vampire situation and unwittingly drinks vervain, which leads to Katherine's capture ("Children of the Damned"). Damon makes a bargain with Emily for Katherine's safety ("History Repeating"). Stefan and Damon are shot trying to rescue Katherine ("Family Ties," "Blood Brothers"). Either one or both of the brothers watch the church burn ("History Repeating" conflicts with "Blood Brothers" on this detail). Before Katherine leaves Mystic Falls, having been released from the church before it was set afire, she gives George Lockwood the moonstone and she sweetly promises (the then-dead) Stefan that they'll be together again ("Memory Lane").

The day after the Battle of Willow Creek — Emily gives the Salvatore brothers their rings; Stefan confronts his father and inadvertently kills him; Damon promises Stefan an eternity of misery ("Blood Brothers").

Shortly thereafter, 1864 — Stefan kills Thomas and Honoria Fell and Johnathan Gilbert (temporarily); Stefan meets Alexia Branson; Damon leaves Stefan in Lexi's care ("The Dinner Party").

1865 — Damon "made sure" vervain won't grow in Mystic Falls ("Family Ties").

Sometime thereafter — Katherine surreptitiously lets the founders know that Emily Bennett is a witch, and she is killed ("The House Guest").

Somehow, Emily's grimoire ends up buried with Giuseppe Salvatore despite the timeline problem . . . ("Children of the Damned").

Sometime thereafter — The Salvatore crypt is built sometime after Giuseppe's burial, but before Zachariah Salvatore's murder ("Children of the Damned," "1912").

The 1900s

1900s — Kol "runs with witches" in New Orleans ("A View to a Kill").

1900? — The Salvatore boarding house is built ("Lost Girls").

July 2, 1910 — Construction begins on Wickery Bridge ("Break On Through").

c. 1910 — Klaus daggers Kol ("Bringing Out the Dead").

1911? — Lexi tries to set up Rose on a date with Stefan ("Rose").

1912 — The brothers see each other for the first time since 1864 for their nephew Zachariah Salvatore's funeral. Samantha Gilbert murdered him as well as another councilman. Sage teaches Damon to seek pleasure in killing. Stefan lets the Ripper out ("1912"). The white oak tree is used to build Wickery Bridge ("Break On Through").

February 11, 1912 — Construction of Wickery Bridge is completed ("Break On Through").

1913? — Mikael runs Klaus out of New Orleans ("The Originals").

1917 — Stefan slaughters a migrant village in Monterey ("As I Lay Dying").

1922 — Samantha Gilbert confesses to her murders and is put in an asylum, where she kills a nurse, a guard, and eventually herself ("1912," "Break On Through").

March 12, 1922 — Stefan is in Chicago and writes in his diary about meeting a woman, presumably Rebekah ("The End of the Affair").

April 1922 — Stefan records in his diary that Lexi found him and is trying to help him again ("The End of the Affair").

June 1924 — According to his diary, Stefan is back feeding on animal blood after his ripper stint ("The End of the Affair").

1935 — Stefan is managing his cravings, and Lexi's project is to get him to laugh ("The End of the Affair").

1942 — The start date for Anna's research into vampire attacks in the Mystic Falls area ("Bloodlines").

1942 — Damon, in New Orleans with Charlotte, gets a visit from his brother and Lexi; Damon kills 12 people in the hopes of breaking Charlotte's sire bond; Stefan leaves to serve in World War II, while Damon stays behind at Lexi's behest ("We'll Always Have Bourbon Street").

1950s — Marcel studies law ("The Originals").

1952 — After 30 years of Lexi's help, Stefan finally begins to feel like himself ("The End of the Affair").

June 12, 1953 — "Uncle" Joseph Salvatore is killed at the Salvatore boarding house, presumably by Damon ("Family Ties," "You're Undead to Me").

1953 — Four people are killed by "animal attacks" in Mystic Falls ("Bloodlines"); that number likely includes Joseph Salvatore.

April 2, 1954 — The first restoration of Wickery Bridge begins, according to the preservation society's sign ("Break On Through").

1962 — Five people are killed by "animal attacks" in Mystic Falls ("Bloodlines").

October 1969 — Stefan meets Sheila Bennett at an antiwar demonstration ("Bloodlines").

August 16, 1972 — Abby Bennett is born, according to the document from the DMV ("The Ties That Bind").

1974 — Three people are killed by "animal attacks" in Mystic Falls ("Bloodlines"). Slater is made a vampire and begins accumulating college degrees ("Katerina").

October 17, 1975 / January 18, 1978 — Isobel Flemming is born: the earlier date is on her driver's license ("A Few Good Men"), the later one on her tombstone ("Know Thy Enemy").

February 4, 1976 — Alaric Saltzman is born ("Break On Through").

1977 — Damon is enjoying himself in New York, Lexi spends six months with him trying to get him to flip his emotions back on; Stefan is in Mystic Falls at the time ("Because the Night").

1980s — Elizabeth Forbes and Kelly Donovan go to high school together ("Lost Girls"); Kelly Donovan and Miranda Sommers are best friends ("There Goes the Neighborhood"). Miranda is also best friends with Abby Bennett ("The Ties that Bind") and Liz Forbes ("Bring It On").

1983 — Anna sees Katherine in Chicago ("Fool Me Once").

Late 1980s? — Elizabeth Forbes and Logan Fell have known each other since he was six ("The Turning Point"). Kelly Donovan babysits Jenna Sommers ("There Goes the Neighborhood").

Spring 1987 — Lexi and Stefan attend a Bon Jovi concert; Katherine stalks Stefan ("Masquerade").

1989? — Damon meets Bree and asks for her help getting into the tomb ("Bloodlines").

August 20, 1991? — Vicki Donovan is born ("Lost Girls").

Early to mid 1990s — Jenna Sommers and Mason Lockwood attend high school together, along with Logan Fell ("Memory Lane").

1993? — Isobel leaves her hometown of Grove Hill; Elena is born in late August/early September ("A Few Good Men"). Caroline is born in the fall ("Our Town").

1994 — Jeremy Gilbert is born ("The Night of the Comet"). Stefan and Damon see each other for the last time before fall 2009 ("Pilot").

March 14, 1994 — Aimee Bradley is born ("Rose").

1996 — Abby lures Mikael away from Mystic Falls, entombs him in a Charlotte cemetery, and stays in North Carolina ("The Reckoning," "The Ties That Bind").

Late 1990s — Logan babysits Caroline ("The Turning Point"); Pastor Young teaches first-grader Tyler Lockwood the importance of teamwork and community ("Memorial").

The 2000s

2001/2? — Ten-year-old Tyler sees his uncle Mason; he doesn't see him again until after Mayor Lockwood's death ("The Return"); Caroline's parents split up ("Bringing Out the Dead").

May 4, 2007 — The date of "death" on Isobel's tombstone ("Know Thy Enemy"); presumably her parents chose the date she disappeared, which conflicts with the timeline established in "Blood Brothers" that suggested Damon turned Isobel in 2008.

2007/2009? — Elena babysits April Young ("Growing Pains").

May 23, 2009 — Elena meets Damon, but he compels her to forget their encounter ("The Departed"). Grayson and Miranda Gilbert die in a car accident ("Pilot"); Stefan rescues Elena ("Bloodlines").

A few days later, 2009 — Elena sees April for the last time before the events of "Memorial" at the funeral of Miranda and Grayson Gilbert ("Memorial").

May–September 2009 — Stefan observes Elena and investigates her family history ("Bloodlines").

Summer 2009 — Matt and Bonnie work as lifeguards together ("The Reckoning").

August 2009 — Katherine compels Jimmy to attack Mason; Mason kills him, which triggers his curse ("Kill or Be Killed").

August 31, 2009 — Mason writes in his journal about how different he's felt since killing Jimmy ("The Sacrifice").

Season One Begins

September 6, 2009 — Damon kills a couple who is driving home from a concert ("Pilot").

September 7, 2009 — First day back to Mystic Falls High ("Pilot").

September 8, 2009 — Damon attacks Vicki during the party by the falls ("Pilot").

September 9, 2009 — The comet passes over Mystic Falls ("The Night of the Comet").

September 10, 2009 — Caroline wakes up with Damon; Stefan tries out for the school football team; Caroline and Damon crash Elena's dinner party with Bonnie and Stefan ("Friday Night Bites").

September 11, 2009 — Stefan gives Elena the vervain-filled necklace; Damon kills Coach Tanner ("Friday Night Bites"). (This date actually was a Friday.)

September 15, 2009 ● — Mason turns into a wolf for the first time ("The Sacrifice").

September 24?, 2009 — The Founders' Ball is held; the date here is based on the original Founders' Ball, which was held on the 24th. Stefan captures Damon and locks him in the cellar ("Family Ties").

September 27?, 2009 — Three days after leaving Elena a cryptic voicemail message, Stefan tries to fix his relationship with her by making dinner for her ("You're Undead to Me").

September 28?, 2009 — The Sexy Suds Car Wash is held at the high school; Damon attacks Vicki and kills her friends; Elena figures out that Stefan is a vampire; Stefan asks her to keep his secret ("You're Undead to Me," "Lost Girls").

September 29?, 2009 — Damon turns Vicki into a vampire; Logan is killed ("Lost Girls").

There's a jump in the timeline here. Between "Lost Girls" and "Haunted" only a few days pass, but "Haunted" takes place at the end of October.

October 31, 2009 — Vicki is staked by Stefan ("Haunted").

Early November 2009 — Bonnie reveals her powers to Elena; Stefan turns 162; Damon kills Lexi ("162 Candles").

Mid-November? 2009 — Emily possesses Bonnie and destroys the crystal; Logan returns, now a vampire. Stefan has been asking Damon for "months" why he returned to Mystic Falls; Alaric mentions to Jeremy that they are halfway through the school semester ("History Repeating").

The following day ● — With a full moon overhead, it's Career Night at Mystic Falls High School; Elena and Stefan have sex for the first time; she discovers the portrait of Katherine; Noah causes her to crash her car ("The Turning Point"). Damon rescues Elena from the car wreck ("Bloodlines").

The following day — Damon takes Elena to Atlanta to visit Bree; Bonnie falls into the tomb and Stefan rescues her ("Bloodlines").

The following day — Elena arrives back in Mystic Falls, and Stefan reveals that he rescued her from the car crash that killed her parents in May and that she is adopted ("Bloodlines").

December? 2009 — The 1950s Decade Dance is held at the high school; Caroline passes a Christmas display in a store window ("Unpleasantville").

Shortly thereafter — Stefan unearths the grimoire that was buried with his father; both Elena and Bonnie are kidnapped ("Children of the Damned").

The following day — The tomb opens; "Duke from Duke" throws a party at the old cemetery where people are wearing winter coats and hats; Sheila Bennett dies ("Fool Me Once").

Christmastime, 2009 — Jenna takes Jeremy and Elena to celebrate the holidays at the lakehouse ("O Come, All Ye Faithful"); this detail conflicts with Elena's assertion in "Crying Wolf" that it is her first time back to the lakehouse since her parents died.

Winter 2010 — An ill-fated hiker tells a tomb vampire named Harper the year; the Bachelor Auction is held at the Grill ("A Few Good Men").

No indication of time of year for "There Goes the Neighborhood" or "Let the Right One In."

One month before Founders' Day ● — Johnathan Gilbert returns to Mystic Falls; the kickoff to Founders' Day party is held on the night of a full moon; Stefan gives in and drinks human blood ("Under Control").

Three weeks or so before Founders' Day — Bonnie returns to Mystic Falls; the Miss Mystic Falls competition is held; Elena and Damon lock up a blood-drunk Stefan ("Miss Mystic Falls").

A few days later — Stefan refuses to eat; Elena convinces him not to commit suicide; Isobel shows up at the Grill ("Blood Brothers").

The following day — The Mystic Falls High students prepare floats for Founders' Day; Elena meets her birth mother, Isobel ("Isobel").

The following day — Isobel gets the Gilbert invention from Elena and gives it to Uncle John ("Isobel").

Founders' Day — The tomb vampires, Anna, and Mayor Lockwood are killed; Tyler, Matt, and Caroline are in a car accident; Katherine impersonates Elena, kisses Damon, and attacks Uncle John ("Founder's Day").

Season Two Events

The following day — Mason returns to Mystic Falls for his brother's wake; that night, Damon "kills" Jeremy and Katherine "kills" Caroline ("The Return").

The following day — Caroline completes her transition to vampirism; the school hosts a carnival ("Brave New World").

Full Moon ● — Alaric, Damon, and Elena go to Duke University. Caroline gets a daylight ring from Bonnie. Mason turns into a werewolf. Tyler discovers the Lockwood secret. ("Bad Moon Rising")

The following day — Caroline wakes up to find Katherine in her bedroom ("Bad Moon Rising").

The following day — (Assuming this is not the same day that Katherine wakes up Caroline in her bedroom, because Katherine's wearing a different outfit when she shows up at the Salvatore boarding house.) Jenna hosts a barbecue; Katherine reveals to Stefan the real story behind the Vampire Purge of 1864 ("Memory Lane").

August 2010 / The following day — The day of the Historical Society Volunteer Picnic; that night, Sheriff Forbes is put in the Salvatore holding cell until the vervain is out of her system ("Kill or Be Killed"). The flashback to "one year ago" in "Kill or Be Killed" is later revealed to have taken place in August 2009 ("The Sacrifice"), meaning the present-day events take place in August 2010. (The timeline is later muddled, because "The Birthday" also takes place in August or early September 2010, a year after the events of the pilot episode.)

Three days later — It takes three days for the vervain to leave Liz's system ("Kill or Be Killed"). The gang sets up for the Masquerade Ball. Mason is tortured and killed by Damon. ("Plan B")

Masquerade Ball — Katherine kills Aimee; Tyler triggers the werewolf curse by accidentally killing Sarah; Katherine is captured and put in the tomb; Elena is kidnapped ("Masquerade").

The following day — Elijah arrives and kills Trevor; Damon and Stefan rescue Elena ("Rose").

The following day — The Martins arrive in Mystic Falls; Elena visits Katherine at the tomb; Rose and Damon visit Slater; Elijah compels Slater to kill himself ("Katerina").

It's not clear how many days, if any, pass between "Katerina" and "The Sacrifice," but since Slater's body is still undiscovered in "The Sacrifice" it's safe to assume the timeline is contiguous.

That night — Late at night, Jonas steals various artifacts from Elena's room ("The Sacrifice").

The following day — Jeremy manages to get the moonstone out of the tomb; Stefan is stuck in the tomb with Katherine; Elijah kills three vampires ("The Sacrifice").

The following day — Tyler calls Mason as he gets ready for the full moon ("By the Light of the Moon"). (Assuming this is a separate day since he's wearing a different shirt than in "The Sacrifice.")

Full Moon ● — Tyler makes his first transformation. Rose is bitten by Jules. ("By the Light of the Moon")

The following day — Jules wakes up in a campground bloodbath; Rose dies ("The Descent").

The following day — The werewolves kidnap and torture Caroline ("Daddy Issues").

The following day — Stefan and Elena go to the lakehouse. Tyler leaves town with Jules. ("Crying Wolf")

The following day — (Assuming it's the next day, since news of Tyler's departure is just spreading.) Elijah is killed (twice). Katherine is freed from the tomb. ("The Dinner Party")

The following day — The Grill burns down; Luka and Jonas Martin are killed ("The House Guest"). Jenna meets Isobel ("Know Thy Enemy").

The following day — Under compulsion, Isobel kills herself; Katherine is kidnapped; Alaric is possessed by Klaus ("Know Thy Enemy").

The 1960s Decade Dance — Bonnie fakes her death to fool Klaus; later that night, Elena takes the dagger out of Elijah ("The Last Dance").

The following day — Elena spends the day with the newly resurrected Elijah, learning the true curse ("Klaus").

The Sacrifice ● — Damon force-feeds Elena his blood; Stefan and Elena go for a climb by the falls; Damon gets bitten by Tyler ("The Last Day"). Klaus breaks the curse, killing Jenna, Jules, and Elena, and transforming into a true werewolf-vampire hybrid ("The Sun Also Rises").

Next morning — Elena and Jeremy bury Jenna and John ("The Sun Also Rises").

The following day — Klaus "kills" Elijah. Jeremy dies but Bonnie resurrects him. Stefan gives himself over to Klaus. ("As I Lay Dying")

By moon cycles, it is two months from Founders' Day to the events of the finale. By time markers within episodes, it is only 26 days.

Season Three Events

Summer — Klaus and Stefan chase werewolves (and kill tons of people), while Elena and Damon track them ("The Birthday").

Day 1 of season three timeline | late August/early September 2010 — Two months after the events of "As I Lay Dying," Elena turns 18; Stefan kills Andie Star ("The Birthday").

Day 2 ● — Elena, Alaric, and Damon track down Stefan in the Smoky Mountains; Klaus's hybrid experiment fails ("The Hybrid").

Day 3 — Caroline is tortured by her father; Elena and Damon go to Chicago; Rebekah is awakened ("The End of the Affair").

Day 4 — In Chicago, Katherine kills Gloria to save Stefan; Damon attacks both Alaric and Bill Forbes at the barbecue at the Lockwoods' ("Disturbing Behavior").

Day 5 — Bill Forbes leaves town; Damon and Katherine go on a road trip; Klaus drags Stefan back to Mystic Falls ("Disturbing Behavior"). That night, Tyler is turned into a hybrid, Stefan is forced to flip the switch, and Katherine and Jeremy locate Mikael ("The Reckoning").

Day 6 and 7 — Katherine tries to revive Mikael but he is unresponsive ("Smells Like Teen Spirit").

Day 8 — The first day of school, established as one year after the events of the pilot. Vicki tries to kill Elena at the Spirit Squad bonfire; Bonnie's magic is used to open the door to this side for the ghosts ("Smells Like Teen Spirit").

Day 9 — The Night of Illumination ("Ghost World").

Day 10 — Elena learns the Original family history from Rebekah; Mikael confronts Stefan and Damon ("Ordinary People").

Day 11 — As part of their plot to fool Klaus, Elena stakes Mikael; Klaus leaves Portland to return to Mystic Falls ("Homecoming").

Homecoming — Rebekah is daggered; Mikael is killed ("Homecoming").

Day 13 — Klaus discovers that his coffins are missing ("Homecoming").

Day 16? — Sunday, likely the one directly following Homecoming Friday. Alaric is run over saving Jeremy; Stefan enlists Bonnie to help him hide the coffins ("The New Deal").

Day 17 — Caroline turns 18; a fundraiser for the Wickery Bridge revitalization is held at the Lockwoods' ("Our Town").

Day 18 — Jeremy leaves Mystic Falls for Denver; Brian Walters is found dead ("Our Town").

Day 19 — Bonnie tracks down her mother; Damon undaggers Elijah ("The Ties That Bind").

Day 20 — Bill Forbes dies; Kol, Finn, Rebekah, and Esther are resurrected ("Bringing Out the Dead").

Day 21 — The Mikaelson family holds a ball ("Dangerous Liaisons").

Day 22 — Esther tries to kill her family; Abby is turned into a vampire ("All My Children").

Day 23 — Alaric spends the day in jail; they realize he is the Mystic Falls Murderer ("1912").

Few days later — Damon, Sage, and Rebekah manipulate each other; Alaric attacks Meredith ("Break On Through").

Next day — Abby leaves Jamie and Bonnie ("Break On Through").

Next day — Bonnie breaks the "united as one" spell; Matt kills Finn; Rebekah tortures Damon ("The Murder of One"). Damon and Elena leave for Denver ("Heart of Darkness").

Next day — Tyler returns; Esther possesses Rebekah ("Heart of Darkness").

Next day — The 1920s Decade Dance ("Do Not Go Gentle").

Next day — Alaric terrorizes the gang; Klaus is desiccated ("Before Sunset"). Late that same night, Elena dies ("The Departed").

By time markers within episodes, it is approximately 31 days between "The Birthday" and "The Departed."

Season Four Events

One year prior to season four — Pastor Young teaches a theology course at Whitmore College and meets Professor Shane ("We All Go a Little Mad Sometimes"). Shane visits the island where Silas is entombed ("Into the Wild").

Three weeks prior to Day 1 — Shane says that the tombstone of Silas is donated to Whitmore College ("We All Go a Little Mad Sometimes").

Day 1 | Morning after Elena dies — Pastor Young and the council take over the town (basically), and Elena becomes a vampire ("Growing Pains").

Day 2 — Shane and Young call each other frequently ("We All Go a Little Mad Sometimes"). The Young farm explodes ("Growing Pains"); Stefan and Elena leave for a learn-to-feed-on-Bambi camping trip ("Memorial").

Day 3 — News of the Young farm explosion hits the newspapers; Stefan and Elena return, and Connor Jordan arrives in town ("Memorial").

Day 4 — The memorial for the 12 dead is held ("Memorial").

Day 5 — Elena returns to school; Rebekah throws a party ("The Rager").

Day 6 — Connor is held prisoner by Klaus; Damon, Elena, and Bonnie go to Whitmore College for the day; Stefan learns about the sire bond ("The Five").

Day 7, Sunday? — Connor takes hostages at the Mystic Grill in an attempt to lure and kill vampires; Klaus excavates Alexander's sword; Elena kills Connor ("The Killer").

Day 8 — Elena suffers from the Hunter's Curse and nearly kills herself; Jeremy activates his hunter status by killing the hybrid Chris ("We All Go a Little Mad Sometimes").

Day 9 — Elena wakes up free from the Hunter's Curse; Stefan and Elena break up ("We All Go a Little Mad Sometimes").

Day 10 — The day before the Miss Mystic Falls competition ("My Brother's Keeper").

Day 11 — At Miss Mystic Falls, Jeremy tries to kill his sister; Elena and Damon sleep together ("My Brother's Keeper").

Day 12 — Damon and Stefan go to New Orleans; Elena finds out she is sired to Damon ("We'll Always Have Bourbon Street").

Day 13 — Damon and Stefan return; Damon and Elena discuss the sire bond ("We'll Always Have Bourbon Street").

Day 14 | December 2010 — At the Winter Wonderland event, Klaus slaughters 12 hybrids and then kills Carol Lockwood ("O Come All Ye Faithful").

Days 15–17 — Damon trains Jeremy at the lakehouse; Klaus quells his urge to kill Stefan ("After School Special").

Day 18 — Rebekah holds the gang hostage at the school; Klaus turns a bar full of people into vampires so Jeremy can kill them ("After School Special").

Day 19 — Matt and Elena return home; Kol compels Damon to kill Jeremy; Stefan and Rebekah consummate their partnership ("Catch Me If You Can").

Day 20 — Day of the 1980s Decade Dance: Jeremy kills Kol, Bonnie traps Klaus in the Gilbert living room. Bonnie uses the new moon to power the spell, which will last three days, four at most. ("A View to a Kill")

Day 21 — The gang travels to Silas island and begin their hike ("Into the Wild").

Day 22 — Jeremy is missing, and the gang spends the day trying to find him ("Into the Wild").

Day 23 — The gang reaches Silas's tomb; Silas kills Jeremy ("Down the Rabbit Hole").

Day 24 — Elena and Stefan return with Jeremy's body; Damon finds Bonnie and brings her back to Mystic Falls; with her emotions turned off, Elena burns down the Gilbert house ("Stand By Me").

Day 27? — It has been a "couple of days" since Elena turned off her emotions: the cheerleading invitational is held at Mystic Falls High, Elena throws an impromptu party at the Salvatores, and leaves that night for New York City with Damon ("Bring It On").

Day 28? — Elena, Damon, and Rebekah spend the day in Manhattan; Caroline kills 12 witches ("Because the Night").

Day 29? — Elena and Rebekah steal Damon's car and head out to find Katherine ("Because the Night").

Day 30? — Elena and Rebekah arrive in Willoughby; Katherine gives Elijah the Cure ("American Gothic").

Day 39? — Elena hasn't killed anyone for "eight or nine days"; Mystic Falls High holds its prom ("Pictures of You").

Day 41? — Klaus and Elijah learn that Hayley is pregnant, and they decide to stay in New Orleans ("The Originals").

Day 42? — Elena, who's been at the Salvatores for days, is tortured back into having feelings ("She's Come Undone").

Day 43? — Liz Forbes says that the blood banks were raided "last month," but it is more like two weeks ago; the veil drops within the Expression triangle ("The Walking Dead").

Day 44? ● **/ June 2011** — It's graduation day at Mystic Falls High ("Graduation"). Since Elena and company started their junior year in 2010, they graduate as the class of 2011.

Gotta love Mystic Falls where it's only 30 days from Christmas to graduation!

Seasons 1, 2, and 3 Recaps

1.01 "Pilot" Stefan and Elena meet on the first day back to school at Mystic Falls High. Vicki Donovan is attacked by Damon in the woods.

1.02 "The Night of the Comet" Damon antagonizes his brother, dangling Vicki off a roof over the town square, as a comet passes over town. Stefan and Elena kiss.

1.03 "Friday Night Bites" Stefan joins the football team, but then Damon kills Coach Tanner, ending the football season prematurely. Caroline debuts her new boyfriend (and penchant for neck scarves): Damon.

1.04 "Family Ties" At the Founders' party, Stefan manages to capture Damon by spiking Caroline's drink with vervain. Vicki leaves Tyler behind for Jeremy Gilbert.

1.05 "You're Undead to Me" It's the Sexy Suds Car Wash! Bonnie sets water on fire. Elena figures out Stefan's a vampire. Damon escapes from the Salvatore holding cell and attacks Vicki as she parties in the graveyard.

1.06 "Lost Girls" The first flashback episode brings us our first glimpse of Katherine and a heck of a lot of backstory on how Stefan and Damon became vampires. Bored, Damon turns Vicki — but not before their classic dance party moment.

1.07 "Haunted" Halloween in Mystic Falls marks the first death of a major character, as Stefan stakes Vicki, on the loose and hungry for Gilbert blood.

1.08 "162 Candles" Stefan's BFF Lexi comes to town on his birthday, the one day he isn't allowed to brood, and Damon kills her to cover up his own bloody tracks. Bonnie reveals to Elena that she's a witch in one of the series' most magical moments.

1.09 "History Repeating" The girls hold a séance and Bonnie is possessed by her ancestor Emily Bennett, who destroys the tomb-opening crystal. Alaric Saltzman makes his debut.

1.10 "The Turning Point" Damon deals with Logan Fell, now a vampire, while Tyler and Jeremy come to blows at the school's Career Fair. Stefan and Elena sleep together for the first time. She discovers Katherine's portrait, takes off, and ends up in an accident, after a vampire in the road causes her to crash her car.

1.11 "Bloodlines" Damon takes Elena on a road trip to Georgia where she gets nice and drunk and saves his life from Lexi's angry ex. Stefan helps Bonnie get her powers back. Elena finds out she's adopted.

1.12 "Unpleasantville" It's the 1950s Decade Dance at MFHS. Uninvited vampires crash the party, but the Salvatore brothers kill Noah. Matt and Caroline kiss.

1.13 "Children of the Damned" Pretending to work with Damon, Elena and Stefan race to find the location of Emily Bennett's grimoire before he can. In flashback we see the events leading up to Katherine's capture. Bonnie and Elena are kidnapped by Ben and Anna.

1.14 "Fool Me Once" The tomb opens — and Katherine isn't in it.

1.15 "A Few Good Men" Damon goes on a bender. A bachelor auction is held at the Grill. Elena finds out that her birth mother is Isobel, Alaric's not-so-dead wife.

1.16 "There Goes the Neighborhood" Caroline and Matt and Elena and Stefan go on a double date. Damon makes out with Matt's mom. Two tomb vampires attack the Salvatores.

1.17 "Let the Right One In" A storm moves into Mystic Falls. Stefan is kidnapped and tortured. Damon, Alaric, and Elena rescue him. Caroline discovers Vicki Donovan's body.

1.18 "Under Control" At the kickoff to Founders' Day party, Stefan tries to manage his thirst for human blood and fails. Tyler makes out with Matt's mom. Uncle John Gilbert arrives with a magic ring.

1.19 "Miss Mystic Falls" Caroline wins Miss Mystic Falls. Stefan attacks Amber Bradley.

1.20 "Blood Brothers" Starving himself in the Salvatore holding cell, Stefan flashes back to the night he and Damon became vampires.

1.21 "Isobel" Elena meets her birth mother, Isobel, who demands the Gilbert device from her. Bonnie pretends to deactivate it.

1.22 "Founder's Day" As the town celebrates its sesquicentennial, the tomb vampires face off with the vampire-hating members of the founding families. Damon kisses Katherine, thinking she's Elena, and Katherine chops off Uncle John's fingers.

2.01 "The Return" The Lockwoods, including Uncle Mason, mourn the mayor. Katherine makes her presence known. Damon snaps Jeremy's neck.

2.02 "Brave New World" Caroline becomes a vampire and kills Carter at the school's carnival.

2.03 "Bad Moon Rising" Alaric, Damon, and Elena go to Duke to investigate werewolves; Tyler learns that Mason is one.

2.04 "Memory Lane" Katherine and Stefan relive some 1864 memories. After Jenna's friendly barbecue, Damon makes an enemy of Mason Lockwood.

2.05 "Kill or Be Killed" At the historical society picnic, Mason and the Salvatore brothers face off; Liz Forbes finds out that Caroline, Damon, and Stefan are vampires.

2.06 "Plan B" The gang finds the moonstone in the bottom of a vervain-filled well. Damon kills Mason. Caroline compels her mother.

2.07 "Masquerade" At the masked ball, Katherine kills Aimee Bradley and orchestrates Sarah's death so Tyler triggers his werewolf curse. She is captured and entombed.

2.08 "Rose" Elena learns about the Originals from her vampire captors Rose and Trevor. Elijah makes an impressive debut.

2.09 "Katerina" Elena turns to the entombed Katherine for answers about being the doppelgänger.

2.10 "The Sacrifice" After Jeremy's botched attempt to get the moonstone from the tomb, Stefan ends up in there with Katherine. Elena tries to turn herself over to Klaus.

2.11 "By the Light of the Moon" Tyler turns into a werewolf. Elijah and Elena make a deal. Jules, in wolf form, bites Rose.

2.12 "The Descent" Rose dies from her werewolf bite.

2.13 "Daddy Issues" The werewolves and vampires face off, with Caroline getting the brunt of the attack. John Gilbert returns to town.

2.14 "Crying Wolf" Stefan and Elena go to the lakehouse; Stefan kills Brady. Bonnie pries information about the sacrifice from Luka.

2.15 "The Dinner Party" While Stefan and Elena talk about his ripper days and the first time he met Lexi, Damon and Andie host a dinner party. Elijah is daggered twice.

2.16 "The House Guest" The unwelcome house guest Katherine proves to be helpful in taking out Jonas. Caroline sings "Eternal Flame," the Mystic Grill burns, and Matt finds out his girlfriend is a vampire.

2.17 "Know Thy Enemy" Katherine double-crosses the Salvatore brothers but is crossed herself by Isobel who is compelled by Klaus who arrives in Mystic Falls . . . in Alaric's body.

2.18 "The Last Dance" At the 1960s Decade Dance, AlariKlaus terrorizes the gang, and Bonnie, using the power of 100 dead witches, fakes her own death.

2.19 "Klaus" Jenna learns about vampires, Elena learns about the Originals and the real curse from Elijah, and Klaus returns to his own body.

2.20 "The Last Day" On the day of the sacrifice, Damon force-feeds Elena his blood to make sure she'll come back to life; Elena tells Stefan how desperately she doesn't want to become a vampire.

2.21 "The Sun Also Rises" The sacrifice takes place: Jules and Jenna are killed, Klaus unleashes his werewolf side, and Damon is bit by Tyler after he rescues him and Caroline.

2.22 "As I Lay Dying" Stefan gives up everything to save his brother from his werewolf bite, becoming a minion to Klaus. After Jeremy is shot dead, Bonnie brings him back to life. Ghosts Anna and Vicki appear to Jeremy.

3.01 "The Birthday" Caroline throws Elena an 18th birthday party, but all she wants to do is find Stefan, who pops into town to kill Andie.

3.02 "The Hybrid" Elena, Alaric, and Damon go mountain-hiking in search of Stefan. Klaus's attempt to turn werewolves into hybrids is an epic failure.

3.03 "The End of the Affair" Stefan finds out that he and Klaus were bosom buddies in the 1920s, and we meet Rebekah, the Original sister. Caroline's dad tortures her.

3.04 "Disturbing Behavior" In Chicago with Klaus and Rebekah, Stefan proves not dastardly enough to fool them into thinking he's on their team. Damon faces off with Bill Forbes.

3.05 "The Reckoning" Senior prank night turns into a horror show, as Klaus turns Tyler into a hybrid and compels Stefan to turn off his emotions. Matt kills himself (temporarily) to see Vicki.

3.06 "Smells Like Teen Spirit" Mystic Falls High is back in session, and Ghost Vicki tries to kill Elena while an emotion-free Stefan is nearly detained by Elena and Alaric.

3.07 "Ghost World" A rift between the mortal realm and the Other Side allows the supernatural dead to return to corporeal form for one night only.

3.08 "Ordinary People" In flashback, we meet the Original family as humans.

3.09 "Homecoming" Klaus ruins homecoming, kills his dad, and frees Stefan from his debt to him. Stefan steals Klaus's coffin collection.

3.10 "The New Deal" Klaus terrorizes the Gilberts, Stefan and Bonnie hide coffins in the witch house, and Jeremy beheads a hybrid.

3.11 "Our Town" Caroline celebrates her birthday with a funeral.

3.12 "The Ties That Bind" Bonnie sees her mother again. Tyler nearly kills Caroline's dad.

3.13 "Bringing Out the Dead" Bill Forbes dies. Elijah returns, as does the rest of the Original family.

3.14 "Dangerous Liaisons" The Mikaelsons throw a ball, and Esther plots to kill her children, enlisting Elena's help.

3.15 "All My Children" The Originals' fight among themselves leads Damon to turn Bonnie's mother into a vampire, in order to save Elena.

3.16 "1912" Damon and Stefan remember the murders that plagued Mystic Falls in 1912 (cue the flashback!), while Elena and Matt unsuccessfully try to pin the current murders on Meredith, not Alaric.

3.17 "Break On Through" Sage, Rebekah, and Damon have a threesome. Evil Alaric tries to murder Meredith, but Elena and Stefan manage to save the day.

3.18 "The Murder of One" Rebekah tortures Damon. Finn is killed, and with him his entire sire line.

3.19 "Heart of Darkness" Stefan and Alaric face their dark sides. In Denver to pick up ghost-talker Jeremy, Damon and Elena make out like crazy.

3.20 "Do Not Go Gentle" The 1920s Decade Dance marks the death of Alaric, lost to Esther's plot to create a super-vamp capable of killing Originals with the last remaining white oak stake turned into an indestructible weapon.

3.21 "Before Sunset" The gang finally manages to desiccate Klaus. Evil Vampire Alaric is on the loose. And Elena, drained of liters of blood, collapses while repainting Jenna's bedroom.

3.22 "The Departed" Elena chooses Stefan. Believing Klaus has been killed, Rebekah forces Matt's truck off the road, and Elena dies — with vampire blood in her system.

Selected Sources

Alonso, Irene Sanz. "Why Do Vampires Prefer Lousiniana?" NeoAmericanist.org. Fall/Winter 2011–2012.

American Friends of The Louvre, aflouvre.org.

"*American Gothic*: About This Artwork," Art Institute Chicago. http://www.artic .edu/aic/collections/artwork/6565#.

Berry, Francis. "Difference Between Modern and Post Modern Art," Postmodern-Art .com. June 26, 2006.

Bierly, Mandi. "*Vampire Diaries* EP Julie Plec Talks the Meaning of Blood-Sharing, This Week's Emotional Final Scene, and What's Next," EW.com. October 19, 2012.

———. "*Vampire Diaries* Hunter Todd Williams Teases This Week's 'Killer' Episode," EW.com. November 7, 2012.

———. "*Vampire Diaries*: Candice Accola Talks Klaus, Miss Mystic Falls, and a Winter Wonderland," EW.com. November 15, 2012.

———. "Julie Plec Talks Potential *Vampire Diaries* Spinoff, 'The Originals' (and Klaus' 'Hard-Partying' Protege Marcel)," EW.com. January 16, 2013.

———. "*Vampire Diaries*: Joseph Morgan and Daniel Gillies on Filming Originals Spin-off Pilot in New Orleans," EW.com. March 29, 2013.

———. "*TVD* Star Daniel Gillies Talks Katherine, Showtime Acquiring His Directorial Debut, and His Next Film," EW.com. April 25, 2013.

———. "*Vampire Diaries*: EP Julie Plec Previews the Season Finale," EW.com. May 2, 2013.

Bring It On. Directed by Peyton Reed, 2000.

Buswell, Robert E. *Encyclopedia of Buddhism*, volume 2. Gale, 2004.

Carroll, Lewis. *Alice's Adventures in Wonderland and Through the Looking-Glass and What Alice Found There*. London: Bloomsbury Publishing, 2003.

Casablanca. Directed by Michael Curtiz, 1942.

Catch Me If You Can. Directed by Steven Spielberg, 2002.

Gelman, Vlada. "*Vampire Diaries* Scoop: Phoebe Tonkin Previews Her Wolfy 'Threat' to Tyler and Caroline," TVLine.com. October 25, 2012.

———. "*Vampire Diaries* Preview: Candice Accola Breaks Down Caroline's Complicated Love Square," TVLine.com. November 14, 2012.

———. "*Vampire Diaries*' Joseph Morgan on the 'Bloody' Midseason Finale and Klaus' 'Game' with Caroline," TVLine.com. December 12, 2012.

———. "*Vampire Diaries* Boss on Stefan's Anger, Jeremy's Killer Urges and Caroline and Tyler's Future," TVLine.com. December 28, 2012.

———. "*Vampire Diaries*' Ian Somerhalder on Elena's Sire Bond, Damon's Angst About the Cure and More," TVLine.com. January 30, 2013.

Guliadis, Theodora. "Exclusive Interview: Joseph Morgan Teases the *Originals* Pilot," VampireDiaries.AlloyEntertainment.com. April 4, 2013.

Griffin, Jennifer. "Claire Holt Talks Rebekah's Fury, Split with Klaus, Working with Phoebe Tonkin & This Season's Giant Game Changer," ScreenSpy.com. October 25, 2012.

Halterman, Jim. "*Vampire Diaries* Exclusive: Julie Plec Teases Finale, The Originals & Surprise Return of . . ." TVFanatic.com. May 8, 2013.

Highfill, Samantha. "No Humanity, No Modesty: *Vampire Diaries* Costume Designer on Elena's Wicked New Wardrobe," EW.com. March 13, 2013.

Highfill, Samantha. "It's the *Vampire Diaries* Prom!," EW.com. April 4, 2013.

HomeOfTheNutty.com/VampireDiaries/Screencaps.

James, E.L. *Fifty Shades of Grey*. New York: Vintage Books, 2011.

Krakauer, Jon. *Into the Wild*. New York: Villard, 1996.

Ladouceur, Liisa. *How to Kill a Vampire*. Toronto: ECW Press, 2013.

La Rosa, Erin. "10 Secrets About *The Vampire Diaries* Spinoff, *The Originals*," Buzzfeed.com. April 24, 2013.

MacKenzie, Carina Adly. "Meet Grace Phipps: The *Vampire Diaries* Ingenue's Nerdy Twitter Secret and Fave 'Supernatural' Brother Revealed," Zap2It.com. October 18, 2012.

———. "*Vampire Diaries* 'Memorial' recap: Julie Plec Talks Elena's First 'Feed' and That Very Special Appearance," Zap2It.com. October 19, 2012.

———. "*The Vampire Diaries*' Candice Accola Dishes on Caroline's Feelings for Klaus and Bond with Stefan," Zap2It.com. November 15, 2012.

———. "*The Vampire Diaries*' EP Julie Plec Talks 'My Brother's Keeper': Damon and Elena Do the Deed — But Are Her Feelings Real?," Zap2It.com. November 29, 2012.

———. "*The Vampire Diaries*' Joseph Morgan Talks Klaus' Priorities and His Place as the Captain of the Klaroline Ship," Zap2It.com. December 12, 2012.

———. "*The Vampire Diaries*' Star Ian Somerhalder Envisions a Future for Damon and Elena: Parties, an Art Gallery, and a Tropical Beach . . . or Not," Zap2It.com. January 30, 2013.

———. "*The Vampire Diaries*' Star Joseph Morgan Dishes on Klaus and Caroline, More 'Revealing' Scenes, and His New Friend on *The Originals*," Zap2It.com. February 13, 2013.

———. "Paul Wesley on *The Vampire Diaries* Set: Could Stefan and Elena Ever Get Back Together?," Zap2It.com. March 14, 2013.

McGrath, Jenny. "Who Is Dead Sara, the Band from *Vampire Diaries* Season 4, Episode 17?," Wetpaint.com. March 21, 2013.

McNeil, Legs with Gillian McCain. *Please Kill Me: The Uncensored Oral History of Punk*. New York: Penguin Books, 1997.

Naoreen, Nuzhat. "Candice Accola Teases Tonight's *Vampire Diaries*, Weighs in on *The Originals* Baby Twist," EW.com. May 2, 2013.

Psycho. Directed by Alfred Hitchcock, 1960.

Rice, Anne. *Interview with the Vampire.* New York: Alfred A. Knopf, 1976.

"Rick Worthy Interview," *Supernatural Radio.* http://supernaturalradio.org/?p=17.

Ross, Robyn. "*Vampire Diaries* Trevino: It's Time for Tyler to Take Charge — But There Will Be Consequences," TVGuide.com. December 12, 2012.

———. "*The Vampire Diaries*' Graham: Bonnie and Kol's Run-In Is One of Her Most Intense Scenes Yet," TVGuide.com. January 30, 2013.

———. "*The Vampire Diaries* Bite: Uh-Oh! Is Damon in Danger?," TVGuide.com. February 13, 2013.

———. "*The Vampire Diaries* Bite: Did Damon and Lexi Hook Up in the '70s?," TVGuide.com. March 20, 2013.

———. "*Vampire Diaries*' Candice Accola: The Final Episodes Will Leave 'Klaroline' Fans Satisfied," TVGuide.com. May 1, 2013.

Shakespeare, William. *Julius Caesar.* InternetShakespeare.uvic.ca.

Shapiro, Michael. "The Great Sumter Rally in Union Square," NYTimes.com. April 19, 2011.

"Silas, A Chief Man Among Brethen," The Master's Prayer Network. MPNHome .net.

Smith, L.J. *The Vampire Diaries: The Awakening* and *The Struggle.* New York: HarperTeen, 2007.

———. *The Vampire Diaries: The Fury* and *Dark Reunion.* New York: HarperTeen, 2007.

Stand By Me. Directed by Rob Reiner, 1986.

Strandagaldur Museum of Icelandic Sorcery & Witchcraft. www.gladrasyning.is.

Swift, Andy. "*Vampire Diaries* Scoop: How Damon & Meredith 'Bond' in Season 4," HollywoodLife.com. October 10, 2012.

———. "*The Vampire Diaries* Scoop: Is Shane Good or Evil? David Alpay Weighs In," HollywoodLife.com. November 29, 2012.

———. "*Vampire Diaries* Scoop: Kat Graham Talks Bonnie & Jeremy's 'Crazy Path,'" HollywoodLife.com. January 24, 2013.

———. "*The Originals* Scoop: Daniel Gillies Previews 'The Beginning of a War,'" HollywoodLife.com. April 24, 2013.

Turchiano, Danielle. "Kat Graham Teases *The Vampire Diaries* Season Four & Meeting Professor Shane," TheExaminer.com. September 19, 2012.

———. "*TVD*'s Julie Plec, Todd Williams & Michael Narducci Tease 'The Killer,'" TheExaminer.com. November 7, 2012.

Twitter.com/CMollere.

Twitter.com/JuliePlec.

"2 Days in the Life of L.A. Rockers Dead Sara," Fuse.TV. March 20, 2013.

The Vampire Diaries. TV Series. Executive Producers Leslie Morgenstein, Bob Levy, Kevin Williamson, Julie Plec. The CW. 2009–.

Vampire-Diaries.net.

A View to a Kill. Directed by John Glen, 1985.

Walker, Dave. "The New Orleans–set 'The Originals' Airs as Possible *Vampire Diaries* Spin-Off," NOLA.com. April 26, 2013.

Wieselman, Jarett. "Phoebe Tonkin Talks *Vampire Diaries*," TheInsider.com. September 6, 2012.

———. "Kat Graham Previews a 'Powerful' Turn of Events," ETOnline.com. January 24, 2013.

———. "*TVD* Star Previews a Rocky Road to the Cure," ETOnline.com. January 31, 2013.

———. "Ian Somerhalder on Damon's Past & Elena's Future," ETOnline.com. March 13, 2013.

———. "*TVD* Boss Talks Sires, Spin-Offs & Graduation," ETOnline.com. May 8, 2013.

Wikipedia.org.

"Wild Great Wall," ChinaTourGuide.com.

"Wyrd Designs: Understanding the Symbols Part 6 — Vegvísir," Patheos.com. August 13, 2010.

Acknowledgments

To the entire gang at ECW Press, thank you for publishing the Love You to Death series, four years running. The beautiful cover art is an original painting by the talented and clever Carolyn McNeillie. Thanks to Erin Creasey for getting our book out into the world; to Sarah Dunn for being our publicist and pal; to the enthusiastic Laura Pastore for her proofread; and to Troy Cunningham and Kendra Martin for making the guts of this book so very attractive. Thanks to *TVD*-convert Nikki Stafford for diligently noting the last stabs of the Gilbert knives for us and also for, like, inventing this episode-guide format with your *Buffy*, *Angel*, and *Lost* companion books.

Gil Adamson, thank you for your genius-as-always edit, excellent marginalia commentary, and demand for more! more! books in this series. It means the world to have your good advice and great jokes cheering us on.

We were admittedly a little nervous when we first reached out to the *TVD* gang with interview requests, so huge thanks to Julie Plec and to Tom Farrell for getting our email into the right inboxes. Thank you to Joshua Butler, Tyler Cook, Caroline Dries, Jose Molina, Dave Perkal, Mike Suby, and Pascal Verschooris for being so keen, responsive, and open with your answers to our millions of questions. And Julie, we are running out of ways to express our thanks to you for being so generous with your time: you went above and beyond to do an interview for this book *and* write its foreword in the midst of your takeover of The CW with your empire of awesomeness. Thank you for valuing what we do.

To the mighty *TVD* family who kept us company while we wrote this book and who've become great friends over the past four years: we raise a Gillies in your honor. (Ask Tash for the recipe. She cares.) Thank you for being so supportive and so goddamn hilarious. To the Vampire-Diaries.net crew — Red, Abby, and Kate — you are the definition of *epic* in every way. Thank you for your unwavering support, honest feedback, and always being there to give us perspective or inappropriately captioned episode stills. And thank you for keeping Vee, in particular, somewhat sane. (Look, you tried.)

Vee is incredibly grateful and humbled to be part of Love You to Death and that is thanks to her friend and co-author, Crissy, who taught her so

much during the process of researching and writing this book, helping her watch the show with a more refined perspective, and always, *always* making her laugh. And Crissy cannot even begin to describe the weight that was lifted from her shoulders when Vee agreed to co-write *Love You to Death 4*. To have a smart, hilarious, expert friend shaping and writing this book with her and inspiring her to step up her game, and to be able to give Vee an outlet for all her *TVD*-related genius — well, there's a beautiful symmetry to that, don't you think? Thank you, Vee, for being a true friend and a wonderful co-author.

And finally to our friends and family who don't know a sire bond from an Expression triangle but are patient with and supportive of us anyway, we love you to death.

Also Available

GET THE eBOOK FREE! At ECW Press, we want you to enjoy *Love You to Death — Season 4* in whatever format you like, whenever you like. Leave your print book at home and take the eBook to go! Purchase the print edition and receive the eBook free. Just send an email to ebook@ecwpress.com and include:

- the book title
- the name of the store where you purchased it
- your receipt number
- your preference of file type: PDF or ePub?

A real person will respond to your email with your eBook attached. And thanks for supporting an independently owned publisher with your purchase!